(continued from front flap)

This book also shows you how to locate, cost and access your information holdings (databases, library collections, corporate records) together with your information handling functions (personal computing, data processing, office automation, couriers) so you'll be able to eliminate redundant efforts and thereby save money.

Here are just some of the book's features:

- Each of the four steps of the information resource discovery process is diagrammed in a concise chart, summarizing the procedures described in the text. Most are illustrated by case examples from the private sector, government, or academia.

- All concepts are illustrated with charts, figures, sample forms, and tables. Every step is guided so you'll find it easy to develop your own InfoMap.

- Examples clearly show how the relative values of information resource entities can be determined with a series of indexes for effectiveness and importance. You'll see how easy it is to assess relative values in a systematic fashion across your entire organization. The entities can then be rank-ordered by value.

- "How-to" flow charts lead you through each of the four key steps of the InfoMap process: inventory, costing, valuing, and synthesizing.

The authors say "the development of policies and programs for the management of information resources *that work* depend fundamentally on knowledge of what, specifically, the resources are." This book will provide you with the tools you need to not only discover that knowledge base, but also to use it to improve the overall performance of your organization.

D1501984

InfoMap:

A Complete Guide to Discovering Corporate Information Resources

InfoMap:
A Complete Guide
to Discovering
Corporate Information
Resources

Cornelius F. Burk, Jr.
&
Forest W. Horton, Jr.

PRENTICE HALL
Englewood Cliffs, New Jersey 07632

Prentice-Hall International, Inc., *London*
Prentice-Hall of Australia, Pty. Ltd., *Sydney*
Prentice-Hall Canada, Inc., *Toronto*
Prentice-Hall of India Private Ltd., *New Delhi*
Prentice-Hall of Japan, Inc., *Tokyo*
Prentice-Hall of Southeast Asia Pte. Ltd., *Singapore*
Editora Prentice-Hall do Brasil Ltda., *Rio de Janeiro*
Prentice-Hall Hispanoamericana, S.A., *Mexico*

10 9 8 7 6 5 4 3 2 1

Library of Congress Cataloging-in-Publication Data

Burk, Cornelius F. (Cornelius Franklin)
  InfoMap: a complete guide to discovering corporate information
resources/Cornelius F. Burk, Jr. & Forest W. Horton, Jr.
    p   cm.
    Bibliography: p.
    Includes index.
    ISBN 0-13-464447-6: $34.95

    1. Information resources management.   I. Horton, Forest W.
II. Title. III. Title: InfoMap.
T58.64.B87 1987
658.4′038—dc19

87-24627
CIP

ISBN 0-13-464447-6

PRENTICE HALL
BUSINESS & PROFESSIONAL DIVISION
A division of Simon & Schuster
Englewood Cliffs, New Jersey 07632

Printed in the United States of America

To Lillian Sale Burk and Cornelius Franklin Burk
and
To Karin and Manuela

PREFACE

How This Book Will Help You

InfoMap guides you through a step-by-step process to discover, map and evaluate the gold mines of the information age: Information resources. By discovering exactly what and where the information resources of your organization are — paper records, computer systems, editorial services, technical databases, couriers and so on — and knowing who uses them, who does not, why, at what cost and with what results, your information can be managed from a position of strength and harnessed for maximum corporate gain. Just as the Chief Financial Officer and the Personnel Director must know where all the dollars and people are and how effectively they are being used, so also the Chief Information Officer must have solid knowledge of all of the corporation's information resources.

If your company or organization remains blithely unaware of the *total* breadth, depth and significance of its information sources, services and systems, it runs several risks. At one level, the risk is waste and inefficiency. Information resources readily available within the firm may lie unused or misused; others in the market-place and the public sector, potentially of strategic importance, may be ignored. We know that millions, even billions, have been wasted by various government agencies because top management did not pay serious attention to information resource management basics like data quality, storage costs, duplication and baseline resource inventories.

At the strategic level, your company risks losing its competitive advantage and its ability to seize new opportunities. Virtually every type of enterprise has been or is being transformed, becoming more and more dependent on its information resources: Mining, manufacturing, banking, insurance, retailing, government services, among many others. Studies show that the return on investment in new information technology and in new sources of strategic information can range up to 1,000 per cent and beyond. But your chances of cashing in on these opportunities, even your survival, will depend on the knowledge you have of your existing corporate information base. That means discovering and mapping all of your information resources. *InfoMap* shows you how.

While most corporate managers acknowledge the critical importance of information to the survival and success of their firms, typically they lack a reliable baseline inventory of what information and tools they already have to generate, acquire, process, store, repackage and disseminate this vital resource. Do you know where your information comes from? Who uses it? How much it costs? Or who is accountable for supply, cost and value? We address these and related questions head-on — not by designing questionnaires, or with wistful admonitions to "manage information as a resource," but by rolling up our sleeves and carefully mapping the resources. That means applying a rigorous methodology: Establishing categories and types of resource entities, describing and counting them, measuring their costs, assessing their values, plotting their relative positions on charts and maps and assessing strengths and weaknesses. Only with this knowledge can the organization get a firm handle on managing information as a corporatewide, results-oriented function.

InfoMap combines theory with practice to bring you flexible, tested methods for discovering corporate information resources. There are four basic steps: First, *surveying*, to identify what you have; second, *costing and valuing*, to establish net worth; third, *analysis*, to locate, map and understand your information resources, and finally *synthesis*, to identify your resource base and evaluate corporate strengths and weaknesses. The central purpose is diagnostic, not prescriptive. Results from the discovery process will tell you what resources you have, what's working well and what's not; but not how to manage.

The main benefits to your organization in discovering all of its information resources are twofold. First, you will be able to more fully exploit what you already have, an immediate and direct payoff. Second, you will establish a basis for more effective management of your corporate information resources, a vital necessity for virtually all firms doing business in the information age. The cost? The time of one or two individuals, using the common-sense, simple forms, tables and charts we provide, over a three-week to three-month period, or longer, depending on the size and nature of your organization and on the particular results you want. There are no technical or other sophisticated requirements.

The discovery process, however, involves more than preparing a simple inventory listing. For the information resources of a large, complex organization, discovery requires some special diagnostic tools, embodied in the mapping techniques we prescribe in detail. We give you a base map, a compass, a set of symbols and coordinates to describe the terrain features, and a special pair of binoculars. You will see more clearly and much farther than you've been able to until now, and bring your information resources into focus in a much more discriminating fashion.

Finally, *InfoMap* is about cost justification, and about balancing information values and benefits with information costs and expenses. It is the first book which explains why and how the information manager might argue: "Given that an information resource has a value of $X and a current cost of $Y, then it must be prudent to invest A% of $X to improve the effectiveness of the resource and to reduce the costs."

A word on scope: Our methods are designed to deal with *formally* defined or recognized information resources, typically named sources, services and systems. They do not encompass *informal* sources, however vital to every decision-maker. (A husband's casual tip to his wife made just before her trip to the brokerage firm may be far more valuable than any of the myriad databases and services offered by the firm.) Nor do our methods map information itself as it is used operationally, minute-by-minute and day-by-day. As we will explain, while information itself can be a resource, our methods do not map the intricate dynamics of everyday flow, handling and use — just its sources, nature, users, suppliers, managers, locations, costs and values. Finally, information certainly has social as well as economic values. While government organizations and others must consider both in formulating information policies, our methods primarily address assessment of the economic aspects.

Who Should Use This Book

InfoMap is aimed primarily at the enterprise's senior information officer and his or her corporate team: Vice-President for Information Systems, VP-Information Services, Chief Information Officer, MIS head or the equivalent. Whatever the titles and labels, the book's appeal, and we hope its value, will be mainly to the company's information managers and other information professionals at the top corporate level and down through the middle echelons of operating departments. While we acknowledge that the book's tone, examples and illustrations mainly are drawn from the corporate world, we believe our approach is equally applicable to government departments and agencies, institutions such as hospitals and colleges, not-for-profit associations and societies and other kinds of organizations.

Imagine where an aspiring Chief Financial Officer in a *Fortune* 500 company would be if, seeking a book on how to discover the company's financial investments, flows and assets, he or she was confronted in the book store with not a single overview of financial management, but instead a dozen specialized books — each dealing with some components of the financial resource management process. In the 1930s and 1940s, the first texts began to appear to help Chief Financial Officers discover and map their corporate financial assets and liabilities. In the 1940s and 1950s, analogous books appeared to help Personnel Directors. Here we put forward a book to guide the Chief Information Officer, or where no CIO exists, to help top management take the first steps in getting a bird'seye view of the breadth, depth and significance of the firm's information resources.

NEIL BURK
WOODY HORTON

Acknowledgments

The main case example, which illustrates many of the steps described, was furnished by CRA Exploration Pty. Limited of Melbourne, Australia. We are grateful to the company for making materials available and to their senior staff who directed the work and later assisted with the manuscript, especially John Collier, CRA Group Executive responsible for CRAE, David Mackenzie, Michael Porter and Jacob Rebek.

During manuscript preparation, encouragement and support to complete the work was received from Kenneth Dye, Auditor General of Canada. Our colleagues offered useful comments and suggestions that added value to the final product. Especially, we thank Bruce Allen, Curtis Fritz, James Henderson, Ronald Kaden, Norman Kyle, Michiel Leenders, Donald Marchand, Joan McKean, Gary North, Michael Ryan, Michael Sutton and Joanne Watt. We are indebted to our editors at Prentice-Hall, especially George Parker and Brian Holding, who guided the project with skill and patience. However, we assume full responsibility for information presented in the published book.

For one of us (Burk), the support of his family was indispensable to seeing the project through to completion. I thank Anne, David and Jennifer for their patience, understanding and good humor; and Dad for his support and kindness, always there when needed. For the other (Horton), family nurture was no less important. I thank Tina, Ingrid and Karin for their understanding and encouragement.

N. B.
W. H.

CONTENTS

PREFACE .... (vii)

Chapter 1 INFORMATION RESOURCES MANAGEMENT ...... (1)

1.1 How this book will help your organization   (4)
1.2 The strategic role of information resources   (5)
    1.2.1 Evolution of information management   (6)
    1.2.2 The current stage of development   (7)
1.3 IRM: The corporate approach to information
       management   (9)
1.4 The nature of information resources   (14)
    1.4.1 Similarities with other resources   (18)
    1.4.2 Differences with other resources   (19)
    1.4.3 The information resource entity (IRE)   (21)
1.5 Context: The importance of understanding the
       business   (25)
1.6 Needed: Information resource mapping methods   (28)
1.7 Overview of the information resource discovery
     process   (31)
1.8 Options for implementation   (34)

Chapter 2 CONDUCTING THE PRELIMINARY INVENTORY .. (39)

2.1 The preliminary inventory project   (40)
    2.1.1 Obtaining top management's support   (42)
    2.1.2 Establishing purpose and scope   (42)
2.2 Defining your resource classification scheme   (44)
    2.2.1 Resource categories and types   (45)
    2.2.2 Examples of classification schemes   (55)
2.3 Collecting and compiling the inventory data   (56)
    2.3.1 Design the inventory data form   (56)
    2.3.2 Collect the data   (60)
    2.3.3 Identify hidden resources   (67)

2.3.4   Main case example   (70)
2.4   Summary of the preliminary resource inventory   (72)

Chapter 3   MEASURING COSTS AND ASSESSING VALUES .... **(75)**

3.1   Concepts of the cost and value of information   (77)
3.2   How to measure costs of an information resource entity   (80)
        3.2.1   Identify cost elements   (80)
        3.2.2   Define costing objectives   (84)
        3.2.3   Select costing methods   (85)
        3.2.4   Measure and rank entities by cost   (86)
3.3   How to assess values of an information resource entity   (91)
        3.3.1   Identify nature of values   (91)
                3.3.1.1   Quality of information itself   (92)
                3.3.1.2   Utility of information
                          holdings   (94)
                3.3.1.3   Impact on organizational
                          productivity   (94)
                3.3.1.4   Impact on organizational effectiveness   (97)
                3.3.1.5   Impact on financial position   (97)
        3.3.2   Assess and rank entity values   (99)
                3.3.2.1   Rate effectiveness   (100)
                3.3.2.2   Determine strategic role of resource
                          entity   (101)
                3.3.2.3   Determine strategic role of activity   (104)
                3.3.2.4   Assess and rank entities by value   (105)
3.4   Relating cost to value   (106)
        3.4.1   Cost/value ratios   (108)
        3.4.2   Discovering unnecessary and excess costs   (111)

Chapter 4   INFORMATION RESOURCE
            MAPPING TECHNIQUES .... **(115)**

4.1   Setting objectives for analysis   (117)
4.2   Locating information users, suppliers, handlers and managers   (118)
        4.2.1   Review typology   (120)
        4.2.2   Select organizational units   (121)
        4.2.3   Construct user worksheet   (122)
        4.2.4   Construct supplier/handler worksheet   (122)
        4.2.5   Construct manager worksheet   (123)
        4.2.6   Analysis of the worksheets   (123)
4.3   Mapping the spectrum of information resources   (138)
        4.3.1   The information spectrum   (138)
        4.3.2   Construct the information resource map   (141)

4.3.3   Analysis of the information map   (145)
4.4   Locating cost data and financial controls   (147)
4.4.1   Review costs of information resource entities   (148)
4.4.2   Relate IREs to corporate financial systems   (148)
4.4.3   Review values of information resource entities   (149)
4.4.4   Determine degree and nature of cost control   (151)
4.5   Observations from the information charts and maps   (151)

Chapter 5   THE CORPORATE
            INFORMATION RESOURCE .... (155)

5.1   Pinpointing your information resources   (156)
5.1.1   Develop resource criteria   (157)
        5.1.1.1   Nature of the information
                  resource entities (IREs)   (158)
        5.1.1.2   Costs of information resource
                  entities   (160)
        5.1.1.3   Values of information
                  resource entities   (160)
        5.1.1.4   Combined criteria   (161)
5.1.2   Identify your information resources   (162)
5.2   How to identify your strengths and weaknesses   (166)
5.2.1   Information holdings   (168)
5.2.2   Information handling functions   (169)
5.2.3   Information accounting and budgeting   (169)
5.2.4   Corporate information management   (171)
5.3   Summary of the information resource discovery process (173)
5.3.1   Step One: Survey   (173)
5.3.2   Step Two: Cost/Value   (173)
5.3.3   Step Three: Analysis   (174)
5.3.4   Step Four: Synthesis   (174)
5.4   Payoffs from the discovery process   (175)

Appendix 1 .... (181)

Case Example: CRA Exploration Pty. Limited,
Melbourne, Australia   (181)

1.1   List of information resource entities (IREs)
      identified in preliminary inventory (74 IREs)   (181)
1.2   Examples of completed preliminary inventory
      data forms (48 IREs)   (184)

Annotated Bibliography .... (235)

Glossary .... (239)

Index .... (247)

InfoMap:
A Complete Guide to Discovering Corporate Information Resources

1

INFORMATION RESOURCES MANAGEMENT

The process of discovering information resources in a large organization can be likened to the process of geographic exploration and discovery that took place in the interior of North America over a century ago. Explorers such as Lewis and Clark, in what is now the western United States, and Palliser in what is now western Canada, were faced with finding their way through and describing huge tracts of uncharted land. Their travels were guided by, at best, only rough ideas of what lay ahead and by crude models of what they might find in the way of native peoples, transportation routes, agricultural lands and mineral resources.[1]

Someone had to make the first trip. Since the "parts as yet unknown" were so immense, the first maps produced were of a reconnaissance nature — sketches of the main features, such as ranges of the Rocky Mountains, the Great Plains, the Columbia River and other major landforms. Although sketchy, the features shown were real and their relative positions made known for the first time. A framework for future, more detailed exploration had been established. A similar challenge — and opportunity — faces those exploring for sources of the raw materials of the Information Age: Information resources.

Just as energy fueled the Industrial Age, so information resources now power the economy in the Information Age. To succeed in the 1980s and beyond, your organization must recognize the strategic dimensions of its information sources, services and systems. The necessary first step for effective management of your information resources is to determine what and where your information resources are.

This book presents an approach and a specific step-by-step method for discovering all of your corporate information resources. The mapping process will survey the gamut, including record centers, computer systems, telecommunication networks, libraries, photocopiers, editorial offices and couriers, whether high-tech or low-tech. As a result, you will be able to separate the strategic information entities from overhead and the nonproductive. Management's full attention can then be focussed on the sources of information critical to your organization's success: Its information resources.

Energy, of course, is still a major resource. Services, manufacturing, transportation, agriculture, mining and many other economic activities depend on the availability of convenient, low-cost and efficient forms of energy to transform raw materials into finished goods and to move goods and services from office, plant, farm and mine through distribution systems to wholesaler, retailer and customer.

The flow and use of energy through the economic infrastructure is managed in a host of ways, each suited to the enterprises and activities being supported. Furniture factories use and manage it one way, airlines another. But to obtain the needed energy, all users depend ultimately on a limited number of specific sources or *reservoirs*: Oil pools, gas fields, coal deposits, nuclear reactors, hydroelectric generators, solar panels, wood lots and so on.

Both the energy flows themselves and the reservoirs from which the energy is derived are regarded by economists as *resources*.[2] The energy flows, in a manufacturing context, are direct factors of production, while the oil pools and other reservoirs are the basic or ultimate sources of supply for these critical factors. Flows may be scarce and many individual sources of supply are exhaustible and nonrenewable. In the oil and gas business, for example, marketing gasoline and other petroleum products (flows) and exploring for new oil and gas pools (sources) are separate but interdependent resource management activities, contributing to a common corporate objective.

In the Information Age, the value of information as a strategic resource emerges. As with energy, the day-to-day use of information itself is managed and handled in a multitude of ways, according to the context of use and application. Likewise, just as energy flows depend on access to finite energy sources, so too does the use by an organization of information depend on access to a limited number of specific information resources. And like energy, critical information flows are replenishable from sources of supply that may not be inexhaustible.

In exploring for and discovering mineral and other tangible resources, there is usually no difficulty in recognizing the sought-after commodity when it is first encountered. For example, if an exploration geologist finds gold-bearing rocks or minerals, they are usually recognized immediately for what they represent — potentially, a commercially viable gold deposit. However, the main targets of the explorer searching for information resources in a large organization are less obvious. Usually the targets are not simply data and information as such. The challenge is to discriminate and isolate from within the organizational complex, the mother lodes — the basic reservoirs that *supply* the data and information critical to the organization's success.

Thus, the elements we seek to discover with our methods are those critical sources of supply, which we will call *corporate information resources*. Throughout the remainder of this book the meaning and import of this phrase will unfold. Two key concepts will serve as beacons to guide our exploration: First, the corporate interest — that is, the well being of the organization as a whole, whether private, governmental or not-for-profit; and second, the resource management concept — managing the sources and supplies which are critical for success. These two basic criteria or filters will be used in screening and examining the many information sources, services and systems you will ultimately discover and map. The filters enable the information explorer to discover what everyone can see but often fails to recognize: The information resource entities of critical importance to the success and profitability of the organization.

Chapter 1 Preview. We begin up front with visualization of what the discovery process will do for your organization. Then, the strategic value of information is explained by describing the evolution of information management over the past century and the current leading edge: *Management of corporate information resources.* We describe the scope and substance of the information resources management (IRM) process in terms of its place in the broader field of information management. The essential nature of a resource is explained and similarities and dissimilarities of information resources with the other resources are listed. To conclude Chapter 1, we explain why more rigorous methods are needed to identify and map organizational information resources.

1.1 HOW THIS BOOK WILL HELP YOUR ORGANIZATION

Before diving into details of the Four Steps of the information resource discovery process and the underlying concepts and considerations, let's visualize how the book could help your organization on various levels.

At the most basic level, the book may convince you and your top managers that information can indeed be viewed — and managed — as an organizational resource. If you do not already accept this premise, the book will lead you to the realization that in most firms information can and does play a strategic, not just a support role. No small discovery.

At another level, use of the methods described in the book will tell you, specifically, which of the multitude of information sources, services and systems used by your organization are *resources* — the reservoirs of information of strategic importance (not all information is a resource). These are the information entities that deserve top management's attention. They are your corporate information resources.

The discovery process will illuminate problems and opportunities related to your current information management practices and policies. For example, it will indicate your relative strengths and weaknesses with respect to information quality, accessibility, performance, use and effectiveness; highlight real dollar costs and waste and reveal inadequate accounting and budgeting practices. The maps, charts and analyses will marshal evidence and point to the possible need in your organization for:

1. Developing a corporate information resources management (IRM) policy;
2. Appointing a Chief Information Officer;
3. Maintaining a systematic inventory of your information resources;
4. Establishing a central information service;
5. Formulating a strategic plan for the management of information resources that is linked directly to business unit plans;
6. Using information resources for strategic competitive advantage; and
7. Addressing other IRM-related issues.

Finally, this book will guide you in applying any of the many specific methods used in the discovery process that individually may benefit your organization. Such methods include designing an inventory form, setting up a classification system for information resources, determining costs, articulating the values of information resources, ranking values, developing criteria for recognizing resources, distinguishing relative strengths and weaknesses and many more.

In short, when the entire information resource discovery process is completed, your organization will have a comprehensive overview of its information sources, services and systems, including knowledge of both the information itself and the means for handling it. You will also expose the existing management framework within which all of this is embedded. Together, these results of the discovery process will form the foundation for the future management and exploitation of your organization's information resources.

1.2   THE STRATEGIC ROLE OF INFORMATION RESOURCES

Donald Marchand and Forest Horton conclude their 1986 book *INFOTRENDS: Profiting from Your Information Resources* with the statement:

> The firms that just survive in the information economy will be the ones that use information resources and computer technologies only as cost-displacement and labor-saving tools. The firms that compete effectively and flourish in the information economy will be the ones that *use information technologies and information resources in strategic ways* to manufacture new and better products, find new markets and enlarge their share of existing markets, and distribute products and services in creative ways. These will be the intelligent organizations of the future.*

[emphasis added]

The strategic significance of information resources provides the most compelling motive for developing methods to identify, cost, value, map and assess information resources. A quick review of the history of information management and a projection into the future will place this need for a mapping process in perspective.

INFOTRENDS: Profiting from Your Information Resources, Donald A. Marchand and Forest W. Horton, Jr., p. 293. Copyright © 1986. John Wiley & Sons, Inc. Reprinted by permission of John Wiley & Sons, Inc.

1.2.1 Evolution of Information Management

The history of information management over the past 100 years shows a progression from a concern for efficiency to a concern for overall business performance, and from playing an operations support function to performing a strategic management function. Five stages can be recognized. Individual organizations evolve from one stage to the next, not by eliminating need for the previous stage (paperwork, after all, is still with us), but rather by absorbing it as the organization moves toward the highest stage of development (Fig. 1-1).

The first of these five stages in the evolution of information management is *Paperwork Management.* Beginning in the late 19th century and lasting until the late 1950s, information management

Figure 1-1. Donald Marchand and Forest Horton's five stages in the development of strategic information management.

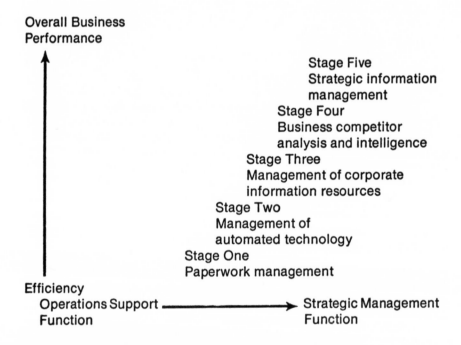

Source: INFOTRENDS: Profiting from Your Information Resources. Donald A. Marchand and Forest W. Horton, Jr., Fig. 5-1. Copyright © 1986. John Wiley & Sons, Inc. Reprinted by permission of John Wiley & Sons, Inc.

was equated with physical paperwork and records management. Information management was a supervisory, clerical and support function. Not many enterprises are still at Stage One, but a few are.

Stage Two, *Management of Corporate Automated Technologies*, focusses on the management of information technologies and technical attributes, mostly at the middle management level. Technical efficiency is the main business objective served. Most firms and industries are currently at this stage.

In Stage Three, *Management of Corporate Information Resources*, the focus is on cost-effective management of information technologies and of both manual and automated information. It is a top management support function with primarily an internal focus. Stage Three represents a decided shift in objectives from, first, a support to a management function in business and, second, from a focus on efficiency to effectiveness. The largest banks are probably good examples of an industry that is moving into Stage Three.

Stage Four, *Business-Competitor Analysis and Intelligence*, is oriented to the business objective of gaining competitive advantage in business unit and corporate strategy. It is dependent on the quality of the intelligence analysis and information collection and processing performed by managers and staff, rather than solely on the use of information tools.

The highest level in this framework, Stage Five, is *Strategic Information Management*. It is primarily focussed on corporate strategy and direction, and emphasizes the quality of decision-making and information use needed to improve overall business performance. The strategic management focus provides linkage to the functional strategies of the business, for example finance, manufacturing, research and development. It is a top management strategic function.[3]

1.2.2 The Current State of Development

Stage Three, *Management of Corporate Information Resources*, is now on the leading edge of information management development, although individual organizations and industries may find themselves at other growth levels. The business objective sought by most organizations today for their information management function is that of cost-effective management and use of information resources and technologies.[4]

This view of the current information management scene implies that most organizations have already recognized, defined and inventoried their *specific* information resources and information assets. Can we assume that this is generally so? Is this the case in your organization? If the answer is "no" to the last question, top and middle managers may not have clear perceptions of what, exactly, their information resources and assets are. One or more of the following situations may exist:

1. Some managers may have difficulty in even visualizing their information as a corporate resource. To them, resources are people, land and other tangible things — but not information.

2. Although the general idea of viewing information as a resource may be accepted, some managers may have no conception of what an information resource entity is, what it looks like or what it does.

3. There may be no corporate-wide policy, approach or system for classifying, categorizing or listing all information resources; consequently, there is no corporate inventory of information resources and assets.

4. Corporate managers may have resisted the chore of developing a baseline inventory of their information resources because vendors promised that turn-key solutions to all of the organization's information management problems were just around the corner.

5. Although some information resource entities may have been identified, management may not know their operating costs or the total investment they represent.

6. Management may not have articulated, or if feasible, measured the value of their information resources and assets.

7. Information assets may not have been recognized as such, capitalized or reported on the balance sheet and in profit-and-loss statements.

8. Top management may lack reliable information on *both* the cost and value of its information resources; if so it cannot assure stockholders and directors that company resource investments represent good value for money.

9. Management may not know who uses what information resources for what purposes; nor who is accountable for the cost and performance of particular entities.

10. The organization may depend entirely on *internal* resources. There is no recognition of the value, cost and effectiveness of *external* information resources.

Other impediments to the cost-effective management of information resources could be added. We believe what has contributed more than anything else to these impediments has been the lack of an *integrative conceptual framework* for managing information as a resource — a view that is large enough and flexible enough to incorporate the entire organization's multiple concerns with its people, systems, facilities, monies and its technologies, and the information embedded throughout.

Past approaches have had one common failing. They are splintered and compartmentalized. It is not enough *just* to admonish information managers to link information plans with strategic business plans. It is not enough *just* to exhort systems designers to make systems "user friendly". And it is not enough *just* to buy the latest smart software and powerful hardware to increase productivity and decision-support. The point of departure in developing a corporate information strategy is to identify how information resources are being used in the firm — here and now. How do they support the business units of the firm *now*? How *should* they support business strategies in the future?

1.3   IRM: THE CORPORATE APPROACH TO INFORMATION MANAGEMENT

Before describing in detail our information resource mapping methodology, let's place it within the broader framework of information management. Information managers of many stripes deal with information in a variety of contexts and with many different motives. All are engaged in information management. Collectively, their attention ranges over an immense and cluttered landscape: From designing micro-chips, operating a piece of equipment or defining data elements for a catalogue, through managing general functional areas such as data processing and library services; coordinating the operation of a family of converging technologies such as computers, telecommunications and office automation and on to managing national information systems and international database services. Somewhere within this terrain lies the corporate interest.

Information resources management (IRM) is the process within the information management arena that serves the *corporate* interest. IRM seeks to harness information for the benefit of the organization as a whole by exploiting, developing and optimizing information resources. The interests of the organization are usually manifested by its corporate goals and objectives. Thus, IRM is the managerial link that connects corporate information resources with the organization's goals and objectives.

Significant and laudable as the corporate interest may be, however, it is not the sole professional or functional focus of the entire field of information management. Information management deals with many issues, serves many masters and is performed in many contexts. As a general topic, it is beyond the scope of our book, but we will describe and identify the broad areas of information management to indicate how IRM — and our discovery process — fit in.

The term "information" does not refer to some solitary monolith. Even with our fragmented and primitive understanding of information — its nature, characteristics, uses, costs and values — we know that a host of distinctions can and should be made. Some dialects of the Inuit of northern Canada distinguish more than 50 words for the two common English words "ice" and "snow".[5] As reflected in the Glossary, information scientists, managers and practitioners have come to recognize a wide variety of "information" genres, and they are gradually developing and refining a growing number of information categories. So when we speak of *managing* information, we should speak of managing certain components, elements or aspects of information — not the whole thing all at once. Just as the Inuit are able to construct their igloos only with blocks of the right varieties of "snow" and "ice," so too are information managers able to apply their kit of management tools only to certain elements of "information," in certain contexts.

The model in Fig. 1-2 isolates the scope of information resources management (IRM) within the broader framework of information management (IM). Four general terms are used in a simple two-level hierarchy, as follows.

Information Management (IM). The most general term refers to application of one or more of the traditional management processes, such as planning, organizing, staffing, directing or controlling, to an

Figure 1-2. A model of the scope of information management.

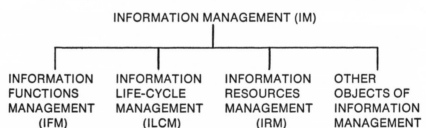

INFORMATION MANAGEMENT (IM)

| INFORMATION FUNCTIONS MANAGEMENT (IFM) | INFORMATION LIFE-CYCLE MANAGEMENT (ILCM) | INFORMATION RESOURCES MANAGEMENT (IRM) | OTHER OBJECTS OF INFORMATION MANAGEMENT |

information entity or entities. Without explicit or implicit qualification, the term information management is neutral; that is, it does not imply any specific entity, context or object of management. Three such objects to which IM processes apply are shown at the second level of the hierarchy.

Information Functions Management (IFM). This area of information management refers to application of the traditional management processes to one or more individual specialized *functional* areas; for instance, data processing, micrographics and records. In this area of IM, attention is focussed mainly on the management of media or conduits for information, not on information itself. For example, management of the micrographics function deals primarily with camera recording equipment and microforms such as microfilm and microfiche.

When information is handled or processed — reproduced, sorted, rearranged, displayed and so on — the activity is sometimes described as "information management." We prefer to describe these activities in terms of what, generically, they actually are or do (e.g. photocopying, data administration, typesetting), reserving the term information management for the application of *management* processes.

Information Life-Cycle Management (ILCM). This area of IM refers to application of the traditional management processes to one or more, or all, of the information *life-cycle* stages, such as acquisition, storage, retrieval, processing and disposal. Emphasis overall in this category is on management of information content, independent of media or conduit. For example, in the records management field, information content, not the media, governs decisions on whether and when records will be archived or purged. Comprehensive and integrated management by a single organization of the entire life-cycle of a particular type of information is not common, but nearly every organization is engaged in the management of some life-cycle stages, especially acquisition, processing and storage. For example, rekeying data at each successive stage is still a common problem. One goal of ILCM is to integrate the life-cycle stages to eliminate the unnecessarily duplicative and redundant re-entry of source data already captured.

Information Resources Management (IRM). Narrowing to the subject of this chapter, IRM refers to the application of traditional management processes, particularly resource management principles, to the stewardship of an organization's information resources and assets. Corporate IRM policies focus on inventorying, defining requirements, costing, valuing and fixing accountability for safe-keeping and results. Application of IRM practices implies that knowledge exists on specific organizational resources. Emphasis overall is on serving the corporate interest; for example, improving a service or product, maximizing cash flow or discovering a new market niche.

Other Objects of Information Management. Although the three areas just described probably cover most of the IM field, information management also deals with other areas. For instance, we manage information *values* (e.g. Table 3-5) and information *assets* (e.g. Fig 3-2). And we apply information management practices to the marketing of information *products and services.*

As summarized in Fig. 1-3, information resources management (IRM) is the process whereby organizations optimize the spending of their information resource dollars to achieve their strategic objectives.[6] Overall, IRM is a *management* process, one of several that most organizations apply. Others in the same category are human resources management (for labor), financial management (for money), real property management (for land and buildings), and material management (for equipment and stores). However, we will not be addressing the "how" of IRM. That is, we will not be prescribing any of the ongoing, operational management processes associated with information resources. Our primary objective is to describe methods that find out what the resources *are*. We believe this knowledge is a prerequisite to dealing with the "how" question. First we should provide top management with the "what" of information resources — their identification, location, cost, value and assessment.

Thus, our interest in Fig. 1-3 is not to explain and elaborate upon the entire IRM process, with all of its ramifications for the multitude of information management functions, roles and responsibilities typically found in most organizations. We will sketch just enough of the general process to place the box labelled "Information Resource Entities" in a management context. Then we will deal exclusively with methods to discover these entities.

The IRM process (Fig. 1-3) balances two opposing forces. One is the demand from individual and corporate users for all of the information deemed necessary — and perhaps then some — to carry out or support the organization's activities. Opposing this potentially unbridled demand for more and better information are resource management principles which are applied to ensure value for

Figure 1-3. IRM chart: The information resources management
process.

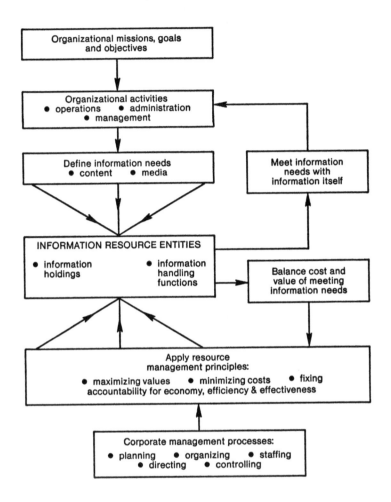

money. Paradoxically, users often, even at the same time, impose
negative demands for information. That is, information available to
the organization, which could or should be used, is *not* sought.
Information overload is another negative demand. Again, these
demands are counteracted by the application of resource management principles. Resource management practices are applied
through the traditional corporate management processes of
planning, organizing, staffing, directing and controlling.[7]

According to the IRM concept, the information resource entities
maintained and used to meet information demands exist solely to

satisfy information requirements defined by corporate users, including users in both operations and administration. Generally, however, most of the organization's information resources exist to support operations since this is where the *strategic* activities are located. All corporate activities, together with the information necessary to achieve them are there to meet organizational missions, goals and objectives, IRM's ultimate driving force.

We have already made reference to problems with terminology in describing information in general and IRM's place within the field of information management. The lexical difficulties within IRM itself are no less troublesome: A lack of specific terms to express certain concepts, the absence of a commonly understood typology for information concepts, multiple definitions of the same term and inconsistent definitions of related terms. To assist readers in sorting out these semantic difficulties, the Glossary lists the technical and specialized terms we have used and selected general terms.[8]

1.4   THE NATURE OF INFORMATION RESOURCES

What and where are your information resources? And by what process can they be identified? Managers must face up to these practical questions if they genuinely accept the concept that information is a costly and valuable resource and one of strategic significance. If a resource, information should be managed in accordance with resource management principles. But exactly what is a resource? And what are the principles of resource management? Finally, managers may ask: What are the basic units of measurement of this "new", intangible resource?

Although most managers usually equate the term resource directly with certain *specific things*, usually tangible items such as people, land and energy, an examination of the evolution of resource management shows us that what we specifically regard as resources derive from *circumstances*, not from the intrinsic nature of the entities. One definition holds that a resource is:

A source of supply, support or aid, especially one held in reserve.[9]

Following this concept, a resource should be thought of fundamentally as a *source* or *reservoir* of something needed or important in the circumstances. A resource is something critical to achieving success and for which there is a real, potential or perceived shortage. For example, such shortages during the past decade — oil and gas, strategic minerals, fresh water and clean air — have brought about the "conserver society" attitude and with it a heightened awareness of the relevance of resource management principles. Optimize, exploit, conserve and enhance are the operative verbs of the '80s.[10]

The history of the resource management function, summarized in Table 1-1, shows that in changing and evolving economic and social circumstances, business and government have come to identify a number of distinctive resources. Like money, labor, land, raw

Table 1-1. Evolution of resource management functions.

Resource	Function	Began	Causes
Money/capital	Financial management	1920s	Heightened investment awareness, capital shortages and depression
People	Personnel management	1930s	Advances in behavioral sciences and social forces (unions, working conditions)
Equipment & supplies; raw materials	Materiel management	1940s	World War II; critical shortage forecasts for strategic stockpiles
Land & buildings	Space & property management	1940s	Need for prudent use of office/plant/laboratory space
Energy	Energy resources management	1970s	OPEC embargo; declining reserves of oil & gas; new alternative sources
Information	Information resources management	1970s	Computers; information explosion; paperwork burden on taxpayers
Knowledge	Knowledge management	1980s	Expert systems; artificial intelligence; economic & cultural value of knowledge

Source: Modified from Forest W. Horton, Jr., *Information Resources Management: Concept and Cases,* (Cleveland, Ohio: Association for Systems Management, 1979, Fig. 2-3). Reprinted with permission.

materials and energy, information has come also to be recognized as a resource, not because of any intrinsic characteristics, but because of the *role* information was beginning to play during the early '60s in government laws and policies (e.g. copyright revision, privacy), in the economy (e.g. the ascendancy of white-collar office workers) and in the success, or failure, of increasingly competitive business organizations.[11]

Narrowing our perspective from an institutional view of the resources of business and government in general, to those of an individual organization, as they might be seen from the top by its Chief Executive Officer, the same logic applies to the identification of *organizational* resources, including information resources. The CEO might ask: What information used by my organization is critical to achieving success? An analysis of (literally) all information holdings and functions within a typical organization, tested against resource criteria, would probably show that only some of its information holdings and functions are in fact resources. The rest is either overhead, of personal interest only or otherwise of little or no value. But in virtually all organizations, we would find a number of specific information entities that would be identified as corporate resources — reservoirs of supply, support or aid critical to the achievement of organizational goals and objectives.

As already pointed out, the information resources management (IRM) process involves, simultaneously, the *meaning* of information — also referred to as "information itself" or information "content" — and the *means* through which information is obtained or delivered, involving generation, processing, storing and so on. When information entities play a critical role, both the information itself and its associated means of delivery or access (broadly, the sources) together constitute the information *resources* of the organization.

Figure 1-4 shows the conceptual and semantic distinctions we are making between "information itself," "information resource entities" and "information resources," and indicates that they originate from the configuration of other resources. The main focus of this book is on the information resource entities — what they are, how to locate them and how to assess their significance to the organization (the IRE concept is described later in 1.4.3). Because the process of inventorying information itself is a function of the unique circumstances of each organization and operation, and the particular use contexts to which the information is put, we cannot deal with it directly as part of our generalized discovery process. On

Figure 1-4. Transformation of resources to information resource entities and to information itself, showing scope of the term information resources.

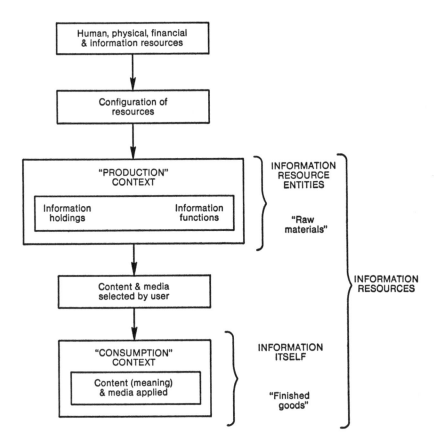

the other hand, we cannot ignore the linkages between the two, because the value of an information resource entity is a direct function of the value of information acquired or produced.

The linkage or relationship in the model (Fig. 1-4) between information itself and information resource entities alludes to the linkage at the practical level between 1) operations and other production activities and 2) management of the resources needed to support those operations. The value of having the right information content at the right time, in the right form and at the right cost, can be realized only to the extent the available resource base permits. Conversely, the maintenance of information holdings and information handling functions which collect, store or provide data of little or no use to the organization represents a waste of funds, time and other scarce resources.

The production of information is both similar to and dissimilar from the production (manufacture) of a physical commodity. However, we believe the generation of information products and services, including those generated by an organization for internal consumption only, can be seen as usefully analogous to the manufacture of physical consumer goods, as illustrated by some of the terms used in Fig. 1-4. In each case, various kinds of raw material resources are procured, stored and then melded together in the manufacturing (production) process. Information resource entities, including both information holdings and information handling functions, are the capital of the information production process; that is, they are the agents or factors of production responsible for the creation of the finished goods for use or consumption by users or consumers.[12]

Unlike most consumer goods, however, the finished information goods "consumed" by users represent a very broad spectrum of customized products because each user assigns a different marketplace utility to the same information product or service, based on the user's unique consumption context. In contrast, the uses of non-information goods and services are much more generic and standardized, and therefore their marketplace utility and price are far easier to ascertain.

While the fundamental nature of information itself in a cognitive sense is a topic beyond the scope of this book, we cannot avoid it entirely. Nor should we, for reasons pointed out above. So now we examine some of the characteristics of information and of the information resource entities from which it is derived, all of which affect our perception of "information as a resource."

1.4.1 Similarities with Other Resources

Our snapshot of the history of resource management (Table 1-1) illustrates the wide range of entities — money, people, space, energy and so on — that over a number of years have come under the resource management umbrella. While sharing certain features, each resource type has its own distinctive characteristics which impose different demands on management methods and skills. For example, there are few similarities among the different basic units of resource measurement — a dollar, a person, a building and a kilowatt hour.

Some have argued that information is so different from the traditional, mostly tangible resources that it defies application of *any* resource management process. However, each of the recognized resources is distinctive in its own right — not only information — and so in this respect information resources are no different. In short, information is in various respects both similar and dissimilar to the other resources.

Among the resource-related characteristics that information shares with the traditional resources, we can list the following:

- Information is acquired at a cost, measurable in dollars.
- Information possesses values, some quantifiable; some is treated as an asset in a financial accounting sense.
- Information "consumption" can be either expensed or capitalized.
- Cost accounting techniques can be applied to help control the costs of information.
- Information has identifiable and measurable characteristics.
- Information has a life-cycle: Requirements definition, collection, transmission, processing, storage, dissemination, use and disposition.
- Information has the capacity to be processed and refined, whereby raw materials (e.g. databases) are transformed into finished products (e.g. published directories).
- Substitutes for specific information are available — some cheaper, some more expensive.
- Choices are available to management in making tradeoffs between different grades, types and prices for information.[13]

These similarities are striking. They suggest that we are indeed dealing with a resource somewhat like the others. To the extent that the characteristics of information are similar to those of other resources, we can apply methods and techniques for the management of information resources that are familiar and workable. However, it is the unique attributes of information that pose the difficulties we have all encountered when first attempting to treat information as a manageable resource.[14]

1.4.2 Differences with Other Resources

What are these unique attributes? Harlan Cleveland provides a vivid description of the unique, sometimes paradoxical qualities of information. These are the attributes, so different from those of the other, mostly tangible resources, that seem to be at the root of our difficulty in dealing with information "as a resource." Yet to manage it we must come to understand, accept, reconcile and exploit all of these characteristics.

> 1. *Information is expandable.* . . . . . information expands as it is used. . . . . . Whole industries have grown up to exploit this characteristic of information: scientific research, technology transfer, computer software . . . . . and agencies for publishing, advertising, public relations and government propaganda . . . . . the facts are never all in. . . . . .

> 2. *Information is compressible.* Paradoxically, this infinitely expandable resource can be concentrated, integrated, summarized — miniaturized, if you will — for easier handling. . . . . .

> 3. *Information is substitutable.* It can replace capital, labor or physical materials. Robotics and automation in factories and offices are displacing workers and thus requiring a transformation of the labor force. . . . . .

> 4. *Information is transportable* — at the speed of light, and, perhaps, through telepathy, faster than that. In less than a century we have been witness to a major dimensional change in both the speed and volume of human activity. . . . . .

> 5. *Information is diffusive.* It tends to leak — and the more it leaks the more we have. Information is aggressive — even imperialistic — in striving to break out of the unnatural bonds of secrecy in which thing-minded people try to imprison it. . . . . . The straightjackets of public secrecy, intellectual property rights and confidentiality of all kinds fit very loosely on this restless resource.

> 6. *Information is sharable.* . . . . . information by nature cannot give rise to exchange transactions, only to *sharing* transactions. *Things* are exchanged: if I give you a flower or sell you my automobile, you have it and I don't. But if I sell you an idea, we both have it. . . . . .

Cleveland concludes that information is, indeed, different in kind from other resources. Nevertheless, it has become "the basic, yet abstract resource".[15]

No wonder that many managers, accustomed to dealing with the traditional resources, are bewildered by admonitions to manage their information *as a resource*! But if they would reflect on the rationale for recognizing land, labor and capital as resources, then they would see that it is the *role* that information plays which distinguishes it as an organizational resource, not its similarities to the other resources. In particular, too much is sometimes made of the need for something to be a tangible "thing" for it to be recognized as a resource.

1.4.3 The Information Resource Entity (IRE)

Given these peculiar characteristics, how should corporate managers go about exercising managerial control of information; or, so to speak, how can they get a handle on it? Many have experienced utter frustration with attempts to manage information, likening it to the task of sweeping feathers out of a room. The endless discussions, the misunderstood semantics and the lack of proven techniques are legend. The solution we are advocating — to carry out a discovery process — is based on the identification of specific information entities used by the organization that we will call *information resource entities*, or IREs for short.

What sort of entities might these be? Basically, an information resource entity or IRE is a configuration of people, things, energy, information and other inputs that has the capacity to create, acquire, provide, process, store or disseminate information; in short, the entities are those information holdings and information handling functions that are, or should be, or could be, managed as organizational resources. In most cases they are specific, named and structured configurations. However, in some situations, some resource entities may be diffused, without structure and unrecognized. Our concept of an information resource entity — a configured amalgam of various "input" resources — may be likened to the view that the primary constituents (resources) of a biological being are the cells, tissues and organs, each a functional entity in its own right, yet forming part of a larger, interconnected living system.

The two essential, interdependent capacities of an information resource entity are: 1) To provide information content, and 2) to store and/or process information. The latter is a function of the medium or conduit used to receive, store or transmit the content. Individual IREs are combinations of content and medium: If all conceivable IREs were arrayed, they would form a spectrum ranging from nearly pure content, such as a collection of top management reports, to nearly pure medium, such as the telephone and mail systems, or to pure medium such as a blank page of paper. The vast majority of information resource entities fall between these end-members, merging imperceptibly according to the relative proportions of content and medium they represent.

In official U.S. Federal Government parlance, the two terms that come closest to the "information resource entity" idea we advance here are: 1) Information system, and 2) information technology facility. The former term is defined as "the organized collection, processing, transmission and dissemination of information in accordance with defined procedures, whether automated or manual." The latter is defined as "an organizationally defined set of personnel, hardware, software and physical facilities, a primary function of which is the operation of information technology."[16]

Thus defined, however, neither term evokes, at least directly, the critical notion of information *content* as a basic constituent of the entity. Both definitions are "systems" and "technology" oriented, ignoring the vast numbers of information sources and services that are neither systems nor based on technology. And, a more glaring omission, ignoring the subject, nature and purpose of the information that is processed.

The general character and scope of what we are calling information resource entities appears to have been first described by Harvard University's Center for Information Policy Research. It developed a series of maps of the information business to portray the total range of business entities in the United States' information industry; about 80 entities are positioned with reference to the extent to which each represents, in one dimension, *content* and *conduit* (or media), and in another dimension, *product* and *service* (Fig. 1-5).[17] Clearly, more than systems and high tech are involved. Later, in Chapter 4, we will apply this technique to construct a map that shows the entire range of information resources within an organization.

Other Concepts of Information Resources. At least two other concepts of what constitutes an "information resource" have been advanced: The "resource input" model, and the "information content" model. The former, used by the U.S. Federal Government within the context of information resources management policies that were developed pursuant to the *Paperwork Reduction Act of 1980*, holds that the basic resource entities, in addition to *information itself*, are *personnel, equipment, funds, technology* and other related resources, which is to say, the resource inputs to information.[18]

Although there is much to favor this straightforward approach, especially since these entities can be directly related to many existing accounting, control and inventory systems, it suffers from the fact that identification of the specific inputs, such as personnel,

Figure 1-5. John McLaughlin and Anne Birinyi's map of the information business, showing the spectrum of information business entities active in the United States.

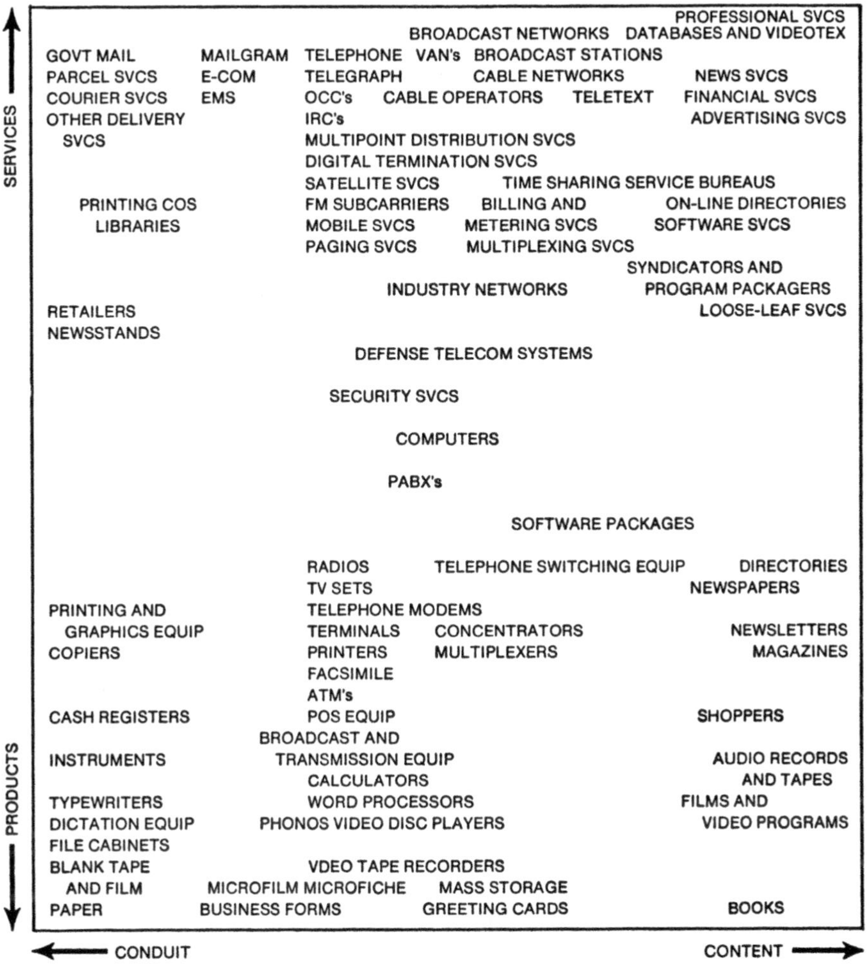

```
                                                         PROFESSIONAL SVCS
                                    BROADCAST NETWORKS  DATABASES AND VIDEOTEX
  GOVT MAIL          MAILGRAM   TELEPHONE  VAN's  BROADCAST STATIONS
  PARCEL SVCS        E-COM      TELEGRAPH        CABLE NETWORKS        NEWS SVCS
  COURIER SVCS       EMS        OCC's   CABLE OPERATORS   TELETEXT   FINANCIAL SVCS
  OTHER DELIVERY                IRC's                                 ADVERTISING SVCS
    SVCS                        MULTIPOINT DISTRIBUTION SVCS
                               DIGITAL TERMINATION SVCS
                               SATELLITE SVCS      TIME SHARING SERVICE BUREAUS
  PRINTING COS                 FM SUBCARRIERS   BILLING AND        ON-LINE DIRECTORIES
    LIBRARIES                  MOBILE SVCS      METERING SVCS      SOFTWARE SVCS
                               PAGING SVCS      MULTIPLEXING SVCS
                                                          SYNDICATORS AND
                               INDUSTRY NETWORKS          PROGRAM PACKAGERS
  RETAILERS                                               LOOSE-LEAF SVCS
  NEWSSTANDS
                               DEFENSE TELECOM SYSTEMS

                               SECURITY SVCS

                                    COMPUTERS

                                PABX's

                                     SOFTWARE PACKAGES

                     RADIOS        TELEPHONE SWITCHING EQUIP    DIRECTORIES
                     TV SETS                                    NEWSPAPERS
  PRINTING AND       TELEPHONE MODEMS
    GRAPHICS EQUIP   TERMINALS   CONCENTRATORS               NEWSLETTERS
  COPIERS            PRINTERS    MULTIPLEXERS                MAGAZINES
                     FACSIMILE
                     ATM's
  CASH REGISTERS     POS EQUIP                              SHOPPERS
                     BROADCAST AND
  INSTRUMENTS        TRANSMISSION EQUIP                     AUDIO RECORDS
                     CALCULATORS                            AND TAPES
  TYPEWRITERS        WORD PROCESSORS                        FILMS AND
  DICTATION EQUIP    PHONOS VIDEO DISC PLAYERS              VIDEO PROGRAMS
  FILE CABINETS
  BLANK TAPE              VDEO TAPE RECORDERS
    AND FILM      MICROFILM MICROFICHE    MASS STORAGE
  PAPER          BUSINESS FORMS       GREETING CARDS        BOOKS
```

CONDUIT ◄———   ———► CONTENT

SERVICES (vertical, top) / PRODUCTS (vertical, bottom)

ATM—Automated Teller Machine; E-COM—Electronic Computer Originated Mail; EMS—Electronic Message Service; IRC—International Record Carrier; OCC—Other Common Carrier; PABX—Private Automatic Branch Exchange; POS—Point-of-State; VAN—Value Added Network

Source: Reprinted with permission from Benjamin M. Compaine's *Understanding New Media: Trends and Issues in Electronic Distribution of Information.* Copyright 1984, Ballinger Publishing Company.

begs the two basic questions of 1) how to know whether a given input resource is related to an *information* entity, and 2) whether or not the information entity so identified, such as a library, is in fact a *corporate resource* or something else, such as overhead.

In order to count all the people, offices, computers, software packages, overhead dollars and so on that form the *inputs* to the organization's *information* entities, we would need an inventory of the sources, services, systems or other information entities that constitute the organization's information resource base. These two views of resources can be related by a simple matrix, shown in Fig. 1-6, which forms a bridge between the traditional resource accounting schemata (e.g. for personnel, space) and the new accounting schema needed for information resources (sources, services and systems). In the not too distant future, new accounting and management structures will be required to explicitly recognize *information* entities, in addition to those of a human, physical and monetary nature.[19]

To continue with our biological metaphor: The "resource input" view of information resources is analogous to considering that the basic organic elements of a living being are water and minerals, as opposed to cells and organs. As it is true that the water/mineral approach misses the essential property of *life* in a biological system, likewise, the people/hardware/software approach to information resources misses the essential property of intellectual content or *meaning*.

The third concept of an information resource holds that only information content, or information itself, constitutes the basic resource entity.[20] Using this model, everything else involved in handling and producing information is ignored, and the management process deals exclusively with the information itself, through management of names, attributes, values and other representational symbols. The main obstacle to managing content in isolation is that content, from a practical management point of view, cannot be arbitrarily divorced from the media or handling functions. Content is inextricably bound with both the container and the source, the central thought expressed in Marshall McLuhan's dictum "the medium is the message."

In short, our concept of information resources includes 1) information itself and 2) information resource entities (IREs). IREs are configurations of people, hardware, materiel, space, software, information and other input resources which we describe broadly as information holdings and information handling functions, or, alternatively, as information sources, services and systems (Fig. 1-4).

Figure 1-6. Information resource matrix. This model links conventional "economic" resources with information resources.

	INFORMATION RESOURCE ENTITIES (IREs)			
	Sources	Services		Systems
		Specific Entities		
	A	B	C	D
Hardware	$	$	$	$
Software	$	$	$	$
Personnel	$	$	$	$
Space	$	$	$	$
Capital	$	$	$	$
Overhead	$	$	$	$
Other cost elements	$	$	$	$
Total dollar costs for each IRE	$	$	$	$

(Left side vertical label: RESOURCE INPUTS)

1.5 CONTEXT: THE IMPORTANCE OF UNDERSTANDING THE BUSINESS

We have described the nature of information resource entities in terms of their similarities and dissimilarities with the traditional resources. To risk belaboring the point, nothing is inherently a resource; in particular, information is not a resource just because it is information. To identify information resources, you must understand the context. This follows from our review of the role of context in the recognition of resources generally (Table 1-1). In more practical terms, you must understand the business before you can be sure of knowing a resource when you see one.

Context plays a pivotal role in the recognition not only of resources of any kind, but in the recognition of information itself and of related concepts such as data, information assets and so on. Scholars such as Robert Taylor have begun to investigate and understand how organizational information environments, or more simply, context, influences or controls the value we place on information. As a minimum, one needs to know what an organization does, who its clientele, customers, constituencies or publics are, and what they demand or expect from the organization (that is, the context), before the value and resource significance of the organization's information can be understood and assessed.[21]

Just as context plays a role in defining resources, so also does the context differentiate data from information, as Gordon Williams clearly illustrates in connection with the application of geological data systems (Fig. 1-7). For our purposes, his diagram illustrates how information resources in one context, say that of a surveying company determining the geographic coordinates and elevation of mine shafts and oil wells, are irrelevant to meeting the information needs of the exploration manager, who is concerned with access to information resources such as geological maps and economic forecasting data, among others. And information resources used by, say, government policy-makers are different again and are of no value to either the exploration manager or the surveying company.[22] We do not want to imply that we believe everyone's information resource needs are so straightforward. To the contrary, they are usually exceedingly diverse. Our point is that the recognition and value of information resources are determined by a particular context, not by an externally imposed logic or the nature of the resource entity alone.

Planning for the acquisition and management of information resources requires sound knowledge of the business. For example, Philip James has described a strategic planning process for information resources in which he emphasizes that the critical first step is to acquire an understanding of the organization being supported. The second step in his methodology is environmental analysis, recognizing that an organization's information resource is imbedded in a complex milieu that includes the business environment

Figure 1-7. Gordon Williams' hierarchy of functional roles in the mineral exploration business, showing a hierarchy of "information" output serving as "data" input at the next higher level.

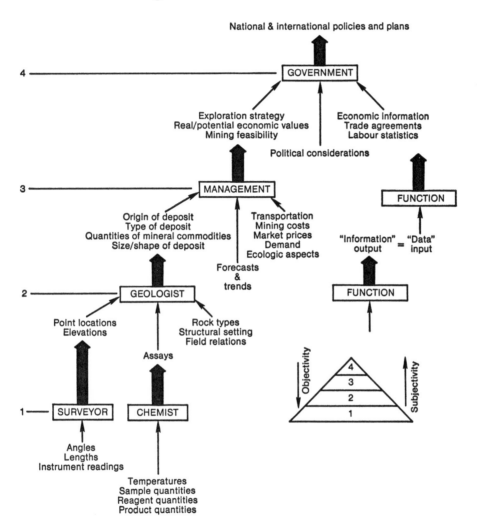

Source: Modified from Gordon D. Williams, "Advantages to Using a Generalized System to Manage Geological Data," in *Computer-Based Systems for Geological Field Data*, (Ottawa, Ont.: Energy, Mines and Resources Canada, 1975). Reproduced with permission of the Minister of Supply and Services Canada.

and marketplace in which it operates; the social, political and
economic environment in which it conducts business and the
information resources management profession.

Thirdly, James addresses synthesis of the results of the first and
second strategic planning steps. He proceeds iteratively with a
consideration of markets, stakeholders, competitors and so forth.
Taking the case of an information systems department, viewed as an
organizational resource, Table 1-2 identifies 14 elements that James'
strategic planning process would address. Clearly, a sound knowledge of the business would be a prerequisite to developing and
carrying out such a planning process.[23]

1.6 NEEDED: INFORMATION RESOURCE MAPPING METHODS

To develop an integrative conceptual framework for the management of information resources we need methods for defining,
identifying, locating and measuring, in short for mapping the
resources. Geoscientists and managers in the mineral and petroleum
industries have long used and depended upon maps to intelligently
and effectively go about their business of exploring for new resources and exploiting those already discovered. Likewise, governments need and use demographic, natural resource and economic
activity maps, among others, to manage national resources. Real
property managers use maps, blueprints and drawings to show
where their lands and buildings are located. Personnel managers
use maps in the form of aptitude tests, biographies and performance
evaluation tools. Maps come in many different shapes and sizes, and
serve many different purposes. They are fundamental to sound
resource management, yet often taken for granted.

To effectively manage information as a resource, we need
equivalent tools for the managers. Maps are needed to evolve a
deeper understanding of the role of information resources in the
firm. To do that we need guideposts and symbols to use maps
efficiently. For example, traditional map symbols for cartographic
maps identify physical, social, economic and political terrain attributes, including different kinds of transportation infrastructures,
boundaries, water bodies, elevation, demographic units, historical
landmarks, and indications of unnavigable and uninhabitable areas.
So we must have legends for information maps to distinguish
information resource attributes and characteristics, and to help us
find our way through the data labyrinth.

Table 1-2. Philip James' elements of strategic planning for an information systems department, as seen from an information resources management perspective.

Market. . . . usually the needs of the organization it supports.

Mission and market share. The department's mission may be to satisfy all information needs . . . or management may prefer to segment the market . . .

Strategic vision. A statement of the department's philosophy and of the long-range goals it seeks to achieve . . .

Objectives. Objectives are specific, quantifiable results that must occur if the department's goals are to be achieved.

Milestones. For each objective, milestones represent the identifiable events en route to its achievement, with planned dates.

Roadblocks. This element includes anything the department foresees as an obstacle to achieving an objective, together with a strategy for minimizing its impact.

Customers and stakeholders. Customers actually buy services . . . Stakeholders have an interest in what the department does and can affect its success . . .

Competitors. . . . those who seek to replace the department in providing for its customers' needs . . .

Strengths and weaknesses. If it is to compete effectively, the department must have a clear understanding of its strengths and weaknesses as well as those of each of its competitors . . .

Opportunities and threats. A key element in the competitive environment is just that: the environment . . . the state of the economy, the state of technology and anything else that could conceivably affect the department's ability to compete . . .

Action plans. The planning process is not complete until action plans . . . are in place . . .

Issues. Many issues surface and are resolved during the planning process. . .

Critical success factors. These are the select factors that must go right if the department is to succeed. They are leading indicators, not trailing indicators such as accounting data.

Scenarios. Often the best way to develop an understanding of the department's strategic vision is through the use of scenarios . . .

Source: Philip N. James, "A Framework for Strategic and Long-Range Information Resource Planning," *Information Strategy*, Fall, 1985. Copyright Auerbach Publishers, Inc. Reprinted with permission.

Legends are needed to distinguish information functions from information holdings; to specify whether input, storage and output media are paper, microform, magnetic disk or drum, floppy disk, coaxial cable, satellite, broad band, optical disk or CD-ROM. Legends are needed to specify the information resource entity in the context of the information life-cycle (creation, intermediate handling and processing to add value, storage or retrieval, communication to users, use and re-use, and final disposition) as well as in the context of management's processes (planning, design and development, budgeting, accounting, control and evaluation).

The field of cartography has been developed over centuries, applying many conventions for formatting and portraying maps of all kinds. Thus, local and global grid systems came into existence. We are familiar with degrees of latitude and longitude and the principal global reference points: The North and South Poles, the Equator and the Royal Observatory at Greenwich. We will put forward several analogous techniques for mapping information resources that may seem crude by comparison — but we believe such maps are helpful to information managers, functional department heads and users in understanding the full complexity and richness of the total organizational information resource.

Until now, most organizations have approached the discovery and mapping challenge with two serious shortcomings. First, many have tended to look at their information resources vertically, typically in a compartmentalized fashion, instead of horizontally, in an integrated fashion. Second, many have conceptualized their information resources as a necessary expense (cost of doing business) instead of a capitalized asset. Consequently, the units they've measured, the aggregates they've distilled and the management reports they've produced to illuminate the costs and values of information, have been badly flawed. For example, the public accounts of the Canadian Federal Government list "information" as an expenditure item, but it includes only publishing, printing, advertising and exposition services. Expenditures on computers, databases, libraries, records and the other information functions and holdings are buried in other accounting categories.[24]

Our methodology for discovering and mapping information resources endeavors to correct these two shortcomings. We look horizontally at the entire spectrum of information resources. Not in some blind, theoretical way that, say, tries to equate mathematically a line of programmer code for an inventory control system with the output from a million-dollar, computer-based enterprise modelling system, but in a common-sense manner that illuminates relative costs and values, using familiar classification schemes, weighting systems and analytical methods.

We deliberately apply a holistic approach to information management, rather than take up the entire array of information assets piecemeal, discipline by discipline, technology by technology, domain by domain. As the reader will know, if one goes to a library or book store to find out about information resources, one is faced with the reality that lexicographers have yet to carve a niche for information resources management. Instead, one is forced to make a choice among a whole array of titles: Books on computers, telecommunications, information systems, human resources, the industrial management of facilities and plant, and books on libraries and information services, among many others.

If your organization wishes to continue managing its information holdings and handling functions as a "necessary overhead expense," then you won't need this book. Or, if your company is content trying to control the dollars it spends for computers, networks, printing and publishing, information centers and so on, on a totally decentralized basis with no overall corporate information management strategy or policy, then you'll probably find the book of marginal value. But if you have decided that your organization must try a fresh approach to getting on top of its information handling, then you owe it to yourself to discover all of your information resources.

1.7 OVERVIEW OF THE INFORMATION RESOURCE DISCOVERY PROCESS

We have developed the concept of the information resource entity (IRE) as the unit of measurement in the information resources management process. IREs are configurations of equipment, technology, personnel, space and other input resources that play individual, "organic" roles in the information life-cycle. Typically they are manifested as named sources, services and systems. The purpose of the information resource discovery process, described in the chapters that follow, is to locate or discover such entities used by, or of potential use to, the organization. Figure 1-8 outlines the four basic steps. In summary, this is what they are.[25]

Figure 1-8. Overview chart: Overview of the information resource discovery process, showing the four steps
described in Chapters 2 to 5.

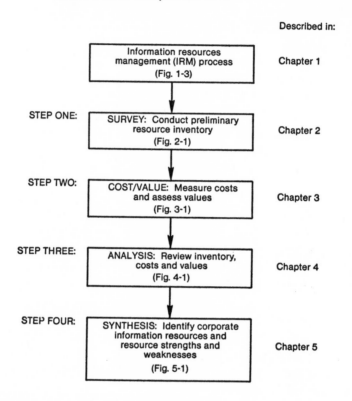

STEP ONE: The first is a *survey*, to find out in a preliminary fashion
what specific resource entities exist within, or are used by the
organization. To organize the data collected, you must develop a
tentative model of the entities you expect to encounter. The
resulting compilation of sources, services and systems will be a
preliminary inventory; preliminary in the sense that the strategic
dimensions are unknown at this point.

STEP TWO: Next, the *cost and value* of the entities identified in the
preliminary survey are examined. Since information costing and
valuing is a new field, particularly as applied to internal corporate
settings, a wide range of approaches, methods and techniques must
be evaluated and applied. The general objective is to derive some
kind of cost/value ratio for each of the entities, even if only rough
approximations.

STEP THREE: In the third step, *analysis*, the inventory and cost/
value data are examined to find out where the resources are

distributed throughout the organization, what the basic nature of each resource entity is and to determine the magnitude and location of costs and values. The various charts and maps produced form springboards for raising pertinent questions on management policies, practices and accountability, in addition to highlighting gaps, overlaps and redundancies among the various holdings and functions identified.

STEP FOUR: In the final step, *synthesis*, the organization's information resources are identified, a sense of their value in relation to cost is obtained and accountability for performance is ascertained. An assessment is carried out of the quality of the identified resources, expressed in terms of relative strengths and weaknesses. Other outputs, byproducts of the resource discovery process, may include illumination of various information management issues, including for example need for a corporate-wide information resources management program.

Our descriptions in Chapters 2 to 5 of the four steps outlined above are encapsulated in flow-chart form in four master charts, providing the reader with general visual guides to each step (Figs. 2-1, 3-1, 4-1, 5-1). Collectively, the charts summarize the entire discovery process.

Case Examples. We will illustrate the various aspects of the information resource discovery process, to the extent possible, with practical examples. However, as the approach has been under gradual development, and is fully explained here for the first time, there are no individual case examples which illustrate the entire process we describe, Steps One through Four, from beginning to end.

The major case study is CRA Exploration Pty. Limited (see Box). We will describe its survey and the resulting preliminary resource inventory (Step One), and certain components of the analysis (Step Three) and synthesis (Step Four) phases. Other case example material, illustrating particular points, will be drawn from the following organizations:

Commission on Federal Paperwork (U.S.)

Department of Energy, Mines and Resources (Canada)

Government of Canada

Smithsonian Institution

U.S. Department of the Army Headquarters

U.S. Environmental Protection Agency

U.S. General Accounting Office

**Case Example:
CRA Exploration Pty. Limited**

This Australian mineral exploration company, which provided the main case example illustrating the information resource discovery process, especially Steps One and Three, is wholly owned by CRA Limited, one of Australia's major industrial corporations. CRA Exploration (or CRAE) manages and conducts exploration for and on behalf of CRA Group's companies. At the time (1982) its activities extended throughout Australia, Papua New Guinea, the South Pacific, New Zealand, Southeast Asia, the North and South American continents and Europe. Its efforts were directed to particularly, but not limited to, the search for copper, lead/zinc, nickel, coal, gold, tin, diamonds and uranium.[26] CRAE had operating divisions located in a number of Australian localities, of which 10 were visited during the case study reported here. Total staff at the time was about 450, primarily geologists, geophysicists, researchers and related support staff such as mineral lease specialists, draftsmen and computer support personnel. Corporate management and administration was provided by a small group headquartered in Melbourne.

The case material reported was carried out by one of us (Burk) during March-April 1982.

1.8 OPTIONS FOR IMPLEMENTATION

At first glance, the complete discovery process may appear long and complex. For some organizations this may be true. We do not minimize the costs, yet in view of the benefits they are probably not unreasonable. Moreover, we do not offer an all-or-nothing approach. We outline three scenarios for implementation:

1. You could travel the complete journey, passing through all regions of all four Steps,
2. You could take a quick trip, a short-cut to reach a specific objective in minimum time, or
3. You could take a scenic route, visiting all sites of interest, but bypassing some.

Each option has its benefits and costs. After reviewing your own situation, you can decide what's best for your organization. Apply only those Steps, techniques, charts and aids that are really needed.

Remember, we are describing the possibilities for a single project only. If you decide to continue any of the resource discovery functions into the future, other considerations would apply.

Option 1: The Complete Journey. To receive the complete range of benefits from our methods, as described earlier in this chapter (1.1), the estimated direct costs would probably be in the $30,000 to $100,000 range. It would likely take about three months to complete in a medium-sized organization of average complexity. One or two individuals would be required on a full-time basis, with access to automated tools. The actual cost would depend mainly on the nature, size and complexity of the organization, and whether the project was staffed internally or by consultants.

Option 2: The Quick Trip. The complete journey may be too long or arduous for some organizations. Perhaps time and resources are simply not available; or maybe your needs dictate that only portions of the mapping process are relevant. Whatever the reasons, there are ways of shortening the journey.

One way to reduce the effort is to restrict the scope of the discovery process, either horizontally or vertically. For example, it could be limited to a certain division or branch of the organization, or certain units could be bypassed. Alternatively, the process could be limited to the upper hierarchical units — or to the lower ones. If these limited efforts are successful, that may be all that is needed, or consideration could be given to expanding the process.

Another way to make a quick trip would be to take short-cuts and concentrate on certain Steps or aspects. The minimum, however, would be to complete Step One: Survey, since the other Steps are based on the preliminary inventory. The time and resources to complete Step One, for average cases, probably would be about three to six weeks' effort by one individual.

Option 3: A Scenic Route. This option will probably be preferred by most. After reviewing the scope and purpose of all Four Steps, match the elements of the process against the knowledge level, problems and needs of your organization. Then design a customized approach and plan. The overall objectives of our methodology will be met if you complete Step One: Survey, apply Step Two: Cost/Value to some, but not necessarily all entities, prepare those charts and maps in Step Three: Analysis that are relevant and, finally, meet your own objectives in Step Four: Synthesis. In short, it is not essential to take the complete journey we describe in order to obtain useful results. We offer a global travel guide: You select the itinerary.

In summary, the pragmatic and flexible approach we are taking to discovering corporate information resources will: 1) Explore for all potential information resource entities (IREs) in the organization; 2) determine their cost and value; 3) map their location and nature and 4) define the organization's corporate information resource base. As in all voyages of discovery, you will encounter surprises — some pleasant, some distressing. But like the explorers of western North America, such as Lewis and Clark, and Palliser, you will at the end of the voyage have established a framework for future resource exploitation. The next four chapters detail how to begin and how to carry out the discovery process.

NOTES

1. "The Making of America: Northern Plains," *National Geographic*, 170(6), December 1986, 13th in a Series of 17 Maps.

2. "Resources," *The Penguin Dictionary of Economics*, 3rd, ed., (1984), 378.

3. Donald A. Marchand and Forest W. Horton, Jr., *INFOTRENDS: Profiting from Your Information Resources*, (New York, N.Y.: John Wiley & Sons, 1986), summarized from pp. 125-134.

4. Ibid., Fig. 5-2.

5. "Language," *The Canadian Encyclopedia* (1985), II, 974.

6. The IRM concept and process have been described and defined in several works, many listed in the Bibliography. This figure attempts to distill what has been written in order to show where "information resources" fit into this management process. The figure is modified from: Cornelius F. Burk, Jr., "Auditing the Management of Information Resources: A Challenge for the '80s," (Ottawa, Ontario: Office of the Auditor General of Canada, October 1984), Discussion Paper 39, Fig. 1.

7. We are using the corporate management model of: R. Alec Mackenzie, "The Management Process in 3-D," *Harvard Business Review*, November-December 1969, Exhibit 1. Mackenzie's concept of management can be summarized as: Achieving objectives through others. We view information resources as one of the "others."

8. Many of the definitions listed in the Glossary were first compiled by: Burk, "Auditing the Management of Information Resources," Appendix 1, and later published in: Cornelius F. Burk, Jr., "Working Definitions of Terms Related to the IRM Concept," *Information Management*, 19(5), May 1985, 8, 22 (Part 1); 19(6), June 1985, 20-21 (Part 2).

9. Reprinted by permission from *The Random House Dictionary of the English Language, Unabridged Edition*, c 1983 by Random House, Inc.

10. For example, Paul S. Bender, *Resource Management: An Alternative View of the Management Process*, (New York, N.Y.: John Wiley & Sons, 1983).

11. Forest W. Horton, Jr., *Information Resources Management: Concept and Cases*, (Cleveland, Ohio: Association for Systems Management, 1979).

12. Morey J. Chick, "Information Value and Cost Measures for Use as Management Tools," *Information Executive*, 1(2), 1984, Fig. 2.

13. Commission on Federal Paperwork, "Information Resources Management Report," (Washington, D.C.: Commission on Federal Paperwork, September 1977), pp. 29-51.

14. For example, Walter L. Carlson, "Information Is Not a Manageable Resource," *The Information Manager*, Summer 1980, 2(2), 6.; and John J. Connell, "The Fallacy of Information Resource Management," *Infosystems*, 1981, 81(5).

15. Excerpted from: Harlan Cleveland, "Information as a Resource," *The Futurist*, December 1982, 34-39. Reprinted with permission of the World Future Society, 4916 St. Elmo Ave., Bethesda, MD 20814.

16. Office of Management and Budget Circular A-130, "Management of Federal Information Resources," *Federal Register*, December 24, 1985, 50(247), p. 52735.

17. John F. McLaughlin with Anne E. Birinyi, "Mapping the Information Business," in *Understanding New Media: Trends and Issues in Electronic Distribution of Information*, ed. Benjamin M. Compaine (Cambridge, Mass,: Ballinger Publishing Company, 1984), Fig. 2-35.

18. Office of Management and Budget Circular A-130, "Management of Federal Information Resources," p. 52735.

19. The impact of the Information Age on business is dealt with in depth by: Donald A. Marchand and Forest W. Horton, Jr., *INFOTRENDS: Profiting from Your Information Resources*, (New York, N.Y.: John Wiley & Sons, 1986).

20. Craig M. Cook and D.W. Fitzpatrick, "IRM: Information Resource Management for the Information Systems Executive," Arthur Young Booklet, 1981.

21. Robert S. Taylor, "Organizational Information Environments," in *Information and the Transformation of Society*, (Amsterdam: North-Holland Publishing, 1982), pp. 309-322.

22. Gordon D. Williams, "Advantages to Using a Generalized System to Manage Geological Data," in *Computer-Based Systems for Geological Field Data*, (Ottawa, Ont.: Energy, Mines and Resources Canada, 1975), Geological Survey of Canada Paper 74-63, Fig. 1.

23. Philip N. James, "A Framework for Strategic and Long-Range Information Resource Planning," *Information Strategy*, Fall 1985, 4-12.

24. "Guide on Financial Administration for Departments and Agencies of the Government of Canada," Amendment No. 17, (Ottawa, Ont.: Treasury Board of Canada, 1985), p. 4.D.4.

25. The original presentation of the discovery process recognized *five* steps. Here we have combined the Costing (no. 2) and Valuing (no. 3) steps as one, calling it Cost/Value (no. 2). See Forest W. Horton, Jr., *The Information Management Workbook: IRM Made Simple*, (Washington, D.C.: Information Management Press, Revised and updated edition, 1985).

26. "Facts about CRA 1982," (Melbourne, Australia: CRA Limited, February 1982), p. 57.

2

CONDUCTING THE PRELIMINARY INVENTORY

The first chapter described the context within which the information resource discovery process can be carried out. Information has been recognized by top management as a corporate resource. Its known or potential strategic value to the organization is recognized, at least in principle even if not fully understood or clearly articulated. The practical issue for corporate managers is: How can resource management principles and practices be applied to *information* resources? We believe that management's first basic step should be to define the organization's existing information resource base. That means, as Step One, conducting an inventory.

The establishment and maintenance of inventories is standard practice in the management of most resources. A counting process of some sort is implicit in the notion of resource management, since only *quantities* can be fully accounted for, itemized, valued and costed, whether the resources are financial (the number of dollars), human (the number of people), real property (the number of square feet) or raw materials (the number of tons). But what units should be recognized and used for measuring and inventorying *information* resources?

The term inventory is usually taken to mean a detailed, itemized list of goods, giving a number of relevant particulars such as stock number, condition or quality, unit of measure and acquisition cost. As applied to resources, the nature of the resource dictates what units are counted. Each kind of resource — whether financial, human, physical or whatever — is listed, measured and described in accordance with its own particular characteristics. For those resources with a long history of stewardship, whole subdisciplines and typologies have evolved. There are recognized standards for classifying the resource, specifying quality, placing a value on it, reporting the value on the balance sheet and so on. However, the process of developing an appropriate and widely used subdiscipline and typology for information resources has just begun.

Chapter 2 Preview. This chapter describes Step One: Survey, the first of four steps required to discover your information resources (Fig. 1-8). To begin, we stress that support from top management is needed. Purpose and scope should be defined. Then we describe how a classification scheme for your information resources can be developed to assist in collecting the inventory data. Using a simple form, summary data concerning each source, service and system are compiled, mostly by interviewing information users, handlers and managers. Means of locating hidden information resources are described. Finally, a case example will be described to illustrate the nature of results you can expect from the preliminary inventory project.

2.1   THE PRELIMINARY INVENTORY PROJECT

During Step One, all information entities used by the organization — sources, services and systems, and other combinations of information content and media — will be identified without prejudice as to their status as organizational resources (Fig. 2-1). By the end of Step One you will have a reasonably complete inventory of all of the organization's information entities, both internal and external. However, only after completing Steps Two, Three and Four of the discovery process will you know with certainty which of these entities are, in fact, *corporate resources*. Thus we call output from Step One a preliminary inventory. It could also be described as an inventory of potential resources — potential in the sense that our knowledge of the entities at this point is incomplete.

In a similar way, certain natural resources, for example deposits of petroleum, are recognized as *potential* resources. These are deposits which are known to exist, or whose existence is inferred, but for which there is insufficient information to pin down their economic viability. Only some of these deposits will later be confirmed as *actual* resources (called "reserves") when it is determined, from additional information on the deposits themselves, from the economics of extracting and selling the resource, govern-

Figure 2-1. Survey chart: Conduct preliminary resource inventory (Step One).

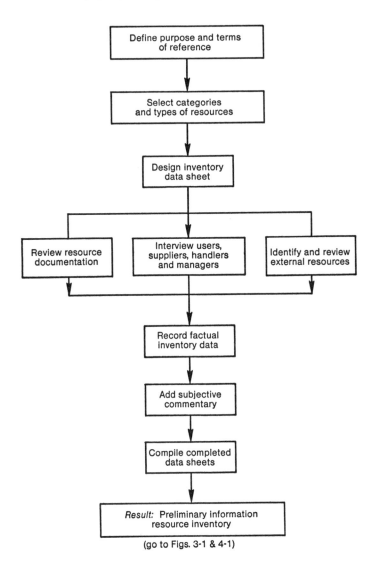

ment policies and so on, that the deposits are in fact economically viable, current *sources* or reservoirs for the commodity in question; for example, crude oil and natural gas.

The process of preparing the preliminary inventory, charted in Fig. 2-1, begins with a decision on the specific purpose and terms of reference, which will be influenced by the organization's current state of knowledge of its information resources, how the inventory will be carried out, who will do it and so on. Next, a concept or model of the information resource entities you expect to discover will be developed and expressed in terms of various categories and types.

You will design a simple one-page form to capture the essential data concerning each potential resource entity. The main sources of data will be interviews with people in the organization, documents collected internally and elsewhere and relevant external organizations. Finally, the inventory data will be collected and compiled. The completed preliminary inventory will take the form of a compilation of the one-page data sheets, sequenced in alphabetical order by entity name.

2.1.1 Obtaining Top Management's Support

As with any endeavor of corporate-wide scope, success in carrying out the preliminary inventory and succeeding steps of the mapping process will depend on an open commitment from top management. To complete the inventory, access will be required to virtually every part of the organization, and authority needed to meet with and interview people occupying a wide range of positions. The essential first step, then, is to secure a mandate from top management.

Top management's decision to proceed will have depended on whether or not it perceives information as a resource, and if so, whether the identification of its information resource base is included in its strategic plans. We assume that management has already made the fundamental decision "to manage information as a resource," and that they are looking for an approach and strategy to translate concept to action.

The mandate from top management will provide the project director with authority to begin the discovery process. *You should not begin until this fundamental support has been assured.* Otherwise, some doors will almost certainly be barred and an open process of peer review of the data collected may be subverted, resulting in incomplete or inaccurate data on the organization's information resources. More important, the recommendations for action made at the conclusion of the mapping process may not be taken seriously by either top management or the staff affected. Someone is bound to ask: "Who said information was a resource, anyway?"

2.1.2 Establishing Purpose and Scope

Within the context of a corporate decision to proceed with an information resource mapping exercise, the purpose and scope of

Step One, the preliminary inventory, should be made explicit. Some factors you should take into account include:

1. *Current knowledge of the organization's resource base:* Advantage should be taken of inventories, surveys and other compilations that may already exist or are being planned or underway. Typically, every company has something of this sort, however preliminary or incomplete, that could serve as a point of departure. These tools could include partial or comprehensive software and hardware inventories, database directories, vendor lists, plans and budgets, administrative manuals and the like.

    On the other hand, a problem with many existing compilations of this sort is that, collectively, they do not reflect a consistent, corporate-wide view of the nature and interrelationships of information resources. So in most cases it's usually best to start from scratch and take a fresh look at the total picture. Many organizations suffer because existing inventory efforts do not add up to much more than a crazy quilt of unintegratable and disconnected lists.

2. *Size and complexity of the organization:* As we explained (1.8), it may be prudent to divide the inventory project into a number of separate "chewable chunks" if geographic, hierarchical, political or sheer size considerations present problems. In such cases, the preliminary inventory could begin with a certain division or branch, a certain geographic region, or deal with a limited range of resource entities, say external and internal databases, or information technology.

3. *Relationship to business and information planning:* As discussed in Chapter 1, the information resource mapping process is, or should be, an element of the organization's strategic and long-term planning. Thus, its purpose and scope should relate explicitly to such plans, making reference to particular issues and concerns; for example: The adequacy or quality of information sources; the use of appropriate information technology; the cost of handling or storing information; the need to provide more competitive services to clientele or improved accountability for quality and price.

Defining purpose and scope of the preliminary inventory should take place somewhere in the corporate planning process; ideally, flowing out of the company's strategic plans. This would ensure that purpose and scope are based on corporate-wide considerations and that they are endorsed by top management.

In the case of *CRA Exploration Pty. Limited*, the Australian mineral exploration company, management undertook to conduct a review of its information handling and analytical tools. The purpose and scope of the preliminary inventory was influenced primarily by the company's need to ensure that its capabilities in information management were adequate to the task of maintaining its competitive position within the mineral industry. Thus, the emphasis of the inventory was on the collection, storage, handling and analysis of technical data, not on the management of administrative information or on the improvement of management processes. The project director visited users, handlers, suppliers and managers of scientific and technical data and information in most of the company's operating divisions.[1]

The purpose of a preliminary inventory undertaken by the *Department of Energy, Mines and Resources* of the Canadian Federal Government was to document for senior management, in budgetary and resource terms, the overall extent of information resources in the department. Emphasis in this example was on determining how much was at stake on the expenditure side, and on investigating the extent to which these resources were subject to information management policies. The scope was as broad as possible, but the depth of the survey was shallow — just deep enough to identify the most obvious resource entities.[2]

A third example is provided by a proposal of the *Smithsonian Institution*, Washington, D.C. to develop an institutional information resource directory. The voluminous and varied materials and collections maintained by SI had led naturally to an equally formidable volume and range of information and data concerning the collections (metadata, or data about data). The basic purpose of the proposed directory was:

> . . . to sustain and encourage the interests of users throughout the Institution by making them aware of the existence of other data and information relevant to their interests and by assisting them in gaining access to that information.

The intended scope of this inventory survey was very broad, encompassing the entire spectrum of activities and subjects dealt with by the Smithsonian, which spans vast segments of man's knowledge.[3]

2.2   DEFINING YOUR RESOURCE CLASSIFICATION SCHEME

All resource managers require some kind of classification scheme for the resource they are managing if they are to intelligently sort and sift through the mountains of detail. For example, financial managers distinguish current and fixed assets and liabilities;

personnel managers differentiate clerical support staff from executives and scientists; inventory managers distinguish control over raw materials from goods-in-process and finished goods inventories and so on.

None of these typologies sprang fully anticipated. Each has evolved over a period of time with experimentation and refinement. For example, even for an area of management as basic as government accounting, it has taken until the mid-'80s for the United States and Canada to *propose* accounting and reporting standards that would permit the respective governments of these countries to publish annual "corporate" financial reports.[4] For their part, information managers are in an even more primitive state, just now becoming aware of the need for a standard typology that would adequately illuminate how organizations are investing and spending their information dollars. Our efforts here to develop and apply some kind of classification scheme are motivated to a large extent by the need for finding ways to break the totality of the information resource into smaller, more manageable components.

Now, let us begin with Step One. With top management's blessing and an agreement on purpose and scope behind us, the first task is to develop a basic classification structure for the resource inventory data. Such a structure is needed now to guide the survey itself and to help organize the collection of data. As the survey proceeds, the structure will probably be modified, and later during analysis (Step Three) it may be refined still further. During Step Three the classification structure will serve another purpose: To provide a framework for the analysis and interpretation of the inventory data. Thus, this first iteration would not be cast in concrete, and the survey director should not feel obligated to find the "right" or "perfect" classification before beginning to collect data.

2.2.1 Resource Categories and Types

Our approach to classifying information resources, and thus to defining the basic unit of resource measurement, is to first categorize all potential resources as *sources, services* or *systems*, then to subdivide each of these *categories* into generic groupings we call *types*, and finally to recognize within each type, specific sources, services and systems which we will call *information resource entities* or IREs (Table 2-1).

Use of the sources-services-systems triad as the basis for classification will cast a wide net over the organization and capture most if not all potential information resources, yet avoid over-

Table 2-1. Basic hierarchical classification structure for information resources.

Categories	Types	Information Resource Entities (IREs)
Sources	Generic groupings	Specific sources
Services	Generic groupings	Specific services
Systems	Generic groupings	Specific systems
Other configurations of content & media	Generic groupings	Specific entities

Source: Modified from Forest W. Horton, Jr., *The Information Management Workbook: IRM Made Simple* (Washington, D.C.: Information Management Press, revised edition 1985). Reprinted with permission.

whelming the survey with masses of confusing detail. Recognition of sources, services and systems as the basic categories reflects our view, as expressed in Chapter 1, that the fundamental entities we are seeking in the discovery process are configurations having an inherent informational quality, not merely the individual labor, hardware, energy or other resource inputs (Fig. 1-6). Moreover, the alternative classification approach of starting from a predetermined, functionally rooted schema of "classes of information" (e.g., marketing, financial, procurement, inventory, etc.) or a schema like the Dewey decimal numbering system for library books, unnecessarily constrains the mapping process by forcing information managers to arbitrarily shoehorn resources into watertight compartments.

Using our basic classification structure, your first essential tasks here are to develop working definitions of the basic categories — the sources, services and systems — and to identify the generic groupings that will constitute the types included within each category. The information resource entities, however, will be identified later, while the survey is in progress.

Information Resource Categories. Here are basic definitions of the three categories of information resources. However, you should not apply the definitions blindly; rather use them as guides to develop definitions tailored to meet the particular requirements and circumstances of *your* organization.

Source: A place, store or person from which information can be obtained. The "stocks of knowledge" maintained or accessed by the organization. The source typically draws its information from pools of holdings: for example, a collection of books, a correspondence file or a database; or from the custodians thereof — for example a librarian, records manager or computer center manager; or from an expert who possesses special knowledge in a subject domain. Sources may be internal or external to the organization: Table 2-2 is an illustrative list of *internal* sources (R & D Department, Purchasing Office, etc.) and the associated internal holdings (Internal R & D reports, Product literature, etc.),[5] while Table 2-3 illustrates *external* information sources.[6]

Service: An activity helpful in acquiring, processing or transmitting information and data or in providing an information product. For example, a courier, computer programming or information locating or delivery service. The activity usually involves people who provide customized assistance. Examples of information services appear in Table 2-4.

System: A structured and integrated series of processes for handling information or data characterized by systematic and repetitive processing of inputs, file updates and outputs. For example, a financial, bibliographic or scientific data system, either manual or automated.

Unlike the predetermined "master list of information classes" approach, sources, services and systems are not mutually exclusive, airtight compartments. However, our experience in using this triad as a broad framework for compiling a preliminary corporate information resource inventory has shown that it does succeed in illuminating, in the broad fashion intended, what and where the organization's information resources are.[7]

A set of subcategories could also be established on the basis of other criteria, for example the distinction between *internal* and *external* resources. It may even be appropriate to *define* the "source" category as comprising only sources of external origin, and to treat internal sources as components of a service or system. However, the validity and utility of subcategories will not usually become evident until after the initial inventory data have been collected; for now, during Step One, the simple threefold scheme will probably suffice.

Table 2-2. Illustrative list of internal information sources and information holdings.

R & D Department

Internal R & D reports
Product literature
Overhead transparencies
Government technical reports
Competitors' technical reports
Conference proceedings
Vendor catalogs
Reprints
Technical journals
Newsletters
Engineering drawings
Industry standards
Manuals and handbooks
Project files
Test results

Purchasing Office

"Commerce Business Daily"
Vendor catalogs
Distributor information
Pricing sheets
Supplier files

Office Manager

Telephone books
Equipment manuals
Personnel skills files, records
 & résumés
Magazine subscription files
Directories
Courier & shipping manuals
Correspondence files
Accounting files

Marketing Department

Census data
Marketing studies
Multi-client consultant reports
Newsletters
International directories

Advertising campaign files
Presentation slides
Videotapes
Audio tape recordings
Marketing journals
Presentations
Proposals
Contracts
Competitors' annual reports

Corporate Offices

Annual reports
Planning magazines
Management society journals
Corporate manuals
Competitors' manuals
Newsletters
Textbooks
Trade association reports
Data processing reports
Business periodicals
Corporate archives
Looseleaf services
Technical reports
Trade publications
Consultants' reports
Audit reports

Computer Department

Data tapes
Program tapes
Equipment manuals
Software manuals
Users' manuals
Suppliers' catalogs
Newsletters
Data processing magazines

Production Department

Vendor catalogs
Equipment manuals
Safety standards

Table 2-2. (Continued)

Production Department (Cont'd)	Case files
Industry standards	Law books
Handbooks	Legal directories
Trade magazines	Looseleaf services
	Legal periodicals
Legal Department	Legal databases
	Newsletters
Export regulations	

Source: Modified from Elizabeth Bole Eddison, "Who Should be in Charge?", *Special Libraries*, 74 (2), April, 1983. Reprinted with permission.

Table 2-3. Illustrative list of external information sources.

Audiovisual libraries	News media stations and companies
Book publishers	Office libraries
Buy and sell bureaus	Ombudsman services
Clearinghouses and exchanges	Passport and visa offices
Community relations offices	Patent and copyright offices
Computer and system centers	Phonograph recordings
Conferences and symposia	Professional societies and trade associations
Consumer information bureaus	Public information offices
Documentation centers	Public libraries
Drug and alcohol rehabilitation centers	Records centers and depositories
Education and training centers	Referral and abstract services
Employment and job assistance centers	Regional resource libraries
Government agencies	Research libraries and centers
Historical associations	School libraries
Information dissemination centers	Serial publishers
Information bureaus	Special book collections
Information analysis centers	Statistical centers
International information networks	Telephone companies
License and permit offices	Trade fairs
Lost and found departments	Traffic, weather, special events bureaus
Magnetic tape libraries	Travel bureaus
Management consultants	Veterans and student assistance centers
Map publishers	

Table 2-3. (Continued)

Market research firms   Visitor centers
Minority information centers   Vital records registries
Museums and archives

Source: Forest W. Horton, Jr., *Information Resources Management: Concept and Cases,* (Cleveland, Ohio: Association
for Systems Management, 1979). Reprinted with permission.

Table 2-4. Illustrative list of information products and services.

Accounting & bookkeeping	Computation services, equipment & supplies	Operations research
Actuarial services	Conference recording services & consultants	Photocopying services
Adding & calculating machines & supplies	Convention services & facilities	Photographic equipment & supplies
Addressing & lettering	Copying & duplicating	Phototypesetting
Advertising services	Correspondence services	Planographers
Aerial photography & surveys	Credit reporting	Printing & binding services & supplies
Analytical services	Delivery services	Programmed instruction
Answering services	Demonstration services	Public opinion pollsters/ analysts
Association management services	Display designers & producers	Radio monitoring
Audiovisual equipment, supplies & services	Economic & social science research	Radiotelephone
Auditing	Educational consultants	Reading improvement
Automatic data processing	Encyclopedias & dictionaries	Security systems for information
Automatic electric typing	Exhibit handling	Surveying
Automatic handwriting machines	Facsimile transmission	Tape recorders
Blueprinting	Ghostwriting services	Technical writing
Bonded messengers	Government information	Telephone answering
Book dealers, printers & publishers	Graphic designers	Television services
Broadcasting	Information bureaus	Testing services
Brokerage information	Information retrieval systems & equipment	Tickets & coupons
Bulletin & directory boards	International conferences	Trademark services
Business forms, systems & consultants	Investment counseling	Transcribing services
Buy & sell exchanges	Job information	Translators & interpreters
Buyers' information service	Keypunch services	Transmitters
Cablegrams	Lecture bureaus	Travel information
Calligraphers	Legislative research	Typesetting
Calling, paging & signaling	Library research & services	Typewriting services
Carbon paper	Lithographic supplies & equipment	Typographers
Cartographers	Magazine & periodical subscription services	Ultrasonic equipment & supplies
Cassettes — audio & videotape	Mailing lists, machines & services	Visa services
Catalogue compilers	Management consultants	Voice-visual-graphic systems
Certified Public Accountants	Maps	Volunteer services information
		Wake-up call services
		Weather information

Table 2-4. (Continued)

Charts	Market research & analysis	Word processing services
City & town guides & maps	Microfilming services,	& supplies
Clipping bureaus	equipment & supplies	Writers
Communications systems,	News services	Yellow pages advertising
equipment & supplies	Office dictating, endorsing	ZIP code information
Composition, offset printing	& other machines	

Source: Forest W. Horton, Jr., *Information Resources Management: Concept and Cases*, (Cleveland, Ohio: Association for Systems Management, 1979). Reprinted with permission.

Information Resource Types. Having defined the resource categories, you should next prepare a list of the generic *types* of information resource entities you are aware of or suspect are present. A good way to begin is to examine lists of resource types prepared by others; then compare them with *your* knowledge of *your* organization. The examples of types in Table 2-5 include an illustration and four actual cases; for instance: abstracting services, library services, computer systems and government publications. Table 2-4, an unstructured, illustrative list of information products and services, reminds us of the broad spectrum of information resources potentially available, and the need for classification and structure.[8]

Two questions concerning the definition of your resource types that are commonly raised at this point are: 1) What level of aggregation (or detail) should I use? and 2) What specific labels or titles should I apply?

If the level of aggregation implicit in the choice of a particular type is too high, important distinctions may be disguised or masked. On the other hand, if the groupings are too narrow or detailed, the big picture may be lost, and the costs prohibitive. There is no pat answer. An optimal level must be sought by trial-and-error as the survey proceeds. We suggest starting at a fairly aggregated level, and then reiterating the process if necessary to successively lower levels until the optimum is reached. You will find that this process is not altogether a bad thing, since it forces a better understanding of the nature of the resources and sharpens your focus on the exploration targets.

As for the language used to label the resource types, there are questions of both substance and style. The terminology you use will

Table 2-5. Example of categories and types of information resource entities (IREs).

1 ILLUSTRATIVE EXAMPLE *Source: Note 9*	2 DEPARTMENT OF ENERGY, MINES AND RESOURCES (CANADA) *Source: Note 10*	3 CRA EXPLORATION PTY. LIMITED (AUSTRALIA) *Source: Note 11*	4 U.S. ENVIRONMENTAL PROTECTION AGENCY *Source: Note 12*	5 SMITHSONIAN INSTITUTION, MUSEUMS PROGRAM *Source: Note 13*
SOURCES Advertising/promotions Consultants/brokers Consumer surveys Credit agencies International Market research News media On-line document delivery Publication subscriptions US Government publications Other *SERVICES* ADP/EDP Audiovisual Drafting/cartographic/graphics Editing/writing/translating Education/training/conferences Facilities management Forms & publications Library/information center Mail & delivery Microforms/COM Photographic Printing/copying Records/archival	*SOURCES* General inquiry centers Libraries Record management centers Sales & distribution centers Scientific & technical information centers *SERVICES* Abstracting & Indexing Computing Copying & duplicating Drafting & cartographic Mail & delivery Photographic Public relations Publishing Telecommunications Word processing *SERVICES* Bibliographic data Economic data Financial data Management information Personnel data Scientific & technical data	*SOURCES* *CRAE Information:* Bibliographic data Drill-log and assay data Exploration reports Geochemical data Geological samples data Geophysical data Management information Maps and charts Mineral lease data Mining information Petroleum information Prospects data Remote sensing data *External Organizations:* Commercial Federal agencies Other CRA Group State agencies Other *SERVICES* Aerial photgraphy Core/sample curation Drafting Geophysical surveying	*ADMINISTRATIVE SUPPORT SYSTEMS* Contracts and grants — procurement control, payments management & status reporting Facilities property management and supplies — facilities inventory, plant maintenance, equipment maintenance scheduling & space utilization Financial — accounting, budgeting & payroll Information services — library & information services, selective dissemination of information, current awareness, abstract journal production & reference services Personnel — personnel services, skills inventory, manpower analysis, position control & strength & salary reporting Program planning and management — program coordination, progress & status reporting, other government reporting, other government coordination & resources management General — safety, security, transportation, equal opportunity, computer scheduling, tape	*SOURCES* *Aerospace Periodical Index* *Dibner Manuscripts Catalogue* *Finder's Guide to Photographic Collections in the SI* *Guide to the Smithsonian Archives* *Information Sources and Services in Aeronomy, Astrophysics & Related Space Sciences* *Museums Studies Program in the United States and Abroad* "Native American Archives" *SITELINE* — SITES newletter *UPDATE* — SITES catalogue *Programs/Projects:* Audiovisual loan program CAL–NBS seminar series Graduate training program for conservators How Museums Can Increase Their Educational Contributions to Their Communities — Study National Museums Act Program Native American Museum Program Museum Practices Internship Program Museum Training Program Smithsonian Oral History Program Smithsonian Training Program in Conservation

Table 2-5. (Continued)

1 ILLUSTRATIVE EXAMPLE	2 DEPARTMENT OF ENERGY, MINES AND RESOURCES (CANADA)	3 CRA EXPLORATION PTY. LIMITED (AUSTRALIA)	4 U.S. ENVIRONMENTAL PROTECTION AGENCY	5 SMITHSONIAN INSTITUTION, MUSEUMS PROGRAM
Source: Note 9	*Source: Note 10*	*Source: Note 11*	*Source: Note 12*	*Source: Note 13*
Statistical/analysis Telecommunications/communications Time sharing Word processing Other *SYSTEMS* Bibliographic Economic/business Financial/accounting Inventory/property Legal/legislative Management MIS Patent/copyright/trademarks Personnel/payroll Purchasing/contracting Quality control Scientific/technical Security/compliance Travel/support Other		Information locating Library Mineral lease information Records management Reporting Reprographics Resource evaluation Systems/programming Other *SYSTEMS* Bibliographic control Communications Computing Drafting/graphics Geoscience data analysis Geoscience data management Image analysis Mineral lease data Prospect information Word processing Other	library management, software development, mailing lists, media production, public inquiries, and any other administrative support system which does not belong elsewhere *MISSION SUPPORT SYSTEMS* Air — air quality, stationary source pollution control, mobile source pollution control programs, emissions & implementation programs Noise — noise abatement & control Pesticides — pesticides regulation Radiation — radiation technology assessment, criteria, standards, surveillance & inspection Solid wastes — solid wastes processing, disposal, resource recovery & solid waste systems management Water — water quality, supply, pollution source control, standards development & implementaiton programs General — multimedia systems, refuse act program, general counsel, media enforcement & any other emission support system which does not belong elsewhere	Visiting Professionals Program Workshop for Native American museum directors *SERVICES* Exhibition Publications Center — Proposed Introductory Gallery — Proposed Museum Reference Center Smithsonian Archaeometry Research Collections and Records Smithsonian Institution Archives Smithsonian Institution Libraries *SYSTEMS* Archives Central Information System Basic Library Card Catalogue and COM catalogue system Conservation abstracts and reports data base "Fingerprints" of materials files In-house accounting system for projects International data base on conservation & treatment Inventory of Smithsonian-produced audiovisual programs Optical reader system Protective coatings data base Smithsonian Institution Bibliographic Information System Survey of scientific drawings and illustrations in NMMH/MOM data base Survey of SI photographs data base Trade catalogue collection data base

reflect the nature and scope of what is being sought, but much of it is also more a question of local usage or corporate culture. For example, with reference to Table 2-5, there are such varying usages as: "copying" *vs* "reprographics," "library" *vs* "information dissemination center," "public relations" *vs* "communications," "data processing" *vs* "computing" and "indexing" *vs* "information locating." The final choices should be based on what the organization feels comfortable with and on achieving the best possible communication with management.

Often the most vexing question to be faced in using the sources-services-systems classification scheme is in deciding, in the case of some types of resources (our generic groupings), whether a type belongs to one particular category or perhaps several. For example, are libraries sources or services? Should computer databases be regarded as systems or sources? Are management information systems more of a source than a system? And so on.

When these and similar questions are posed in general or as abstractions, there are no theoretical answers (underscoring once more our primitive understanding and an inadequate typology for information resources). At the practical level, however, the answers to such questions can be approached by focussing on the context. For example, when developing your classification scheme, don't think about libraries *in general*, but about the specific libraries in, or used by, *your* organization. Are they perceived by their users (or managers) primarily as *sources*, or are they viewed as *services*? Or, put another way, is the *value* of the libraries used by your organization based primarily on what they have that is accessed directly by patrons (a source), or primarily on what the staff does (a service)? Or perhaps both. More and more libraries are becoming active information-seeking helpers as the "information center" catches hold, rather than serving as dormant archival repositories. Which type does your organization have or use?

Nevertheless, there will be cases in which it appears equally logical to place an information resource type (e.g. library) in one category as in another; moreover, it is also possible that some members of a type belong in more than one category. For example, the main library is a service, while subsidiary libraries serve as repositories for specialized collections and are therefore sources. In these cases, the label should be placed in both categories. What matters is that the type *has been identified* and these resource entities will be inventoried.

2.2.2 Examples of Classification Schemes

The five examples of classification schemes shown in Table 2-5 include an illustrative example and four specific cases. They exemplify a range of approaches applied in a diversity of contexts. All use sources, services and systems as the basic categories, although one (No. 4) deals only with systems.

The illustrative example (No. 1) provides a good starting point. It shows a representative list of resource types expressed in generic terms; most organizations would have most of these types. Many also appear in the other, specific cases, but there the resource types tend to use labels that relate more directly to the business of the organization. For example, the mineral exploration company (No. 3) includes various geoscience data types, the government environmental agency (No. 4) selected systems dealing with phenomena such as pesticides and radiation, while the museum example (No. 5) is ultra-specific (their types appear in many instances to be specific resource entities).

In the CRA Exploration example (No. 3), the sources category consists mainly of various types of data and information, rather than organizations, facilities or places. This categorization reflects one of the main objectives of this survey, to *establish* the sources of key data and information types. As we shall see, much of it was widely dispersed and not usually associated with any specific or obvious physical facility or facilities. To meet the particular objectives of this inventory, the types under the sources category were selected to designate various kinds of data and information, regardless of their physical, geographical or organizational aspects. Thus, types of sources can be viewed, at one extreme, as basically information itself, as in this case, or at the other, as information in various aggregated forms; for example, record centers, archives or libraries.

At this stage, the main purpose of the examples in Table 2-5 is to illustrate how broad classification schemes can be set up to help focus the survey effort. The question is whether your scheme is broad enough to capture all potential resource entities, without being so general as to overlook important distinctions. Later, when the inventory is compiled, the concepts and names of the resource types will probably be modified to more accurately show what you actually found. Still later, during the analysis phase (Step Three) you will use the classification scheme as a framework for analyzing the preliminary inventory.

The study and classification of types, or typology, is fundamental to the development of sound methodology. While we do not minimize its significance, we cannot pursue it in greater depth. One of our hopes is that future development of a more rigorous typology for information resources will be among the benefits of extending application of the sources-services-systems triad to its practical limits, as we are attempting in the information resource discovery process.

2.3   COLLECTING AND COMPILING THE INVENTORY DATA

Now you are ready to collect and compile some data. Within the framework of the information resource categories and types you have selected, you will design an inventory data form; obtain and collect the data through interviews with users, suppliers, handlers and managers; scan documentation and obtain other data from external organizations. The factual material concerning each potential resource entity will be compiled on a data form and supplemented, as appropriate, with subjective commentary. Finally, the data sheets will be sequenced to produce the preliminary information resource inventory (Fig. 2-1).

2.3.1   Design the Inventory Data Form

Data collected from the preliminary inventory should be summarized and compiled on a standardized, one-page form (or its electronic equivalent). The form should be designed to highlight the salient features of each specific source, service, system or other entity encountered. The form's utility and power will derive from its succinctness and the overview it provides, both of the individual entity and later collectively when the inventory is completed, rather than from masses of detail and analysis concerning an individual resource entity.

Using the model inventory data form (Fig. 2-2) as a rough guide, the survey director should design a form suited to the purpose and scope of the inventory to be conducted. If necessary, headings should be modified to match the corporate culture. Other fields can be added or deleted. However, we do not recommend expanding the form much beyond the scope of this model, even if more data are readily at hand, as this might obscure the essential qualities of the entity being described.

If a hardcopy (paper) form is used, the amount of information that could be placed in each field would be limited. However, if an

Figure 2-2. Suggested content for inventory data form. Data could be compiled manually on a form or on its equivalent in a word processor. For examples of completed forms, see Appendix 1.

Identification (ID) Number:	Category:	Type:	Resource Name:
Location:	Organizational Unit:	Resource Manager:	Operating Contact:
Concise Statement of Goals/Missions/Purposes Supported:			
Description of Contents, Operations and Uses:			
Comments and Observations:			
Evaluation:			
Primary Inputs:	Primary Outputs:		Holdings/Storage Media:
Prepared by/Date:	Reviewed by/Date:		Approved by/Date:

electronic word processor is used, as it was in the main case example (Appendix 1), then fields can be conveniently expanded, contracted or eliminated as desired. Brief explanations of each of the fields shown in Fig. 2-2 follow. Examples of completed forms can be seen in Appendix 1.

Identification (ID) Number: A unique number is useful for identification, sorting and analytical purposes. It could be arbitrarily assigned as resource entities are encountered or assigned retroactively to reflect some desired sequence such as alphabetic order of the Resource Names.

Category: The broadest classification level; either a Source, Service or System (Table 2-1).

Type: The secondary classification level; a generic grouping of information resource entities selected for purposes of the inventory (Table 2-1). For example, "libraries," "government publications," "printing services," "word processors," "custom-coded software," "local area networks."

Resource Name: A proper descriptive or generic name for the information resource entity (IRE), usually a named source, service or system (Table 2-1). For example, "Public Library X," "Drafting System Y," "Online Database Service Z."

Location: The geographic location of the focal point or center of the named resource entity. For some organizations the location might refer to a city, or for others it could refer to a floor, room or building location. For example, "Melbourne," "10th Floor, XYZ Building," "Room 654."

Organizational Unit: The name of the division, branch, section or other unit within the organizational hierarchy in which the focal point or center of the resource entity is located. For example, "Geophysics Branch," "Accounts Receivable Section."

Resource Manager: The name of the person responsible or accountable for managing the named resource entity.

Operating Contact: The name and telephone number of a person from whom authoritative information about the resource entity could be obtained.

Concise Statement of Goals/Missions/Purposes Supported: The immediate and corporate end or ends served by the resource entity. The broad operational context(s) in which information resources are used. See Appendix 1 for examples.

Description of Contents, Operations and Uses: If a source, what the information contents are and who maintains them; if a service, what functions are performed and by whom or, if a system, what information is processed for what purpose and by whom. A statement on who the users and beneficiaries are should also be recorded. See Appendix 1 for examples.

Comments and Observations: An optional field, to provide for knowledgeable remarks on any other aspect — for example on role, uniqueness, relevance or relationships to other resource entities; or plans for enhancing, upgrading or discontinuing the entity. See Appendix 1 for examples.

Evaluation: An optional field, not usually used in the preliminary inventory, since at this stage of the discovery process there is usually enough to do without doing an assessment. Moreover, the inventory process should not be viewed as an audit or inspection because staff may well see the inventory as a disguised effort to cut budgets and personnel. See Appendix 1 for examples.

Primary Inputs: The sources (from where?) and nature (what?) of the data or information "received" by the resource entity; for example, "field offices, geological descriptions." Content, formats and media should also be noted; for example, "notebooks and logs."

Primary Outputs: The nature (what?) of data or information "produced" by the resource entity; for example, "graphs, histograms and trend lines." Content, formats and media should also be noted; for example, "floppy disks."

Holdings/Storage Media: The medium or media used to handle or store the information itself; for example, "disk and paper."

Inventory data should be readily available in most organizations and for most information resource entities for all fields except for "Comments and Observations" and "Evaluation," which are more subjective and judgmental in nature. In the main case example (Appendix 1), only about half the entities identified had one or both of these two entries completed. For the other fields, there may be a few situations in which an entry would not be applicable; for example, if the resource entity is widely dispersed throughout the organization, there would be no entry for "Resource Manager" or "Operating Contact."

The model data form in Figure 2-2 is the one actually used in the main case example (Appendix 1).[14] We are not aware of other examples of this type of form; i.e., one applicable to a broadly based inventory of all information resources. However, there are many examples of forms, formats and database management systems (DBMSs) designed with the same objectives of summary and synthesis, that deal with particular categories of information resources. For example, in the case of computer-readable databases there are numerous directories and inventories on the market and in the literature offering particular formats that provide for synoptic overviews.[15]

In the case of information systems (one of our three major resource categories), we can point to the example of a résumé form developed in the early '70s by the *U.S. Environmental Protection Agency*, reproduced in Fig. 2-3.[16]

2.3.2 Collect the Data

The major source of data for the inventory normally will be interviews with those in the organization involved in *using, handling, supplying, managing* and *counseling on* information. By making frequent reference to the model of these five information communities (Fig. 2-4), you will help keep their respective roles in perspective as the interrogation and fact-finding proceeds. Keep asking yourself: Am I speaking with a user, supplier, handler or manager? Understanding roles and functions will in turn help in isolating the resource entities you are seeking. Later, in Chapter 4, we will use these distinctions to form a basis for analyzing the preliminary inventory.[17] The two other important sources of inventory data are documents obtained from those interviewed and from external organizations that provide, or could provide, information resources to the organization (Fig. 2-1).

To the extent possible in the circumstances, interviews should be held in accordance with a plan, prepared jointly by the project director and management. However, inventory projects of this nature cannot be entirely preplanned, since they are, to a large extent, forays into "parts as yet unknown." However, some factors you should consider in drawing up a rough plan include:

1. How the organization is structured.
2. Who its key personnel are.
3. What its objectives are, including objectives of the various organizational units.
4. Existing lists or compilations of information services, systems, personnel and so on; internal evaluation and audit reports.
5. Agreement with management on the purpose, scope, budget and time available; the project director and management should share common expectations.
6. A schedule for the key meetings, arranged for in advance *by management*.

Figure 2-3. Information systems résumé used by U.S. Environmental Protection Agency.

INFORMATION SYSTEMS RÉSUMÉ

1. SYSTEM ACRONYM

2. SYSTEM NAME

3. SYSTEM ID

4. STATUS
   a. ☐ OPERATIONAL
   b. ☐ DEVELOPMENTAL

5. YEAR IMPLEMENTED 19

6. YEAR OF LATEST REVISION 19

7. SYSTEM JUSTIFICATION OR AUTHORITY
   a. ☐ KNOWN (STATE SOURCE)
   b. ☐ UNKNOWN

8. ANNUAL SYSTEM OPERATING COST (TO NEAREST $1000)

9. TYPE OF SYSTEM
   AUTOMATED   a. ☐ GO TO ITEM 10
   MANUAL   b. ☐ GO TO ITEM 15

10. EQUIPMENT UTILIZED (INCLUDE BOTH PERIPHERALS AND CPUS IF APPLICABLE)
    a. (NAME)   b. ORG. AND LOCATIONS WHERE INSTALLED

    (USE ATTACHED BLUE SHEET FOR EXTRA SPACE)

11. PROGRAMMING LANGUAGES USED
    a. ☐ COBOL   e. ☐ ASSEMBLY   i. ☐ IRS
    b. ☐ FORTRAN   f. ☐ ALC   j. ☐ OTHER
    c. ☐ PL/1   g. ☐ AUTO CODER   (SPECIFY)
    d. ☐ BASIC   h. ☐ RPG

12. SYSTEM CHARACTERISTICS (CHECK ALL APPROPRIATE BOXES)
    INPUT   d. ☐ BATCH   g. ☐ DIGITAL
    a. ☐ KEYBOARD   ENVIRONMENT   h. ☐ ANALOG
    b. ☐ CRT   e. ☐ ON-LINE   OUTPUT
    c. ☐ SENSOR   f. ☐ REAL-TIME   i. ☐ PRINTER

    j. ☐ CRT   SOFTWARE   q. ☐ LOCALLY DEVELOPED
    k. ☐ PAPER TAPE n. ☐ SPECIALIZED   r. ☐ OTHER (SPECIFY)
    l. ☐ MAG TAPE   o. ☐ GENERALIZED
    m. ☐ PLOTTER   p. ☐ NATIONALLY DEVELOPED

13. MAX. CORE REQ. FOR LARGEST PROGRAM
    NO. OF BYTES _____
    IF OVERLAY _____ PERCENT

14. NUMBER OF APPLICATIONS
    a. ☐ PROGRAMS OPERATIONAL
    b. ☐ UNDER DEVELOPMENT

15. SIZE OF LARGEST FILE
    NO. OF RECORDS _____
    AVG. BYTES/RECORD _____
    OR
    AVG. CHARACTERS/RECORD _____

16. SYSTEM DEVELOPED BY
    a. ☐ LOCAL STAFF
    b. ☐ OTHER (SPECIFY ORGANIZATION)

17. SYSTEM OPERATOR
    a. ☐ LOCAL STAFF
    b. ☐ OTHER (SPECIFY ORGANIZATION)

18. OTHER SYSTEMS FURNISHING INPUT
    1. _____
    2. _____
    3. _____

19. OTHER SYSTEMS RECEIVING OUTPUT
    1. _____
    2. _____
    3. _____

20. SYSTEM MANAGER'S NAME; TITLE; ORGANIZATION NAME; CODE; AND ADDRESS

    20a. TEL. NO.
         AREA CODE
         EXT.
    20b. PARENT ORGANIZATION
    20c. GOVT. AGENCY

Figure 2-3. (Continued)

INFORMATION SYSTEMS RÉSUMÉ (Continued)

21. ALTERNATE CONTACT FOR SYSTEM	21a. ORGANIZATION	21.b TEL.NO. AREA CODE EXT.

22. SYSTEM OBJECTIVES (DESCRIBE ANY CHANGES FROM ORIGINAL SYSTEM OBJECTIVES IF KNOWN) (USE ATTACHED BLUE SHEET FOR EXTRA SPACE)

23. MAJOR DATA OR INFORMATION ELEMENTS MAINTAINED BY SYSTEM (USE ATTACHED BLUE SHEET FOR ADDITIONAL INFORMATION ELEMENTS)

1. _____
2. _____
3. _____
4. _____
5. _____

6. _____
7. _____
8. _____
9. _____
10. _____

24. KEY OR SIGNIFICANT PROCESSING STEPS (USE ATTACHED BLUE SHEET FOR EXTRA SPACE)

25.1. TITLE OF INPUT SOURCE DOCUMENT

25.2. METHOD OF INPUT

a. ☐ CARDS	d. ☐ MAG. TAPE	f. ☐ PAPER TAPE	i. ☐ OTHER (SPECIFY)
b. ☐ DOCUMENT	e. ☐ LOCAL TERMINAL	g. ☐ OCR	
c. ☐ SENSOR	DISPLAY	h. ☐ MARK SENSE	

25.3. NAME OF SYSTEM/ORGANIZATION PROVIDING INPUT

25.4. UPDATE FREQUENCY

a. ☐ ANNUAL	d. ☐ MONTHLY	g. ☐ OTHER (SPECIFY)
b. ☐ SEMI-ANNUAL	e. ☐ WEEKLY	
c. ☐ QUARTERLY	f. ☐ DAILY	

26.1. TITLE OF INPUT/OUTPUT DOCUMENTS

26.2 METHOD OF INPUT
a. ☐ CARDS
b. ☐ DOCUMENT
c. ☐ SENSOR
d. ☐ MAG. TAPE
e. ☐ LOCAL TERMINAL DISPLAY
f. ☐ PAPER TAPE
g. ☐ OCR
h. ☐ MARK SENSE
i. ☐ OTHER (SPECIFY)

26.3. NAME OF SYSTEM/ORGANIZATION PROVIDING INPUT

26.4. UPDATE FREQUENCY
a. ☐ ANNUAL
b. ☐ SEMI-ANNUAL
c. ☐ QUARTERLY
d. ☐ MONTHLY
e. ☐ WEEKLY
f. ☐ DAILY
g. ☐ OTHER (SPECIFY)

35.1. TITLE OF OUTPUT/REPORTS

35.2. FORM OF OUTPUT
a. ☐ COMPUTER PRINTOUT
b. ☐ MAGNETIC TAPE
c. ☐ PUNCHED CARDS
d. ☐ PAPER TAPE
e. ☐ LOCAL TERMINAL DISPLAY
f. ☐ TYPED/PRINTED
g. ☐ MICROFILM
h. ☐ PLOTTER
i. ☐ OTHER (SPECIFY)

35.3. FREQUENCY
a. ☐ ANNUAL
b. ☐ SEMI-ANNUAL
c. ☐ QUARTERLY
d. ☐ MONTHLY
e. ☐ WEEKLY
f. ☐ DAILY
g. ☐ OTHER (SPECIFY)

35.4. PRINCIPAL USER ORGANIZATIONS
a.
b.
c.
d.

OUTPUT USES

36.1. TITLE OF OUTPUT/REPORT

36.2. FORM OF OUTPUT
a. ☐ COMPUTER PRINTOUT
b. ☐ MAGNETIC TAPE
c. ☐ PUNCHED CARDS
d. ☐ PAPER TAPE
e. ☐ LOCAL TERMINAL DISPLAY
f. ☐ TYPED/PRINTED
g. ☐ MICROFILM
h. ☐ PLOTTER
i. ☐ OTHER (SPECIFY)

36.3. FREQUENCY
a. ☐ ANNUAL
b. ☐ SEMI-ANNUAL
c. ☐ QUARTERLY
d. ☐ MONTHLY
e. ☐ WEEKLY
f. ☐ DAILY
g. ☐ OTHER (SPECIFY)

36.4. PRINCIPAL USER ORGANIZATIONS
a.
b.
c.
d.

OUTPUT USES

(USE ATTACHED BLUE SHEET FOR ADDITIONAL OUTPUT AND NUMBER 37-45 FOR EACH)

Figure 2-3. (Continued)

INFORMATION SYSTEMS RESUME (Continued)

56. DOCUMENTATION

a. SYSTEM FLOWCHART	☐ NO	☐ YES	d. FILE LAYOUTS	☐ NO	☐ YES
b. SYSTEM DESCRIPTION	☐ NO	☐ YES	e. CODE DESCRIPTION	☐ NO	☐ YES
c. SAMPLE OF OUTPUT REPORT	☐ NO	☐ YES	f. MANUAL FORMS/RECORDS	☐ NO	☐ YES

(FOR ALL YES BOXES CHECKED, PLEASE ATTACH COPIES TO THIS RESUME)

57. ADDITIONAL COMMENTS

58. a. FORM PREPARED BY
NAME
DATE

b. FORM REVIEWED BY
NAME
DATE

EPA—S4

Source: U.S. Environmental Protection Agency, "Directory of Information Resources", (Washington, D.C.: EPA Management Information Systems, 1973).

Figure 2-4. A model of communities, roles and functions in information management. Another community, information counselors, assists the four shown.

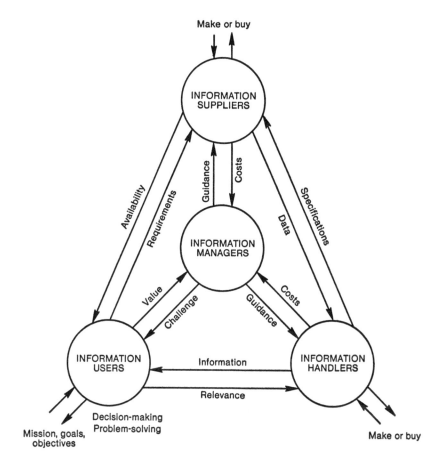

ROLES IN INFORMATION MANAGEMENT

Source: Forest W. Horton, Jr., *The Information Management Workbook: IRM Made Simple*, (Washington, D.C.: Information Management Press, revised edition 1985), Fig. 1-2. Reprinted with permission

Once the first few interviews have been held (we will not dwell on interviewing techniques), the director will gradually become immersed in the organization's information world: Confronted with its information management problems; referred to a host of other people, systems and so on; told of past successes and horror stories and offered all manner of recommendations and unsolicited advice. On the face of it, a tangled web indeed.

To steer your way through this onslaught of detail and confusion, keep your objective firmly in sight: To obtain the specific information needed to complete the various fields of the Inventory Data Form, including both facts and subjective commentary (Fig. 2-2). Above all, remember that your main task is to look for and identify the organization's potential *information resource entities*. Many entities will be obvious and well-known, but typically there will be others not so obvious at the beginning, and perhaps not recognized at all until several interviews have been completed. A special type, which we call hidden resources, is even more obscure, yet often among the most significant. This type will be treated separately in the next section.

You will find a second important source of inventory information in the various *documents* collected in the course of interviewing and following up leads. Of likely primary interest are internal reports, such as proposals to develop systems, evaluations and operational and strategic plans. Other documents of interest include consultants' reports, promotional and trade literature and even newspaper reports bearing on information issues of concern to the company or department. Some of these external sources may shed light on the existence of potential information resources.

External organizations, including private-sector service companies, government agencies — and even competitors, provide the third main source of data for the inventory form. There is a wealth of information resources "out there," many unknown and untapped by the organization.[18] However, within the tight time constraints of a typical resource survey, all relevant products and services probably could not even be scanned, much less evaluated. Some effort should be made to determine whether the organization has a mechanism to make itself aware of external resources, and, if not, to point out some examples of the values and benefits of resources located outside the organization.

The data collection process is illustrated by the *CRA Exploration* case. Over a 24-calendar-day period, about 60 people were visited and interviewed, located in 10 of the company's 24 Australian offices. These individuals represented most of the company's operating divisions, plus headquarters. Priority was given to seeing as many varied types of information handling activities as possible, without missing what the company itself considered its most important activities.

In the circumstances, it was not possible to see and visit *every* office, operation or person with a role in the company's information activities. But the sampling was sufficient to meet the objective of obtaining an overview of strengths and weaknesses, and to provide a basis for addressing key problems and opportunities.

The interview data were recorded in handwritten note form and analyzed. Appropriate portions were transferred to the Inventory Data Forms (Appendix 1), mostly toward the end of the survey. Separate files were kept for all documents collected during the survey which were later included as an appendix to the final report. Telephone calls and visits were made to several external organizations initially unknown to the director, to supplement knowledge of relevant external resources already known.

As illustrated in Appendix 1, the final compilation of 74 potential resource entities was assembled in alphabetical order by entity name and the identification (ID) numbers changed to match this sequence. This proved to be a convenient order for purposes of presentation and, later, for analysis and synthesis (Chapters 4 and 5). We will describe the inventory as a whole after we deal first with the matter of "hidden" resources.

2.3.3 Identify Hidden Resources

The main objective of the information resource discovery process is identification of configured resource entities — not information itself. Yet, as we have defined the "information resource" concept (Fig. 1-4), information itself can also be a corporate resource. Moreover, the information resources management process (Fig. 1-2) dictates that expenditures for the resource entities should be justified in terms of meeting corporate information needs, which in turn should be linked to achieving corporate goals and objectives.

Thus, all of the information actually used by the organization should, in theory, be linked to and mirrored by, specific resource entities. An inventory of these entities should reflect the information actually used. How then do we deal with cases in which major volumes of information, critical to the organization, and therefore clearly resources, are not linked with, or do not "come from" any obvious and identifiable resource entity? We describe such resources as hidden — hidden in the sense that they are not manifested as, or linked to, clearly identifiable sources. If ignored or overlooked in the inventory process, there would be no reflection in the inventory of the existence of what could be some of the organization's major resources.

An important assumption held in applying the sources-services-systems classification approach (Table 2-1) is that *all* information resource entities (IREs) would be recognizable in these terms. The IREs would all have some degree of concreteness, structure and organization, to a point where normally they all could be identified with a name or descriptive label — the ABC Service, the XYZ System and so on. In particular, a Source would imply a place, person or thing having limited physical dimensions.

Another assumption usually made when scanning an organization's information resource base is that all of the information content actually used, especially in its main line of business operations, "comes from" some well-structured and organized source (Fig. 1-4).

You should carefully test these two assumptions; namely, that sources of information are all neatly structured, configured entities, and that all critical information comes from such entities. You may be led to instances where, as in our main case example, information itself, clearly a corporate resource, does not all "come from" clearly demarcated sources, but instead some is widely dispersed, unstructured and, figuratively speaking, just lying around the organization, largely unattended by anyone or anything: A hidden resource. Former Vice-President Hubert Humphrey, for example, was fond of saying that he was fearful the key to unlocking the secrets of cancer was lying somewhere in a filing cabinet. In a similar vein, many a mineral exploration manager has wondered how many undiscovered ore deposits lay buried in the company's own files.

As the preliminary inventory proceeds, and resource entities are identified, the results should be matched with the information and data actually required and used by the organization, especially for "bread and butter" purposes. You should trace the origins of these critical data by asking members of the user community (Fig. 2-4): Where does your critical information come from? If there are no obvious matching sources, services or systems, you may have located a hidden resource. Such critical information should be identified with a descriptive label, classified as a "source" entity on an Inventory Data Form, and then described and commented upon as if it were a concrete source.

For example, in the *CRA Exploration* case, the company made extensive use of various types of geoscience data and information (Table 2-6). (Here and elsewhere, "ID" numbers refer to the Identification (ID) Numbers for the resource entities recorded in Appendix 1.) A number of the data types important for exploration purposes, for example *Drill-log and assay data* (ID 12), were

Table 2-6. Summary of preliminary information resource inventory: CRA Exploration Pty. Limited (CRAE) case example.

Categories:	Types:	Number of Information Resource Entities (IREs):			
		Internal	*External*	*Not Used*	*Total*
SOURCES	*CRAE Information:*				
	Bibliographic data	1			1
	Drill-log and assay data	1			1
	Exploration reports	1			1
	Geochemical data	1			1
	Geological samples data	1			1
	Geophysical data	1			1
	Management information	2			2
	Maps and charts	1			1
	Mineral lease data	1			1
	Mining information	1			1
	Petroleum information	1			1
	Prospects data	1			1
	Remote sensing data	1			1
	External Organizations:				
	Commercial		3	2	5
	Federal agencies		2		2
	Other CRA Group				0
	State agencies		5		5
	Other				0
SERVICES	Aerial photography		1		1
	Core/samples curation	1			1
	Drafting				0
	Geophysical surveying				0
	Information locating	6	1	2	9
	Library		2		2
	Mineral lease information		1		1
	Records management				0
	Reporting		1		1
	Reprographics	2			2
	Resource evaluation			3	3
	Systems/programming		2	2	4
	Other				0
SYSTEMS	Bibliographic control	2	3		5
	Communications		4		4
	Computing	1			1
	Drafting/graphics	2	1		3
	Geoscience data analysis	2			2
	Geoscience data management	4		1	5
	Image analysis	1			1
	Mineral lease data	1			1
	Prospect information	1			1
	Word processing	1			1
	Other				0
	Total IREs:	38	26	10	74

Source: CRA Exploration Pty. Limited case study, conducted during March-April, 1982 — parts of which are reported here with the company's permission.

dispersed in various company reports and files. In a practical sense there was no single source for these particular data. Although many of the *documents* in which the actual data were located were controlled by a bibliographic system, there was at that time no service or system dedicated to locating and retrieving this particular type of actual *data* within the documents and elsewhere.

Another category of information resource falling under the hidden label, but of a different nature, is represented by the *external* sources, services and systems that are either unknown to, unseen by, unappreciated by or unused by the organization. Here, they are hidden due to ignorance or lack of insight. Even *internal* entities may be hidden in a similar fashion, although (one would hope) to a lesser degree. For example, the preliminary inventory of *CRA Exploration* (Table 2-6) identified 10 external sources and services that appeared to be of potential value, but which were not then being used (e.g., ID 5, 42, 46, 55, 62).

2.3.4 Main Case Example

We have already made reference to the example of *CRA Exploration Pty. Limited*, the Australian mineral exploration company. Here we provide an overview and summary of this, our main case example. It illustrates most of the elements involved in Step One, conducting a preliminary information resource inventory.

Selected portions of the preliminary information resource inventory itself are provided in detail in Appendix 1. A summary is given in Table 2-6. The CRAE inventory project revealed a wide spectrum of entities, ranging from the commonplace, such as *Mail service* (ID 37), to sophisticated high-tech systems for analyzing geoscience data (e.g., *Magnetic data analysis system*, ID 43). The overview and summary (Table 2-6) shows the total range of resource types and the number of entities, 74 in all, broken down by: 1) Entities developed and managed within the company (Internal), 2) those obtained by the company from outside (External) and 3) other external resources available to the company, but not actually used at the time of the survey (Not Used). Discounting the Not Used category, 59 per cent of the entities inventoried were Internal and 41 per cent were External.

In Chapter 4 we will describe some analytical techniques, using portions of this case example, which will shed more light on the nature of the entities identified, their interrelationships and some management issues they pose. For the time being we will limit our comments to the classification or typological aspects of the completed preliminary inventory.

Looking at the classification scheme adopted, note that some of the types shown in Table 2-6 have no corresponding Resource Entities (i.e., *Other CRA Group, Geophysical surveying, Records management*). This reflects instances where resource types were anticipated before the survey began, but never actually encountered. The labels *Mineral lease data* and *Mineral lease information* provide an example of the case where entities concerning a single topic or subject must be classified in more than one category, in this case all three. Thus in the Sources category, *Mineral lease data* (ID 43) refers to those lease data which are "lying around" the organization, not associated with a structured source, service or system. Under the Services category, *Mineral lease information* (ID 44) includes an external, commercial service providing this type of information, while under the Systems category *Mineral lease data* (ID 59) includes an internal, computer-based system for handling these data.

Many of the types and entities within the sources category (Table 2-6) are not, as the term "source" implies, physically discrete places, organizations or persons, but are simply types of data and information located within the company, occurring largely in an unstructured form: The hidden resources we described earlier. Examples are *Maps and charts* (ID 39), *Drill-log and assay data* (ID 12) and *Geochemical data* (ID 24). For these cases, the name of the entity is the same as that used for type. While from a classification or typological point of view this is a crude solution, a great deal more time would have been needed to determine, more precisely, the nature and location of *all* the files, drawings, reports, notebooks, films and other packages of data and information in which this content was housed.

Other information resource types identified in the sources category (e.g., *Geological samples data*, ID 29; *Remote sensing data*, ID 61), while given a generic label, were actually highly centralized, and could have been given a specific organizational name. But to meet the objectives of this particular survey, it was more instructive to include them alongside all the other data types identified.

In the systems category, under the type Computing, one might have expected to see more than one entity identified. Indeed, the data form (ID 7) notes five computer installations in five different locations. However, all systems were physically similar and performed similar functions. At this stage it did not seem profitable to isolate details of their differences as five separate entities.

2.4 SUMMARY OF THE PRELIMINARY RESOURCE INVENTORY

The preliminary inventory, the main output of Step One of the information resource discovery process (Figs. 1-8, 2-1), is an itemized list of named information resource entities, showing type, location, "owner," purpose and nature, and for some entities, quality. In essence, it is a conventional inventory, no different in principle from one maintained by a drug store or supermarket.

The big difference, of course, is the nature of what is counted. For a supermarket, there is no problem with defining, recognizing, counting and comparing such goods containers as cans, bottles and boxes. The "containers" or units of measure of information, however, are not so tractable. So in beginning an inventory of information resources, much of our energies must be spent in *defining* the nature, shape and size of the containers; then we worry about whether we will be able to *recognize* the containers when we see them; still later, we may actually *find* them. All this effort must be expended before being able to look inside to savor and compare the contents!

One purpose of creating the information resource inventory is to enable the shop manager and his or her customers to know what kinds of information are "on the shelf" (Are we out of current marketing statistics today?), and then to be in a position to compare the quality, price and informational value of competing products. For example, which results in the best value: Using our scientists' time to index reports, buying an online bibliographic service or doing nothing? This question cannot be answered until the cost and value dimensions have been considered in Chapter 3, but the shop manager and his customers should at least have the benefit of knowing if there are any bibliographic services "on the shelf" or not.

The preliminary inventory, illustrated in Appendix 1, takes the form of a sequential listing of information resource entities — numbered, named and characterized by their essential qualities. Each entity is described in a standard format, taking up about one page or its electronic equivalent, and sorted by one of the data fields such as entity name. For the first inventory project, the format should be concise, the data fields few, but the number of entities described as large as reasonably possible. If, as a result of completing the resource mapping process, second and third iterations are carried out, leading to establishment of a permanent, updatable inventory, each iteration will become more detailed and accurate, and more focussed on the business. It would probably include fewer, but more significant entries.

In summary, the following basic information would be included in the preliminary inventory:

1. Name of potential information resource entity.
2. Category and type.
3. Geographic and organizational location.
4. Manager's name.
5. Contact for additional information.
6. Objectives supported.
7. Description of contents, functions and users.
8. Primary inputs and outputs.
9. Media employed.
10. Comments and evaluation of project director (optional).
11. Signoff signatures and dates.

Inventories of all kinds, such as this case example, too often are regarded in a perfunctory rather than a dynamic or strategic vein. That is, they are undertaken typically to check up on the physical status and safekeeping of assets: The warehousing supervisor periodically inventories items in the bins and on the pallets for which he is responsible; banks count cash in their vaults; property officers count equipment for which they are responsible and so forth.

In the succeeding chapters, however, we will try to emphasize that a preliminary inventory of the organization's information resources should be undertaken, not only to establish a beginning baseline, should it be the first of its kind, but also, for strategic purposes, to reconnoiter the information terrain, and thus take the first steps in drawing the organization's information resource map. With it, the firm will be in a better position to assess the adequacy of its present resource base and to plan for meeting future information needs.

. . . .

Now you have a preliminary inventory: A reasonably complete listing of the specific information resource entities your organization uses or could use, including both internal and external resource entities. Next, in Chapter 3, we turn our attention to another facet of the discovery process, measurement of the costs of these entities and assessment of their values.

NOTES

1. Information here and elsewhere throughout the book on the CRA Exploration Pty. Limited case study originated with one of us (Burk) in a study conducted during March-April 1982, parts of which are reported here with the company's permission.

2. Cornelius F. Burk, Jr., "Management of Departmental Information Resources: Report to EMR Executive Committee," (Ottawa, Ontario: Department of Energy, Mines and Resources, March 25, 1980).

3. Smithsonian Institution, "A Smithsonian Institution Directory of Information Resources: A Proposal," (Washington, D.C.: Office of Information Resource Management, Smithsonian Institution, August 16, 1984), p. 2. Reprinted with permission.

4. Office of the Auditor General of Canada and United States General Accounting Office, *Federal Government Reporting Study*, (Ottawa, Ontario and Washington, D.C.: Office of the Auditor General of Canada and United States General Accounting Office, 1986).

5. Elizabeth Bole Eddison, "Who Should Be In-Charge?", *Special Libraries*, 74(2), April 1983, Fig. 1.

6. Forest W. Horton, Jr., *Information Resources Management: Concept and Cases*, (Cleveland, Ohio: Association for Systems Management, 1979), Fig. 4-5.

7. The sources-services-systems classification scheme was first described by Horton in the early '70s in the context of describing a "systems approach" to the management of information: Forest W. Horton,Jr., *How to Harness Information Resources: A Systems Approach*, (Cleveland, Ohio: Association for Systems Management, 1974), pp. 15-16.

8. Horton, *Information Resources Management*, Fig. 4-5.

9. Forest W. Horton, Jr., *The Information Management Workbook: IRM Made Simple*, (Washington, D.C.: Information Management Press, revised edition 1985), Fig. 2-1.

10. Burk, "Departmental Information Resources," Table 1.

11. See Note 1.

12. U.S. Environmental Protection Agency, *Environmental Information Systems Directory: An Inventory of Administrative and Environmental Mission Support Systems with Indexes*, (Washington, D.C.: U.S. Environmental Protection Agency, June 1973), pp. iii-iv.

13. Smithsonian Institution, "Smithsonian Directory," Appendix A, pp. 8-9. Reprinted with permission.

14. This form is based on one published earlier by: Horton, *Workbook*, Fig. 2-6.

15. For example, with respect to databases covering a particular discipline: Cornelius F. Burk, Jr., "A Worldwide List of Source and Reference Databases in the Geosciences," *Database*, 5(2), 11-21.

16. U.S. Environmental Protection Agency, "Directory of Information Resources," (Washington, D.C.: EPA Management Information Systems, 1973). See also U.S. Environmental Protection Agency, *Environmental Systems Directory*, pp. xiii-xvi.

17. Horton, *Workbook*, Fig. 1-2.

18. For example, online databases: Forest W. Horton, Jr. "Tapping External Data Sources," *Computerworld*, August 15, 1983, 1-10 (In Depth).

3

MEASURING COSTS
AND ASSESSING
VALUES

The preliminary information resource inventory, described in Chapter 2, has provided you with a list of the full range of information resource entities (IREs) used by your organization. The next step in the discovery process, Step Two, will determine the costs associated with each IRE, and in a parallel fashion, assess their values (Fig. 1-8). The general objective of Step Two is to find out, approximately, how costly and how valuable each IRE is. Cost and value may be expressed in either qualitative, relative or quantitative terms, depending on a variety of factors. Knowledge of costs and values, and the relationship between the two, will be used in later steps of the mapping process as criteria for determining which of the IREs identified in the preliminary inventory are corporate information resources, which should be considered overhead and which represent waste.

Like other resources, information is acquired, used and reused, stored and disposed of, at a cost. Many companies and government agencies — virtually all organizations — have already recognized, or are quickly coming to appreciate, the magnitude of their information investments and costs and the impact they have on corporate fiscal management. Survey results reported by the Institute for Information Management, for example, show that some major companies are spending as much as 80 per cent of their payroll and related overhead costs on creating and maintaining information.[1] One purpose of Step Two, to be described in this chapter, is to suggest approaches to management for breaking down these massive, total costs by relating them to costs associated with meaningful, more digestible portions: Information resource entities (IREs).

Offsetting the costs of each information resource entity, are its values and benefits. Often taken for granted or even ignored, values also should be examined, assessed and taken into account. While more difficult, or often impossible to quantify in conventional dollar terms, there are other ways to express values. Values must be articulated, in some fashion or other, if we are to satisfy the basic resource management principles of minimizing costs and maximizing values (Fig. 1-3).

In addressing questions of the cost and value of information in this chapter, we will not stray far beyond our immediate concern, the preliminary information resource inventory. In particular, the areas of budgeting and accounting for information, while matters of vital concern to the ongoing management of most organizations, are beyond the scope of the information resource discovery process we are describing (as are all ongoing information management functions). We also eschew the even broader issues of the information business and the information economy. Our focus will remain on costing and valuing the IREs we have identified in the preliminary inventory.

On the other hand, the approaches, methods and specific techniques that you will apply or use are drawn from the domains of accounting, budgeting, financial management, business and economics. Unfortunately, only a few ready-made solutions are at hand. Information costing and valuing, while in today's context subjects of strategic significance to most organizations, are still underdeveloped fields. Traditional economic theory and accounting practice have thus far been unable to accommodate "information entities" in the asset and liability columns of the corporate balance sheet, much less to rigorously account for the cost and value of underlying information resource investments.

Chapter 3 Preview. In this chapter we describe approaches and methods for measuring the costs associated with each of the IREs identified by the preliminary inventory project; describe approaches and ways of assessing values associated with these entities; show how IREs can be ranked by their cost and by their value and, finally, we suggest ways to relate cost and value in the form of ratios. Our assumption is that the value of a resource should equal or exceed its cost. If not (as Robert Browning might have put it), what's a manager for?

3.1 CONCEPTS OF THE COST AND VALUE OF INFORMATION

Our approach to evaluating the preliminary inventory will be to examine each entity individually and to consider separately 1) its cost and 2) its value; then we will relate the two. In the Chart summarizing the process (Fig. 3-1), the word "measure" is used in connection with costs, while "assess" is used with values, with the intention of implying that, by and large, most *costs* can be quantified in dollar terms, while most *values* can be determined only qualita-

Figure 3-1. Cost/Value chart: Measure costs and assess values (Step Two).

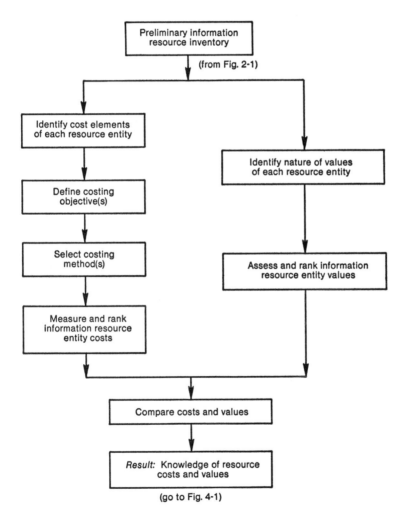

tively or in relative terms. However, as will be illustrated, we can also expect cases involving qualitative assessments of costs and quantitative measurements of values.

It's axiomatic that in order to manage any resource intelligently we must know both its cost and value. A business would certainly risk disaster if it did not know the *cost* of its labor, materials and overhead; so would other kinds of organizations in both the private and public sectors. In addition, managers would be in grave risk if they did not have ways of assessing the *value* of resources available to their organization. Similarly, investors must be cognizant of the current and future values of their enterprises, both in return-on-investment terms and in capital worth terms.

At this point, some working definitions of terms will help clarify the basic distinctions that should be made between the concepts of cost and value. The terms we will define are:

Cost	Information cost
Value	Information value
Price	Information price
Benefit	Information benefit

Our definitions are not presented as new proposals, nor as dogma from the accounting or economics disciplines. They merely reflect and convey some basic distinctions you should make when costing and valuing information resources.

Cost: An outlay, expenditure or price paid to acquire, construct or manufacture capital assets and commodities, as well as other expenses incurred for running an organization and accomplishing institutional missions, goals and objectives. Costs include expenditures for raw materials, direct labor and other related expenses, as well as depreciation and amortization of capital assets.

Information cost: The costs incurred in acquiring and/or producing information, as well as storing and maintaining it, using it, communicating it and disposing of it. Included are the costs of the input resources used to produce information (Fig. 1-6), and other related expenses incurred in production, storage and dissemination. From an accounting standpoint, this production is similar to the production (manufacture) of a physical commodity. Both involve converting something "raw" (unfinished) to a finished product by applying resources such as direct labor, equipment, overhead and information in order to add value to it (Fig. 1-4).

Value: Monetary, attributed, intrinsic, and/or relative worth, merit, usefulness, importance, and/or utility of a good, service, product, principle, item or entity. The value of something can be evidenced by a willingness or need to barter in exchange for, or otherwise need to use or have it available for use or for other purposes. We use the term "value" in its colloquial sense, not as defined formally by economists.

Information value: The value attributed to information produced or acquired by organizations, entities and persons, and delivered in the form of an information product or service.[2] The values may be realized immediately or at some later time. For example, the values attached to information created by scientific research are often realized long after it is created. The risk of realizing future values must be weighed against present and continuing costs of creating, storing and accessing it.

Perhaps the most straightforward criterion of information values is the willingness to pay for information. However, unwillingness to pay doesn't necessarily mean one places no value on the information sought. Other criteria of information value include those based on social, political and personal considerations. These, however, tend to be values associated with information itself, as opposed to the information resource entities from which it is derived.[3]

A number of other terms refer to concepts closely related to, or identified with, cost and value. Our working definitions further clarify the distinction between cost and value:

Price: The quantity of one thing that is exchanged or demanded in barter or sale for another. The amount of money given or set as a consideration for sale of a specified thing. The terms for the sale of which something is done or undertaken.

Information price: The price attached to an information product, service, system or source, either produced in-house or acquired externally, at the time of sale, based in part on costs for acquiring the raw materials (the data itself and the resources involved in their production and handling), and in part on value-added services undertaken at intermediate processing stages; or the transfer price attached by one internal organizational unit for "sale" of an information product or service, to another.

Benefit: Something that promotes well-being. An advantage. Useful assistance. Something worthwhile, rewarding or profitable. Expected return on investment.

Information benefit: The long-term gain or ultimate purpose to be derived from the production/acquisition and use of an information product or service.

With these working definitions in mind, we can begin Step Two: Measuring the costs and assessing the values of entities identified in the preliminary information resource inventory (Fig. 2-1).

3.2   HOW TO MEASURE COSTS OF AN INFORMATION RESOURCE ENTITY

As set out in Fig. 3-1, we will determine the costs associated with an information resource entity in four stages. The first is identification of the *elements* of cost that can or should be considered — that is, to define precisely what "cost" means for each entity. Next, an *objective* for costing should be specified, so that we are clear about whether we are looking for, say, the total investment to date, current direct operating costs, replacement costs, amortized costs or some other aspect of cost. Third, we must select an appropriate *method* or methods to ascertain the costs of the entity; lastly, the costs are *measured*.

Our methodology for determining costs and values does not supplant established practices in cost accounting. Knowledge, methods and standards on this subject are readily available from the accounting profession. Our purpose is to help bridge the gap between cost accounting practices and their application to the management of information resources and assets. What we offer is some insight into *what* costs to consider accounting for; we will not dwell on *how* to account for them.

3.2.1   Identify Cost Elements

Having identified an individual information resource entity, say a library or a computer system, you must now decide what elements making up the entity to consider in defining the cost. A number of factors will influence what elements can be used: The nature of the resource entity, your knowledge of its components and how they work, the availability and quality of cost data on the elements selected, the time and resources available to make the measurement and others.

However cost may be defined in particular cases, what matters is that you make the cost elements explicit. These decisions will influence the costing stages that follow, and later in the discovery process will affect judgments made during analysis (Step Three) and synthesis (Step Four).

A number of typical cost elements are listed in Table 3-1. They were selected as representative elements that would commonly be important components of various information resource entities. The

Table 3-1. Some categories and elements of cost of information resource entities.

Elements	Commonly Applicable Resource Categories		
	Source	Service	System
Functional Elements: Examples			
Editing	X	X	
Facilities management			X
Feasibility studies			X
Indexing	X	X	
Information acquisition	X	X	
Information disposal	X		
Information dissemination	X	X	
Information production	X	X	X
Inventory	X		
Maintenance		X	X
Operations		X	X
Photocopying	X		
Postal and courier	X	X	
Storage	X		
Telecommunications	X	X	X
Training			X
Translation	X	X	
Transportation		X	
Travel	X	X	
Writing	X		
Resource Elements: Examples			
Administrative overhead	X	X	X
Brokerage fees	X		
Capital			X
Computer hardware	X	X	X
Computer software	X	X	X
Consulting fees		X	X
Information	X	X	X
Labor (personnel)	X	X	X
Paper	X	X	
Real property (space)	X	X	X
Service fees		X	
Subscription fees	X		
Supplies	X	X	X
Temporal Elements: Examples			
Depreciation		X	X
Development			X
Life-cycle stages	X		X
Long-term fixed (sunk) costs	X	X	X
Processing steps		X	X
Rental fees		X	X

three categories of cost elements reflect three general sources of cost: Doing something (Functional elements), using something (Resource elements) and using time (Temporal elements). Obviously, many more elements would be required, at various levels of detail and complexity, to cover all conceivable elements of all resource entities. The table merely suggests different types of elements and levels of detail that could be considered in particular cases. Since the purpose of this Step of the mapping process is to obtain an *overview* of costs and values across the organization, not a detailed analysis of individual entities, you should limit the cost elements selected for a particular IRE to those that are basic; for example, direct labor, materials, hardware acquisitions, contracted services and the like.

Many of the cost elements you identify as the important ones would be applicable only to certain information resource entities; others, for example labor, would apply to nearly all of them. While we have not listed in Table 3-1 any information *types* or *entities* to which the various cost elements might apply, entries (X) are shown under the resource *categories* (source, service and system) to suggest that you might find it useful in some cases to prepare such an analysis at a detailed, entity level.

Our three case examples are all drawn from large governmental organizations. One example breaks down cost components for a narrow, single function, photocopying. Another illustrates cost elements recognized by an entire organization. The third example deals with cost elements for information technology facilities.

1. *Photocopying, Government of Canada.* For most organizations, the cost of photocopying is just another component of administrative overhead, not usually accorded special attention. However, where the organization is large and complex, even the cost elements associated with photocopying deserve attention. For example, the Government of Canada spent about $Cdn 50 million per year on photocopying during the early '80s. To arrive at a government-wide estimate, the Auditor General identified the five cost elements of photocopying detailed in Table 3-2.[4]

2. *Headquarters, U.S. Department of the Army (HQDA).* In its study on the design of an information management program for HQDA, Arthur Young & Company recommended that the following information handling entities be recognized as information cost elements (mainly functional elements) of the organization, and that the total direct costs incurred for each, including salaries, materiel, equipment purchases, rentals and so forth, be accounted for:

Table 3-2. Cost elements used to estimate total annual costs for photocopying by the Government of Canada. About 6,250 photocopiers were being used.

Cost Element	Amount ($Cdn 000)
Rented copiers — including rental and supplies	24,240
Purchased copiers — including amortization (straight-line, 60 months), maintenance and supplies	2,300
Full-time operators — assuming payroll cost of $20,000 a year for each operator	3,400
User-operators (convenience copiers) — assuming 10 copies and 2 minutes a trip and salary cost of $15,000 a year	18,530
Space — assuming 5 square meters per machine @ $100 per square meter	3,120
TOTAL	$51,590

Source: "Management of Photocopying," in *Report of the Auditor General of Canada to the House of Commons*, (Ottawa, Ontario: Auditor General of Canada, 1981). Reprinted with permission.

- Computer centers and EDP activities.
- Telecommunications networks, centers and related activities, including message centers.
- Printing, copying and publication activities, facilities and programs.
- Paperwork management programs, including reports, forms and records management activities.
- MIS staffs and information systems staffs.
- Libraries, information centers, records depositories, clearing-houses, document rooms and related facilities.
- Word processing pools.
- Statistical programs.

- Other related information programs, activities, facilities and networks which collect, transmit, store, retrieve or otherwise manipulate data, documents and information.[5]

3. *Office of Management and Budget (OMB), U.S. Federal Government.* For information technology facilities within the U.S. Federal Government as a whole, OMB defines "full costs" as comprising:

  - *Personnel*, including salaries, overtime and fringe benefits of civilian and military personnel; training and travel.

  - *Equipment*, including depreciation for owned, capitalized equipment; equipment rental or lease and direct expenses for non-capitalized equipment.

  - *Software*, including depreciation for capitalized costs of developing, converting or acquiring software; rental of software and direct expenses for noncapitalized acquisition of software.

  - *Supplies*, including office supplies; data processing materials and miscellaneous expenses.

  - *Contracted services*, including technical and consulting services; equipment maintenance; data entry support; operations support; facilities management; maintenance of software and telecommunications network services.

  - *Space occupancy*, including rental and lease of buildings, general office furniture and equipment; building maintenance; heating, air conditioning and other utilities; telephone services; power conditioning and distribution equipment and alternative power sources and building security and custodial services.

  - *Intra-agency services*, including normal agency support services that are paid by the installation.

  - *Interagency services*, including services provided by other agencies and departments that are paid by the installation.[6]

3.2.2 Define Costing Objectives

After you have decided on the number and kinds of costs elements to be evaluated, you should next set an objective for the costing exercise. For example, you may want answers to questions such as: Cost over what period of time; costs for whom; direct or indirect costs? Or some other such general question. The objective set out at the beginning of the mapping process may dictate, for example, that only current-year costs are relevant; that sunk costs must (or need not) be calculated or that life-cycle costs for certain types of information must (or need not) be determined.

The costing objective specified at this stage will influence what specific costing methods are relevant and useful. Moreover, having an objective will make collection of the cost data more efficient.

3.2.3 Select Costing Methods

Organizations will in most cases find that no single method for measuring cost will suffice for each and every IRE listed in the preliminary inventory. There is a strong likelihood that one method or approach may be adequate for a large cluster of potential resource entities (for example, direct costing for products sold in the commercial marketplace; life-cycle costing for internally developed information systems), while other methods are necessary for other clusters. The costing methods and costs we will describe briefly are:

Direct costing	Cost finding
Adsorption (imputed) costing	Life-cycle costing
Standard costing	Opportunity costs
Cost estimating	Qualitative (nonfinancial) costs

Various costing methods are available, each appropriate to different objectives and circumstances. The brief descriptions below provide some flavor of their scope and potential. You should refer to standard accounting texts for technical definitions and for details of methods and their application.

Direct Costing. This method is based on determining those costs obviously traceable to a unit of output or a segment of operations; for example, the information centers of the Department of Energy, Mines and Resources listed in Table 3-4. Total units of raw materials, direct labor hours, raw material unit price, direct labor hourly rate and variable overhead (indirect costs) should go into the calculation.

Adsorption (Imputed) Costing. Where no actual cash outlay is involved, and as a consequence there is no record of costs in the financial records, costs may be imputed. Adsorption costing can be important in cost studies involving comparisons between alternatives — say, a computer-based process versus a manual one.

Standard Costing. Standard costs are rigorously defined, predetermined costs — established measures expressed in terms of definite specifications and applicable within a given area or to a given situation. They are established in terms of the purpose that they are primarily to serve. Standard costing may be applied to routine or well-established functions such as order processing, printing, calculation and storage, or for the acquisition of standard information products such as directories, supplies and business forms.

Cost Estimating. Estimated costs are also predetermined costs, but differ from standard costs in that less care and objectivity are employed in their measurement. Cost estimating involves identifying informational transactions and specifying their units of measure. For example, in administrative areas, units of measure such as cost per personnel action, cost per inquiry, cost per service call, cost per square foot of office space and so on are traditionally used.

Cost Finding. Largely because of rapidly changing technology, some organizations may find the application of formal cost accounting methods too difficult or time-consuming, usually for the reason that their baselines keep shifting and the parameters (e.g., price-performance ratios) are too volatile. Under such conditions, the organization may have to use cost-finding techniques. In this instance we are unable to start with a clear identification and unit of measure for an information transaction; we must, instead, "find" the cost by indirect methods, such as imputation or inference.

Life-Cycle Costing. The information life-cycle concept holds that information is created, passes through various stages of development and ultimately is destroyed or purged. When the concept is applied to specific information, stages can be identified such as requirements definition, collection, processing, storage and so on. Life-cycle costing (and valuing) identifies the costs (and values) associated with each stage, arrays them over the "lifespan" of the information, and calculates a total cost (and value).

Opportunity Costs. Taking a decision to spend or invest in a particular information resource entity or entities exacts the cost of foregoing the benefits of alternative investments. The significance of opportunity costs in the case of information resource investments is heightened by the increasing number of options for meeting information needs and the risks of making a poor choice. Even doing nothing can have a cost if opportunities are not seized.

Qualitative (Nonfinancial) Costs. Burdens involved in maintaining information resources may be exclusively or largely nonquantifiable. For example, the toll taken by "technostress" and "computerphobia" can be real and serious, yet not easily measured in monetary terms. We urge that for each IRE, consideration be given to applying a "hassle factor" judgment that would later be taken into consideration when cost/value relationships are examined.

3.2.4 Measure and Rank Entities by Cost

The last stage of the costing exercise (Fig. 3-1) is to measure the costs, and then to rank the entities in order of decreasing cost. The cost data actually compiled would depend on the objectives and cost elements already decided upon. Unfortunately, however, the cost data we want are frequently difficult to compile because many of the monetary costs of information are relegated to overhead or subsumed in other, noninformation accounting entities. It is not uncommon to draw a blank at this point, or at best to find only partial data. However, if the major cost elements have been correctly identified, then, as a last resort, you can apply a cost-finding approach to yield rough approximations.

Next, list your entities in decreasing order of cost. Ranking resource entities in this way can highlight where in the organization, and for what purposes, your organization's information dollars are being spent. Even if full costs for some of the resource entities, such as data processing (a function, not usually an IRE), are already known, chances are that management will see for the first time how these known costs relate to other information expenditures (and perhaps learn what the others are), and reveal an estimate of *total* costs for its information resources. From a resource mapping point of view, especially if a costing exercise has never been carried out before, even rough approximations can provide new insights for your managers.

As an illustrative example (Table 3-3), we have categorized costs into four broad classes: High cost, medium cost, low cost and little or no cost. The number of categories and class intervals should be selected on the basis of the ranges you encounter. Note that in this illustration some costs are not comparable; for example, "Development" and "Operations," but often such data are all that may be available during the discovery process. Nor are *all* costs necessarily accounted for. For instance, even if public libraries are "free" to the organization, there is a cost to the organization of "using" them; thus some libraries may be significantly less costly. "Use costs" for many of the identified potential resources are, of course, significant in their own right and can exceed the cost of the resource itself (e.g., cost of purchasing a personal computer *vs* cost of using it).

A basic objective of mapping information costs is often to simply highlight the order of magnitude, or even the existence of information costs, without primary concern for accuracy or comprehensiveness. For an example in this category, we can again cite the *Department of Energy, Mines and Resources* (Canada) case.

To arrive quickly at an estimate of *minimum* annual expenditures for information resources, an inventory was prepared of the department's information centers — those divisions, branches or

Table 3-3. Illustrative example of ranking of selected resource entities by overall cost to the organization.

Cost Category	Information Resource Entity	Cost Measure
HIGH COST	Computer System A	Development
Over $1 million	Computer System B	Operations
	Records Center	Operations
MEDIUM COST	Editorial Office	Estimate
$500,00 to $999,000	Financial Control System	Development
	Marketing Database	Annual fees
	Personal Computers	Purchase
	Telecommunications Network	Operations
	Word Processing Pool	Operations
LOW COST	Conference Facilities	Overhead allocation
Under $500,000	Courier Service	Contract
	Photocopiers	Rental fees
	Supplier Index	Operations
LITTLE OR NO COST	Government directories	—
	Public libraries	—

other organizational units devoted to acquiring, processing, storing and/or disseminating information products or services (Table 3-4).

The 18 centers identified had budgets totalling $Cdn 15.4 million and 471 person-years. In addition, another $9.8 million was to be spent on computing. The total of $25.2 million represented about 18 per cent of the department's salary and operating budget. While these cost elements represented only a portion, perhaps a small portion, of EMR's total base of information resources, they had not previously been isolated and reported in resource terms. Knowledge of a *minimum* cost, related to clearly defined organizational units, was the first step in recognizing the budgetary significance of the department's information resources.[7]

Table 3-4. Operating costs and person-years (PYs) of information centers, Department of Energy, Mines and Resources (Canada).

Information Center	1979-80 Resources		Main Activities**							
	Cdn $000	PYs	P	S	L	B	T	P	R	C
Science & Technology Sector										
Technology Information Div Can Ctr Mining & Metallurgy	1,089	34	X			X	X	X		
Geological Information Division Geological Survey of Canada	2,699	95	X	X	X	X	X			
Geol [ISPG] Info Subdivision Geological Survey of Canada	558	22	X	X	X		X			
Canada Map Office Surveys & Mapping Branch	766	34	X							
National Air Photo Library Surveys & Mapping Branch	259	15	X	X						
Information Service Surveys & Mapping Branch	168	7			X		X			
Automated Cartography Center Surveys & Mapping Branch	535*	8								X
Technical Information Service Can Ctr for Remote Sensing	210	3	X			X	X	X		
CCRS Computing Center Can Ctr for Remote Sensing	748*	12								X
Library Earth Physics Branch	111	3			X					
Can Ctr for Geoscience Data	278	5				X				
Mineral Policy Sector										
Information Systems Division	1,086	38	X		X					
Energy Sector										
Energy Communications Division	4,796	18	X				X	X		
Administration Sector										
Information EMR Branch	1,672	60	X				X			
Computer Science Center	141*	97								X
Information & Sales Center	35	3	X							
Headquarters Records Office	208	13							X	
Departmental Manuals & Directives	81	4	X						X	
DEPARTMENTAL TOTALS:	$15,437	471	7	5	8	4	6	2	2	3

*Full costs less revenue.

**P = publishing, S = sales, L = library, B = bibliographic, T = scientific and technical information services, P = public relations, R = records management, C = computing.

Source: Cornelius F. Burk, Jr., "Management of Departmental Information Resources: Report to EMR Executive Committee," (Ottawa, Ontario: Department of Energy, Mines and Resources, March 25, 1980). Reprinted with permission.

Another case example deals with costs related to a single information resource entity — a large information system called STORET, designed and operated by the *U.S. Environmental Protection Agency* (EPA).

After over 10 years' operations, a review of EPA's costs for STORET was called for by passage of the *Clean Water Act of 1972.* Costs had risen appreciably due to enhanced technology which had replaced batch operations with remote terminals, thereby increasing access sites from 1 to 300. New legislation had created additional demands for information on water quality assessment and water quality management, all requiring new files and analysis routines. Included were files on programs for water standards, water quality violations, permit applications, inventories, sources of pollution and fish kills by pollutants, among others.

The review indicated that when access to STORET became decentralized, the only costs paid by its Federal and state user agencies were for their remote terminals. For this small cost, each agency was able to access, share, process and store a wide range of data, some unrelated to water quality, such as land, timber and wildlife management data. EPA's computer costs rose from $434,000 in 1971 to $1.2 million the next year and to $3.0 million in 1973.

The evaluation of STORET's costs covered development and operations, including personnel, computer support, data reduction and conversion. Operational costs were reported by system component and use. Comparisons were made with costs incurred by other large systems in government and the private sector. The evaluation report concluded that:

- Total costs for STORET were unknown.
- Cost elements had not been defined or measured.
- No periodical assessments had been undertaken to determine whether STORET could be operated more efficiently.
- The provision of "free" services by the Federal Government to the States had never been addressed as a high-level policy issue.

These and other findings led to a number of recommendations and technical and management decisions dealing with file management techniques, storage costs, archiving capabilities, contracting arrangements and user charges; and with the need for a cost accounting system to discriminate between development and operations and internal and external users, to track cost trends, determine volume/cost relationships and to relate the cost of STORET to EPA's total information resources budget.[8]

3.3 HOW TO ASSESS VALUES OF AN INFORMATION RESOURCE ENTITY

Before describing the valuing process, let us briefly review why it is necessary. We have set out to examine information entities on the premise that "information is a resource," so we need means for determining the *role* that specific information actually plays, and we need to understand its significance to the organization as a whole. Measures of value are required that would establish which information entities, if any, should be treated and managed as organizational resources. The measuring methods used need not be elaborate or designed to yield precise results. Our purpose here is to discover and sketch the information landscape, not to closely analyze and measure individual terrain features. We want just enough information on value to allow us, with a reasonable degree of confidence, to place it on the corporate information map.

Determining the *values* of information is, in many cases, a formidable task, one that only recently has attracted serious attention from scholars, economists and managers. We have no illusions about the difficulty. On the other hand, we are not prepared to throw up our hands in despair. While there are, as yet, no generally available and applicable methods to quantitatively measure value with precision, resource management principles require us to take the approximate value of information into account.

Accepting for the time being that there are no fully objective methods for measuring value, analogous to those applied to costs, we will approach assessment of the value dimension on two other fronts: 1) by describing the *nature* of the values associated with a resource entity, and 2) by determining the *relative* value of the entity.

The 19th century European explorers of western North America had no objective methods for measuring the eventual worth (or value) of the minerals, forests and waters over which they traversed, but they could and did subjectively describe their general nature and quality, and indicated where they were located. Implicit in their descriptions was the notion of value or potential value. Such "soft" information provided the incentives for others to later exploit and ultimately measure and realize these values in economic and social terms.

3.3.1 Identify Nature of Values

When, in a particular context, content and media combine to evoke a response, we have "information." In a sense, value is implicit in the response and thus in the very notion of information. By understanding the *nature* of the values that we attach to information (that is, to answer the question: *What* makes this information of value?) we not only are better able to see information resources for what they are, but we are better equipped to seek out those information resources having the values that match our needs.

To help you describe the nature of the values of your information resources, we have compiled in Table 3-5 a list of elements of value, organized in two broad groups: First, values related closely to information itself (Quality of Information Itself, Utility of Information Holdings), and second, values related to the impact of information resources on particular organizational attributes (Productivity, Effectiveness, Financial Position). This is not a complete list. Many others, known and imagined, could have been added to each category — and there are other categories of values; for example, the impact on strategic activities (as opposed to administrative activities), or values associated with information-handling capabilities.

As with the determination of information costs, our list of elements of value should stimulate and orient development of measures of value appropriate to your own situation. The purpose of the table, analogous to the table used to help identify elements of cost (Table 3-1), is to provide some guidance and help in answering the question, for each information resource entity: What makes this IRE of value to my organization? Alternatively, Why is it of value; or why of no value; or why of negative value?

For purposes of the information resource discovery process, you are seeking knowledge of what the elements of value *are* for each entity. Do not try to measure *how much* of whatever qualities are identified may be present. In the stage that follows you will compare and *rank* IREs by their overall value.

To emphasize the nature of information values, we have grouped the elements shown in Table 3-5 into five categories, each a broad criterion of value. The five criteria form a rough hierarchy, from the most detailed to the most general. To use this table, or another customized to meet your needs, ask yourself, for each IRE in your inventory: Which elements of value most closely reflect the values of critical importance to my organization? Then tabulate the answers for all IREs. You will have articulated, verbally, the main values associated with each entity. Now, let's look at Table 3-5.

3.3.1.1 Quality of Information Itself. Information values in all contexts usually include one or more of these "conventional" attributes. The context dictates which specific values are important.

Table 3-5. Some categories and elements of value of information resource entities.

Quality of Information Itself: Examples

Accuracy	Precision
Comprehensiveness	Relevance
Credibility	Reliability
Currency	Simplicity
Pertinence	Validity

Utility of Information Holdings: Examples

Accessibility, intellectual	Format and presentation
Accessibility, physical	Frequency of use
Adaptability	Physical stability
Browsability	Reproducibility
Ease of access	Selectivity
Ease of use	Unreproducibility
Flexibility	

Impact on Organizational Productivity: Examples

Greater returns for employees and management	Reducing "noise"
	Reducing uncertainty
Improvement in decision-making	Stimulation
Improvement of product quality	Timeliness of actions
Improvement of working conditions	Time-saving
More efficient operations	Withholding unneeded information
Obtaining needed goods and services	

Impact on Organizational Effectiveness: Examples

Finding new markets	More harmonious relationships
Improved customer satisfaction	Part of a product
Meeting goals and objectives	Part of a service
Meeting responsibilities	Product differentiation

Impact on Financial Position: Examples

Cost reduction	Exploitability of existing assets
Cost saving	Improved profits
Creation of new assets	Insurable interest
Displacement of more expensive resource inputs	Lost opportunity cost
	Return on investment (ROI)

Note the inherent conflict between some, such as *simplicity* and *comprehensiveness*, or *currency* and *accuracy*. Tradeoffs must be made to enhance any given value element. For instance, one overriding value of a daily newspaper is *currency*, while a major value of a monthly periodical dealing with the same basic information may be *reliability* and *validity*. Not only cannot all three values normally be achieved to the same degree at the same time, but they should not, because we are deliberately trading one information value attribute for another.

3.3.1.2   Utility of Information Holdings. Moving from values associated with "quality" to those of "utility" is fundamentally more a difference in degree than a difference in kind. Here, however, the emphasis is on the *processibility* or *manipulatibilty* of information. As the criterion name implies, these values are related to the physical, electronic and logistical attributes of holdings — files, records, dossiers, databases, disks, reels, fiche and the like, as stored in paper, electronic, magnetic, film, optical disk or other media.

Again, maximizing any one value is usually achieved at the expense of another. Examples include *physical accessibility* vs *selectivity, browsability* vs *ease of access* and *reproducibility* vs *ease of use.* The context has a fundamental bearing on which values are important. In one context, a value element such as *reproducibility* may be highly desirable (e.g., copying programs for personal computers), while in another context the opposite value, *unreproducibility,* may be paramount (e.g., safeguarding treasure maps or stock certificates).

Robert Taylor has identified a wide spectrum of elements of value by applying a value-added model to the information life-cycle (Table 3-6). His model relates a number of elements of value, mostly belonging to our Utility category (Table 3-5), to user needs and to specific processes (e.g., "indexing") that add the values (e.g., "item identification").[9]

3.3.1.3   Impact on Organizational Productivity. The meaning of the Industrial Age concept of productivity to its Information Age equivalent translates roughly as "working smarter, not just harder." The strategic deployment of information resource entities accounts for many of the dramatic improvements in organizational productivity (and to numerous failures where misapplied) that have become recognized as hallmarks for success (or failure) in the economy.[10]

Table 3-6. Robert Taylor's value-added model, relating information value elements (center column) with user needs and value-added processes.

User Criteria of Choice (User Needs)	Interface (Values Added)	System (Value-Added Processes: Examples)
Ease of Use	Browsing Formatting Interfacing I (Mediation) Interfacing II (Orientation) Ordering Physical accessibility	Grouping similar data Highlighting important terms Instructing for user sophistication Providing access to terminal Writing good instructions

Reducing Noise	Access I (Item
	  identification)
	Access II (Subject
	  description)
	Access III (Subject
	  summary)
	Linkage
	
	Precision
	Selectivity
		Indexing
		
		Vocabulary control
		
		Writing executive summaries
		
		Ranking output for subject
		  relevance

Quality	Accuracy Comprehensiveness Currency Reliability Validity	Editing Updating Verifying data input Comparing similar data for discrepancies Evaluating data

Adaptability	Closeness to problem
	
	Flexibility
	
	Simplicity
	
	Stimulatory
		Formulating decision
		  options
		Writing speeches for
		  executives
		Ranking output for problem
		  relevance
		Interpreting data

Time-saving	Response speed	Reduction of processing time
Cost-saving	Cost-saving	Lower conect-time price

Source: Robert S. Taylor, "Information Values in Decision Contexts," *Information Management Review*, Summer 1985. This paper was based on Taylor's book: *Value-Added Processes in Information Systems*, (Norwood, New Jersey, Ablex Publishing Corporation, 1986). Reprinted with permission.

The value elements in this category are those known or perceived to bear directly on productivity of the organization. Of course other categories of values, like Quality and Utility, also affect productivity, but less directly. The significance and impact of information resources on improving productivity in various contexts — office, factory, laboratory and for business in general — have already been elaborated upon.[11]

The *U.S. Paperwork Commission*, in its value/burden study, noted that value, particularly where social value must be taken into account, can rarely be quantified. Consequently, it approached the problem of determining the values of paperwork and information by expressing what the values *are*. The Commission reported the following elements of value, expressed in terms of information's *impact* on government operations and policy-making. Most fall in our Productivity category. Thus information "of value" is that information which:

- Contributes to the effective operations of an agency.
- Is collected in a cost/effective manner for the agency.
- Helps policy-makers set priorities and/or agendas.
- Introduces a new idea or innovation into government.
- Helps an administrator/policy-maker justify his/her program or record of performance.
- Helps to assess public reaction to policy options being considered by policy-makers.
- Provides part of a research base for future planning.
- Helps administrators/policy-makers in formulating marketing strategies for executive, congressional and public presentations.
- Is required to administer programs.[12]

One could easily transform most of these governmental values into parallel scenarios involving individual agencies and private-sector organizations, although the mix in emphasis as between the social and economic dimensions may differ.

The second case example illustrates how value can be expressed quantitatively, in dollars and cents. Peter Sassone and Perry Schwartz studied four departments in two unidentified *Fortune 500 organizations* (two marketing, one legal, and one engineering department, involving 587 individuals) and applied quantitative methods to measure productivity gains attributable to office auto-mation (OA) systems. They used "work profile analysis" and the "hedonic wage model" to establish a baseline activity profile which could then be compared to the new profile, created after introduction of office automation systems.

Each profile reflects the various employee classes (managers, junior professionals, secretaries, etc.) and the percentage of time each class spends on "higher-value," "lower-value" and "no-value" work. The intended effect of OA systems is to increase time spent by each class on higher-value activities and decrease time spent on the others. Using salaries as implicit measures of value and loaded hourly costs of the five employee classifications, the model calculates the overall difference in value, expressed as dollars, between the baseline and post-OA profiles. This difference is a quantitative measure of value of the productivity gains.[13]

3.3.1.4 Impact on Organizational Effectiveness.

This category of elements relates values directly to organizational outputs — whatever the organization provides, produces or accomplishes. Of course, all of the previous categories contribute also, but here values are related directly to effectiveness. This impact is most obvious where information is an integral part of, or the entire service or product marketed by the organization; the information resource entities directly responsible for such information have values related to the benefits realized by sale or production of the product or service in question.

As we've mentioned, in the case of governmental or other public services, the value of information resource entities may be directly related to the level of service to the public, or to meeting statutory or other responsibilities (social values).

3.3.1.5 Impact on Financial Position.

Values in this category directly impact the organization's financial position, including its profitability and level of expenditures. Use of an information resource entity may result in cost reduction, by replacing a more costly alternative (e.g., using an automated teller machine (ATM) *vs* a bank teller), or in cost saving, by avoiding certain costs altogether (e.g., using electronic funds transfer (EFT) systems).

An information resource entity may be the principal factor of production in a process designed to yield a particular return on investment or profit. David Vincent has argued that the value of information to a company should be measured in terms of its *investment* value; that is, its potential to yield future benefits to the organization. Corporate information resources can be described and reported in financial statements under the category "Other assets," as illustrated schematically by Vincent (Fig. 3-2).[14]

The commercial value of information products and services is of course a measure of value of information. Approaches and techniques for the pricing of information for commercial and marketing

Figure 3-2. David Vincent's schematic illustration reporting information as an asset on the balance sheet.

N. Consolidated Balance Sheet Details

	December 31,	
Assets	1983	1982
Trade and other receivables		
Trade, less allowances	$ 720.5	$ 710.9
Unbilled and other	445.3	467.2
Total	$1,165.8	$1,178.1
Inventories		
Finished goods	$ 497.3	$ 486.5
Work in process	593.7	611.6
Raw materials and purchased parts	739.6	575.1
Total	$1,830.6	$1,673.2
Finance and related receivables		
Total finance and related receivables	$4,311.5	$4,408.1
Less: Unearned income	754.3	887.2
Allowance for losses	383.5	388.2
Net finance and related receivables	$5,449.3	$5,683.5
Other assets		
Information	$ 483.4	$ 501.9
Deferred charges	593.1	587.6
Investments — affiliates	435.7	405.4
Total	$1,512.2	$1,494.9

Source: David R. Vincent, "Information on the Bottom Line," Computerworld, September 26, 1983, p. 1 (In Depth). Copyright 1984 by SW Communications, Inc., Framingham, MA 01701.

purposes, however, are beyond our scope. Topics in this area would include marketplace pricing, marginal revenue, marginal cost pricing and so on.

3.3.2 Assess and Rank Entity Values

Having examined the *nature* of the values associated with each IRE, your next step is to compare and *rank* all information resource entities with one another in terms of their overall value to the organization (Table 3-1).

Various methods for ranking the values of your information resources could be used. As an example, we will outline portions of the method described in Eugene Bedell's 1985 book *The Computer Solution: Strategies for Success in the Information Age.*[15] Although developed for computer systems, parts of Bedell's methodology are well-suited to evaluating other kinds of information resource entities and thus are applicable to meeting needs of our mapping process. This example, described more fully in *The Computer Solution*, is based on three ratings:

1. A rating of the *effectiveness* with which the information resource entity supports the activity or activities it was designed to support;
2. A rating of the *strategic importance* of the resource entity in carrying out this activity;
3. A rating of the *strategic importance* to the organization of the activity supported.

Typically, an organization will have a number of activities, each supported by various information resource entities. In the simplest case, only one activity would be involved — that of the organization itself, in which case the two strategic importance ratings (2 and 3) would collapse into one. In more complex organizations, we might have to deal with a hierarchy or network of separate activities. For purposes of outlining Bedell's methods, a simple organizational structure is assumed, but his approach could be expanded to deal with more complex situations.

The objective of Bedell's method of direct interest to our mapping process is to develop numerical indexes that would allow you to *rank* your entities by their value, in a manner analogous to the ranking of entities by cost (Table 3-3). Using excerpts from *The Computer Solution*, here are descriptions of the four steps of interest, which we label: 1. Rate Effectiveness, 2. Rate Strategic Role of Resource Entity, 3. Determine Strategic Role of Activity and 4. Assess and Rank Entities by Value.

3.3.2.1 Rate Effectiveness. The first part of Bedell's formula for assessing and ranking value is a measure of the *effectiveness* with which the system, or more broadly for our purposes, the information resource entity, supports the activity or activities intended. For each IRE, Bedell would ask: "How effectively does a particular [resource entity] support the activity it was built to support?"[16] The activity in question could range from a minor administrative function to a major operational activity, to the organization as a whole.

Applying Bedell's definition of an effective system, we would say that an information resource entity is "effective" if it meets stated information requirements and is functionally effective and technically adequate within the context of the activity it supports.[17] Context matters. As Bedell notes:

> A system that might be rated highly effective by one activity in one organization may be rated nearly useless by a similar activity in another organization. . . . . Even within the same organization, different activities might rate the effectiveness of the same system differently. . . . . A system is effective or ineffective based on the needs of the activity it is supporting.[18]

To measure effectiveness, Bedell applies a scale of values to arrive at an index. In our application we call it the Resource Effectiveness (RE) Index (equivalent to Bedell's ESA Index). However, the particular scale you use should be worded and quantified to meet your own circumstances. The following scale, excerpted from *The Computer Solution* and amended to meet our broader application, provides a basic standard: A direct measure that rates resource effectiveness on a scale from 10, as the most effective, to 0, as least effective.

> *10: Highly Effective.* The [resource meets information requirements], is functionally appropriate [and] technically adequate. . . . . Little or no additional work or investment is required on the [resource], other than routine maintenance. Specifically, the [entity] provides the right [kind and] amount of information [content, media and functionality] to support the activity it was designed to support; the information [quality is adequate] for the purpose intended and it is provided in a timely enough fashion to be useful. . . . .

> *5: Moderately Effective.* The [resource entity] provides reasonable support to the activity, but substantial improvements are necessary to improve [the degree to which it meets information requirements], functional appropriateness [or] technical quality . . . . . Despite required improvements, however, [resource entities] that fall in this category generally do not need to be replaced.

1: Ineffective. The [resource entity] provides support to the activity it was designed to support, but ineffectively. . . . . the enhancements required to improve [it] are so extensive that, in the long term, the [entity] will have to be replaced with a better [one].

0: No Support. No [resource entity] is currently [available], or the [entity] that is [available] is so ineffective as to be worthless. . . . . This category also includes [resources] that the organization [has access to, but] is not currently using.[19]

Table 3-7 illustrates application of Bedell's method to assessing the relative value of information resource entities. The entities are drawn from the *CRA Exploration* case and six actual "activities" are identified. However, the numeric values for the three indexes are hypothetical and, while reasonable, are presented solely for purposes of illustrating the method. Moreover, the list of CRAE activities and resource entities is not comprehensive.

The table illustrates several points. Note that an information resource entity (e.g., *Exploration reports index, Computer systems*) can support more than one activity. Some activities (e.g., Research and Development) may use virtually all of the organization's information entities at one time or another, while others (e.g., Property Administration) would almost always use only a limited number of IREs.

More specifically, Column B illustrates use of the Resource Effectiveness (RE) Index. A "0" rating for one of the examples means in this case that the entity was not being used by the company, *not* that it was inherently ineffective.

3.3.2.2   Determine Strategic Role of Resource Entity. The second part of Eugene Bedell's formula we are using to rank the value of information resource entities involves a measure of the *strategic importance* of the resource entity with respect to the activity or activities it is intended to support. For each activity supported by an information resource entity, we ask Bedell's question: "How important is a particular [IRE] to the activity it was [acquired or built] to support?" Later we will ask one of his follow-up questions: "How important is the activity in question to the organization?"[20]

By "importance," Bedell means strategic importance — the importance of something, say a computer system or an information source, to achieving the objectives of the organization or one of its components. As with so many other facets of information management, context plays an overriding role in determining what is

Table 3-7. Calculation of hypothetical Value Indexes for information resource entities selected from the CRA Exploration case (Appendix 1). The numeric ratings are reasonable but shown for illustrative purposes only.

A Activity Supported/ Information Resource Entity (IRE)	B Resource Effectiveness (RE) Index	C Importance to Activity (IA) Index	D Importance to Organ'n (IO) Index	E Value Index **
Mineral Exploration:				
Airborne geophysical survey				
index (ID 2)	9	5	10	450
Computer systems (ID 7)	7	10	10	700
Drill-log and assay data (ID 12)	8	10	10	800
Drill-log data system (ID 13)	0	5	10	0
Exploration information service				
B (ID 15)	5	5	10	250
Exploration information service				
C (ID 16)	7	5	10	350
Exploration reports index				
(ID 18)	5	5	10	250
Field data coding system				
(ID 23)	5	5	10	250
Geochemical data (ID 24)	8	10	10	800
Geophysical data (ID 30)	8	10	10	800
Magnetic data analysis system				
(ID 36)	8	5	10	400
Maps and charts (ID 39)	8	10	10	800
Prospects data (ID 58)	8	10	10	800
Petroleum Exploration:				
Exploration well index (ID 19)	5	5	6	150
Maps and charts (ID 39)	8	5	6	240
Petroleum information (ID 54)	5	5	6	150
Property Administration:				
Maps and charts (ID 39)	8	5	8	320
Mineral lease data (ID 43)	8	10	8	640
Mining Development:				
Drill-log data system (ID 13)	0	5	4	0
Mining information (ID 47)	5	1	4	20
Research and Development:				
Computer systems (ID 7)	6	5	8	240
Exploration information service				
C (ID 16)	8	5	8	320
Exploration reports index				
(ID 18)	8	5	8	320
Image analysis slide catalog				
(ID 31)	5	1	8	40
Library service (ID 35)	1	1	8	8

Table 3-7. (Continued)

Office Administration:

Computer service bureau B (ID 6)	1	1	2	2
Microform reader-printers (ID 40)	10	1	2	20
Telex system (ID 73)	5	5	2	50
Word processors (ID 74)	8	5	2	80

**Value Index = RE Index X IA Index X IO Index.

Note: "ID" numbers refer to information resource entities described in Appendix 1.

meant. For example, a resource of strategic importance to a particular activity, say an inventory system supporting materiel management, would probably not be considered strategic by the company as a whole.

To measure the importance of the resource entity to the activity supported, we can adapt and apply Bedell's scale of factors to determine the Importance to Activity (IA) Index (equivalent to Bedell's ISA Index). The index is a direct assessment of the strategic role played by an information resource in a particular context. The IA Index can range from 10, indicating the greatest strategic importance, to 0, the lowest.

> *10: Strategic Factor.* A particular [resource entity] is a strategic factor for an activity if it is *absolutely essential* in achieving significant strategic objectives of the activity. For example, if it is an important strategic objective that a bank provide competitive retail banking services at outlying locations, then an automated teller system may be absolutely essential . . . .

> *5: Major Support Factor.* [An IRE] is a major support factor if it is not absolutely essential to the activity in achieving important strategic objectives, but can, or already does, play a vital role in supporting the activity. Alternatives to the [resource] would be far less convenient or effective, would be more costly or would cause major disruptions to install. . . . .

> *1: Minor Support Factor.* [An entity] is a minor support factor if it helps the activity achieve its strategic objectives but reasonable alternatives are available that are not significantly more costly, less convenient or less effective, and that would not significantly disrupt operations.

> *0: Not Useful.* [An information resource entity] is not useful if the activity does not derive benefits from its use. It should be removed.[21]

Column C in Table 3-7 illustrates application of this factor scale to establish hypothetical IA Indexes for a number of information resource entities selected from the *CRA Exploration* case.

3.3.2.3 Determine Strategic Role of Activity: The third and final index needed to rank values is one that would measure the *strategic importance* of the activity supported by the information resource entity.

As emphasized by Bedell, such an evaluation has nothing whatever to do with information systems, nor with resource entities or information managers. The selection of activities and their evaluation in strategic terms would come from management: "An activity's strategic importance is based solely on its contribution in achieving the organization's strategic objectives."[22] Bedell's scale of activities, excerpted below, can be used to obtain an Importance to the Organization (IO) Index for each activity (equivalent to Bedell's IAO Index).

> *10: Critically Strategic Activity.* An activity is critically strategic if it must achieve outstanding performance on its strategic objectives for the organization as a whole to achieve its long-term goals. Outstanding performance is performance that is difficult to achieve. It may involve improving or changing current performance levels or sustaining a past performance level that was unusually high and difficult to accomplish. The key here is that an activity that must produce hard-to-achieve, outstanding performance (implying it is unlikely to occur without significant effort and resources applied) is critically strategic. . . . .
>
> *8: Strategic Activity.* An activity is strategic if it must accomplish most of its strategic objectives for the organization's long-term goals to be achieved. The important difference between strategic and critically strategic is that outstanding performance is not required. . . . .
>
> *6: Contributory Activity.* An activity may *directly* contribute to meeting the organization's long-term goals, but the organization may still succeed even if the activity fails to achieve a substantial portion of its strategic objectives. An example of a contributory activity is a small division of a large organization. . . . .
>
> *4: Support Activity.* Activities that do not directly work to achieve the organization's goals but that support critically strategic and strategic activities in achieving their objectives, and whose failure will not prevent the organization from attaining its long-term goals, are termed support activities. The key is that support activities contribute only indirectly to the organization's long-term goals. . . . .

2: Overhead Activities. Activities that must be done but that do not contribute directly to achieving the organization's long-term goals, are classified as overhead activities. Certain accounting, government and financial reporting, employee benefits administration and legal activities are examples. . . . . It is not that the organization can function without them but that they do not contribute to achieving the organization's long-term goals except [indirectly].

0: Detrimental Activities. Detrimental activities are those that work against achieving the organization's long-term goals. Such activities should be removed as soon as possible. . . . .[23]

By rating the strategic importance of the organization's various activities and linking these or similar ratings with the IREs identified by the preliminary inventory, you will forge a vital link between the IREs and the goals and objectives of your organization. As we described in Chapter 1, such a link is fundamental to making the information resources management (IRM) process an operational reality (Fig. 1-3).

Column D in Table 3-7 illustrates, hypothetically, how Importance to Organization (IO) Indexes could be applied to a number of activities (Mineral Exploration, Property Administration, etc.) related to various IREs. Note that all information resource entities supporting a particular activity are given the same IO Index rating.

3.3.2.4 Assess and Rank Entities by Value. Using Bedell's method you have now determined three indexes for each resource entity: The Resource Effectiveness (RE) Index, the Importance to Activity (IA) Index and the Importance to Organization (IO) Index. The relative value of an entity to the organization as a whole can be obtained by multiplying the three indexes to create a fourth, which we call the Value Index (equivalent to Bedell's EIO Index).[24] If the numeric scales suggested above were used, each ranging from 0 to 10, Value Indexes would have a range of 0 to 1000.

Having developed Value Indexes for all resource entities across the organization, you are now able to compare and rank their values. For reconnaissance mapping purposes, we are not interested in fine distinctions. Rather, we are looking for overall, meaningful differences that would isolate and group resource entities in terms of broad categories of value.

By applying a rating scheme for values across the entire organization, you will be able to see, at least roughly, the *relative values* of your IREs. They will be related by a framework of Value Indexes that take into account three factors: The effectiveness of an

IRE in supporting activities, the strategic importance of the entity's role in so doing and the strategic importance of the activity itself to the organization.

In Table 3-7, hypothetical Index Values are calculated and shown in Column E for selected entities supporting the five activities. These results are in turn summarized in Table 3-8 in terms of four categories of value: High, Medium, Low and Nil. Entities supporting more than one activity, such as *Computer systems*, are shown in the highest-ranking category only, to reflect their overall value to the organization.

Not surprisingly, nearly all "high value" entities in our example support the activity of highest strategic importance, Mineral Exploration (Table 3-8). However, some entities supporting this activity have lower values because they have a low Resource Effectiveness Index (e.g., *Drill-log data system* (ID 13)) and/or have a low Importance to Activity Index. Since the rankings are based on hypothetical indexes, we will not speculate on their real-world significance; it would not be difficult, however, in an actual case, to conjure up lengthy discussions on why this entity ranked here, another over there and so on.

Tables such as 3-7 and 3-8 can pose many questions and, perhaps, shed some light. It would be instructive to analyze circumstances related to resource entities that combine high index values for strategic importance (IA and IO Indexes) and low index values for effectiveness (RE Indexes). Additional questions would be raised for these or other interesting combinations of index values, when the *costs* for each entity are brought into the picture, as we will do in the next section.

3.4 RELATING COST TO VALUE

As we described in Chapter 1, the principles of resource management require information managers to pay particular attention to the relation between the cost and the value of information resource entities for which they are responsible (Fig. 1-3). In this chapter we have outlined ways of measuring costs and assessing values. Now we can examine the two side by side. Or, metaphorically, we can place cost on one end of a balance beam and value on the other.

Yet it is no easier to rationalize the cost of information resources in terms of their values than it is for stocks, houses, vacations, orthodontics or fur coats. Is anything worth the price? Decisions to buy or to forego the opportunity, however, can be made more

Table 3-8. Hypothetical ranking of selected information resource entities by overall value to the organization, as
measured by Value Indexes (see Table 3-7). Listed
alphabetically within categories.

Value Category	Information Resource Entities	
HIGH VALUE Value Index: 500-1000	Computer systems (ID 7) Drill-log and assay data (ID 12) Geochemical data (ID 24) (ID 23) Geophysical data (ID 30)	Maps and charts (ID 39) Mineral lease data (ID 43) Prospects data (ID 58)
MEDIUM VALUE Value Index: 100-490	Airborne geophysical survey index (ID 2) Exploration information service B (ID 15) Exploration information service C (ID 16)	Exploration reports index (ID 18) Exploration well index (ID 19) Field data coding system (ID 23)
LOW VALUE Value Index: 2-90	Image analysis slide catalogue (ID 25) Library service (ID 35) Microform reader-printers (ID 40) Mining information (ID 47)	Telex system (ID 73) Word processors (ID 74)
NIL VALUE Value Index: 0	Drill-log data system (ID 13)	

Note: "ID" numbers refer to information resource entities described in
Appendix 1.

objectively, if not necessarily more easily, if all costs are in plain view, and at the same time the benefits are known and understood. This basic principle of commerce applies equally to the acquisition and maintenance of information resources. But in far too many cases neither the costs nor the values and benefits are known or, if known, they are not seen in juxtaposition.

While we offer no new formula or criterion for determining, in the context of your organization, whether the cost of a particular information resource entity is less than, equals or exceeds its value, the foregoing review of costs and values suggests ways in which the two can be more clearly and more closely related.

3.4.1 Cost/Value Ratios

One obvious way to relate one variable with another is to bring them together in a ratio. Information cost/value ratios are somewhat analogous to business and financial ratios. There is implicit recognition that the absolute or other measure of two variables, examined one at a time, is often not as significant as a ratio of the two. For example, financial managers use debt-to-equity, turnover, return on earnings and other such ratios. These might be seen to have their approximate informational equivalents. Based on the types of measurement and analysis described to this point, four categories of cost/value ratios suggest themselves, as listed in Table 3-9. To our knowledge, only the first category, Monetary, has actually been applied in practical cases. The utility of the other three remains to be explored.

Monetary Ratios. Where information products and services are sold in the marketplace, the selling price is of course a quantitative, monetary measure of value (Robert Taylor's "exchange value"). The values of such products and services could be related directly to the cost of producing or providing them. Their ratio would be a numeric index reflecting the relation of one to the other. Although our book deals only with costs and values internal to the organization, not with the marketplace, internal analogues in the form of cost-recovery and charge-back mechanisms can, in a similar way, be used to determine quantitative cost/value indexes.

Sassone and Schwartz' method, described earlier in the case example of the impact of office automation systems on improving productivity (3.3.1.3), is an example of how quantitative measures of both cost and value can be calculated and then compared as a numeric ratio. Unfortunately, quantitative measures of *both* cost and value are rarely available. More commonly, the measure of value must be presented in other ways.[25]

Table 3-9. Suggested categories and types of cost/value ratios for information resource entitites.

Categories	Measures of Cost	Indicators of Value	Types of Cost/Value Ratios
MONETARY	Monetary unit	Monetary unit	Numeric index
RANK ORDER	Rank order of costs	Rank order of values	Ratio of indexes
	Range: Most costly to least costly	Range: Most valuable to least valuable	
ACTIVITY	Effort/burden	Use/success	Ratio of activities
	Range: High to Low	Range: High to Low	
DESCRIPTIVE	Description of costs	Description of values	Qualitative "ratio"
	Range: Qualitative	Range: Qualitative	

Rank-Order Ratios. Using our second category of cost/value ratios, you can compare the two indexes created to reflect the rank order of cost and value, respectively (e.g., Tables 3-3, 3-7). Such ratios could be compared meaningfully only if the indexes had been developed on a consistent basis across the entire organization. Rank-order ratios might reveal, for example, that the values of some types of information entities greatly exceed their costs, as compared with other types in the organization.

The higher the rank-order ratio, the more cost-effective the resource entity. For example:

Rank Order of Cost	Rank Order of Value	Rank-Order Cost/Value Ratio
4	1	4
2	2	1
1	4	0.25

Activity Ratios. Information handling functions commonly can be measured in terms of activities; e.g., handling requests, filing dossiers, etc. In this category, you can relate some measure of effort, burden or resource input (the "cost") with a relevant measure of productive use, benefit, success or desired output (the "value"). The units measured would vary from case to case; possibilities include the number of documents, number of transactions or number of files. For example:

- The ratio of information collected to information actually used;
- The ratio of information handled to information that achieves bottom-line results;
- The paperwork and information-handling intensity in selected, comparable activities or work flows, and an information/paper-work intensity ratio;[26]
- The ratio of the number of searches to the number of successful "hits" in online searching of a database;
- The ratio of dormant files to active files in a records center.

Descriptive "Ratios." In this category, you simply compare qualitative or quantitative measures of cost with qualitative measures of value. Such measures can be objective in nature, even if qualitative, or they may be highly subjective. In the latter case, the Delphi method or peer evaluation can sometimes be applied to force rankings of cost and/or value, or to develop a judgment on overall cost-effectiveness, using a group of experts or peers with special knowledge of and competency in the resources in question.[27] For example:

Expression of Cost	:	**Expression of Value**
Low staff morale	:	Critical functions performed
$246,000	:	Improved decisions by management resulting in savings
$34,000	:	Physical security of sensitive information preventing loss
"Computerphobia"	:	Timeliness of information delivery
$120,000	:	Satisfied customers resulting in new business

3.4.2 Discovering Unnecessary and Excess Costs

Without straying too far into the domain of management, we conclude our discussion of the relation between the cost and value of information by pointing to those situations in which cost far outweighs value. One of the benefits of the systematic identification of the costs and values of information in an organization is discovery of what Morey Chick of the U.S. General Accounting Office (GAO) describes as "unnecessary and excess costs," or more simply: Waste. Chick points out that some of this waste could be eliminated immediately — to everyone's benefit — by eliminating, for example, a resource entity that supports an activity having no strategic or other importance for the organization.

Unnecessary costs are those that simply should not be incurred. They can be reduced by management because they are variable or semivariable in nature. Certain fixed costs, often attributed to depreciation of capitalized assets acquired or constructed for use over a relatively short period of time (3-5 years), can also be reduced in the short term if they fit this category. Such unnecessary costs could be eliminated at the end of the useful life of the capitalized asset, or sooner. The trend towards shorter useful lives of software and hardware, caused in part by rapid advances in information technology, may result in a more "variable" nature in some "fixed cost" categories, because decisions to continue to incur them will have to be made more frequently.

Excess costs apply to long-term, fixed costs of operation (also called sunk costs). They are allocable to the production of information that, in general, has little or no value. These excess costs, often referred to in terms of efficiency or productivity losses, cannot be immediately reduced, but the facilities commonly can be applied to more productive activities, including the production of more valuable information. This waste can usually be eliminated or reduced, eventually.[28]

The *U.S. General Accounting Office (GAO)* has demonstrated in its reports the impact that information management problems, including waste, can have on achieving Federal agency missions, goals and objectives. GAO findings identified the following categories of problems that involved the reduction or elimination of *values*, and the burden of unnecessary and excess *costs*:

- *Data and information use difficulties:* Information and data access problems and poorly designed or nonstandard output.

- *Data quality problems:* Incomplete, inaccurate, obsolete, untimely or inconsistent data and/or information.

- *Data storage problems:* Unnecessary storage of information beyond its useful life, and premature data destruction.

- *Duplications in data processing:* The collection, processing, output and/or dissemination of data and information that duplicates data in the same or other systems, or systems that duplicate the support of a program or function.

- *Nonuse of needed information:* Failure to use available and needed information or failure to acquire or produce it.

- *Software problems:* Application software containing incorrect, obsolete or otherwise inappropriate processing criteria, and/or inadequate technical controls over data in software.

- *Unnecessary data processing:* The processing and output of data and information that is not needed, and unnecessary data processing steps.[29]

. . . .

With completion of Steps One (Survey) and Two (Cost/Value), you have completed the essential fact-finding portion of the information resource discovery process. Your potential resources have been identified, individually described, costed and valued. Now you are ready to analyze the facts.

NOTES

1. David R. Vincent, "Information on the Bottom Line," *Computerworld*, August 13, 1984, 25-32 (In Depth).

2. Morey J. Chick was among the first to point out the need for better, more precise definitions related to the cost and value of information. The definitions given here are taken from his work, "The Cost of Information," *The GAO Review*, Summer 1973, 52-62; and "Information Value and Cost Measures for Use as Management Tools," *Information Executive*, 1(2) (1984) 48-49.

3. Sena H. Black and Donald A. Marchand, "Assessing the Value of Information in Organizations: A Challenge for the 1980s," *The Information Society Journal*, (1)3, (1982), pp. 191-225.

4. "Management of Photocopying," in *Report of the Auditor General of Canada to the House of Commons*, (Ottawa, Ontario: Auditor General of Canada, 1981), Chapter 4, p. 97.

5. U.S. Department of the Army, "The Design of an Information Management Program for Headquarters, Department of the Army, Phase 2, Detailed Report," (Washington, D.C.: Arthur Young & Company, February 26, 1980), Contract No. MDA 903 78-C-0483, pp. 92-93.

6. Office of Management and Budget, "Management of Federal Information Resources; Final Publication of OMB Circular A-130," *Federal Register*, December 24, 1985, (50)247, 52741.

7. Cornelius F. Burk, Jr., "Management of Departmental Information Resources: Report to EMR Executive Committee," (Ottawa, Ontario: Department of Energy, Mines and Resources, March 25, 1980), Appendix 1.

8. "Improving the Management and Capitalization Base of STORET," (Washington, D.C.: U.S. Environmental Protection Agency, 1973).

9. Robert S. Taylor, "Information Values in Decision Contexts," *Information Management Review*, Summer 1985, 1(1), Table 2. This paper was based on Taylor's book: *Value-Added Processes in Information Systems*, (Norwood, N.J.: Ablex Publishing Corporation, 1986).

10. Donald A. Marchand and Forest W. Horton, Jr., *INFOTRENDS: Profiting from Your Information Resources*, (New York, N.Y.: John Wiley & Sons, 1986), Chapter 8.

11. Forest W. Horton, Jr., *Information Resources Management: Harnessing Information Assets for Productivity Gains in the Office, Factory and Laboratory*, (Englewood Cliffs, N.J.: Prentice-Hall, Inc., 1985).

12. U.S. Commission on Federal Paperwork, *Information Value/Burden Assessment*, (Washington, D.C.: Commission on Federal Paperwork, 1977), pp. 21-22.

13. Peter G. Sassone and A. Perry Schwartz, "Cost-Justifying OA," *Datamation*, February 15, 1986, 32(2), 83-88. Reprinted with permission of DATAMATION magazine. Copyright by Technical Publishing Company, 1986. All rights reserved.

14. David R. Vincent, "Information on the Bottom Line," *Computerworld*, August 13, 1984, pp. 25-32 (In Depth); and "Information as Corporate Asset," *Computerworld*, September 26, 1983, 1-12 (In Depth).

15. Eugene F. Bedell, *The Computer Solution: Strategies for Success in the Information Age*, (Homewood, Illinois: Dow Jones-Irwin, 1985), Chapter 3. Copyright 1985 Eugene F. Bedell. Excerpts reprinted with permission of Eugene F. Bedell.

16. Ibid., p. 35.

17. Ibid., p. 38.

18. Ibid., p. 40.

19. Ibid., pp. 39-40.

20. Ibid., pp. 35-36.

21. Ibid., pp. 37-38.

22. Ibid., p. 45.

23. Ibid., pp. 45-47.

24. Ibid., p. 44.

25. Sassone and Schwartz, *"Cost-Justifying OA."*

26. Forest W. Horton, Jr., "Budgeting and Accounting for Information," *The Government Accountants Journal*, Spring 1979, XXVIII (1), 28.

27. Phillip Ein-Dor and Carl R. Jones, *Information Systems Management: Analytical Tools and Techniques*, (New York, N.Y.: Elsevier, 1985), pp. 31, 33-34.

28. Chick, "Information Value and Cost Measures," 53.

29. Ibid., Fig. 7.

4

INFORMATION
RESOURCE MAPPING
TECHNIQUES

Having reconnoitered the organization's information landscape, taking note of potential resources and making rough estimates of their cost and value, the explorer's next task is to fashion a set of charts and maps that will summarize what he or she has seen and provide a framework for assessing their significance. For the 19th century explorers of western North America, making isolated observations in the prairies, mountain ranges, river valleys and by the Pacific Ocean was one thing. But plotting their relative positions on a map and in so doing to reveal, say, a new transportation route through a previously unknown mountain pass, was something else. Maps help to elucidate the strategic significance of fundamental relationships.

The first two Steps of the discovery process generate a great deal of factual information. For example, our main case example (Appendix 1) lists 74 individual sources, services and systems, each with a general description (Step One of the process); the cost/value analysis that follows produces additional information (Step Two). Now, in Step Three, we will organize and present this array of data in ways that relate the potential information resource entities identified in the preliminary inventory to the structure, functions and management of the organization, and relate all entities to each other through a common grid or framework. In brief, we will map the organization's information resources.

When mapped, studied and analyzed, the roles and inter-relationships of the information entities will become known and better understood, their significance to the organization appreciated — perhaps for the first time — and management will be in a position to determine which of these information entities are, in fact, *organizational resources.*

The identification of the organization's information resources, in specific business and management-oriented terms, is the overriding objective of the discovery process. There are, however, additional benefits. During construction of the various lists, charts and maps described in this chapter (and later as they are studied and analyzed), a variety of management problems and opportunities may be revealed. For example, we may see previously unknown or unexpected gaps and unnecessary overlaps in our information holdings and functions, the absence of management policies and accountability, surprisingly high costs, unknown costs for major functions, undervalued assets and mismatched information and business plans; or we may discover hidden or unexploited resources.

This chapter describes Step Three: The *analysis* phase of the discovery process (Fig. 1-8). Basic mapping and charting techniques will be described, their rationale explained and, where possible, practical examples offered. Some of the techniques are new, described here possibly for the first time. Bearing in mind that we are exploring new ground, the reader is encouraged to question the merits of this or that procedure, even a technique as a whole. Moreover, at this stage, the long-term benefits of using these techniques have not been fully documented and proven. Nevertheless, in the spirit of exploration, we will accept some risks and forge ahead using whatever methods and tools are at hand in order to discover what and where our information resources are, and to thereby place ourselves in a position to manage information *as a resource.*

Chapter 4 Preview. The chapter suggests a variety of objectives that might be pursued during the analysis step. Then it describes three main analytical techniques: First, to chart where in the organization's structure the information entities are located, expressed in terms of where their users, suppliers/handlers and managers are located; second, to map on one page the total spectrum of information resource entities identified by the preliminary inventory and third, to chart the magnitude, nature and location of costs and financial controls associated with the information resource entities. Finally, for each of these general techniques, some guidelines are offered for analyzing the results.

4.1 SETTING OBJECTIVES FOR ANALYSIS

Within the framework of the overall purpose and scope of the discovery process you established at the outset in Step One, the survey director should now focus attention on what he or she hopes to achieve through analysis of the inventory and cost/value data. We have stressed that your purpose overall is *discovery* of your information resources, not finding new or better ways to manage them. That must come later. However, as additional benefits, a range of purely business and managerial purposes is also usually served by the various outputs and knowledge acquired as a result of the discovery process.

Thus, in addition to the primary objective of discovering all of your information resources, complementary objectives that might be pursued during the analysis step could include, for example:

- Identification of *criteria* for recognizing the specific sources, services and systems that should be managed as organizational resources.
- Identification of relative *strengths and weaknesses* in how the organization creates or acquires, handles, stores, uses and reuses and disseminates its data and information.
- Location of *where* in the organizational structure information *costs* are incurred and information *values* are realized.
- *Discrimination* of information costs by, for example, purposes or activities supported, by department, by equipment and handling media or by general information service.
- Determination of the general *nature and characteristics* of the organization's information resource entities.
- Determination of where *accountability* lies for information quality, timeliness, costs, planning, budgeting, etc.
- Assessment of the *adequacy* of the existing resource base to meet current and expected future information needs.
- Assessment of the *need* for improved, upgraded or expanded information management policies for the organization.

Your organization would not necessarily pursue all of these objectives, and others more appropriate to your circumstances could be added. It is important, however, to establish explicit objectives in order to focus the effort involved in the analysis of the preliminary inventory. With them established, we can begin Step Three: Analysis (Fig. 4-1).

Figure 4-1. Analysis chart: Review preliminary inventory, costs and values (Step Three).

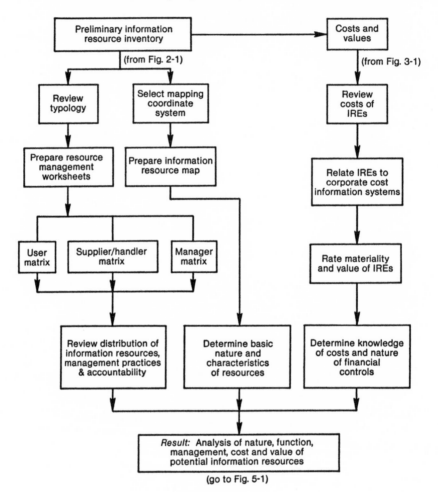

4.2   LOCATING INFORMATION USERS, SUPPLIERS, HANDLERS AND MANAGERS

The purpose of the first mapping technique we will describe is to *locate* all of the entities previously identified in the preliminary information resource inventory (Step One). By "locate," we mean determining where in the organizational structure the three main information communities (or players) related to each entity are located; namely, the *users, handlers and/or suppliers* and *managers.* At first glance this may seem like a roundabout way of locating something, but it is necessary because of the characteristics of information and of information resource entities (IREs) as we described in Chapter 1. Even seemingly self-contained, highly visible entities such as a computer center or library may include critical elements, such as terminals, networks and their users which are physically located in places well beyond the center or library building.

Recall that what we are seeking to discover are essentially *configurations* of various physical and other kinds of input resources, not the individual, tangible input resources that make up the configurations (Fig. 1-4). Some of the latter — things, such as computer hardware, could of course be located in the conventional, spatial sense, but most information resource entities transcend traditional administrative, physical and spatial boundaries. For example, think of the difficulty of stating precisely where the telephone system is *physically* located, including all of its handsets, switch boxes, business offices, microwave towers, cables and such, not to mention its operators, line workers and customers. The address of the telephone company's head office does not specify the physical location of the telephone *system.*

To overcome this problem of locating information resource entities in a physical sense, we will employ a series of simple two-dimensional matrices that show where within the organization the three main information players or communities are located. Each matrix, a model of which is shown in Fig. 4-2, is called an *information resource worksheet.*[1] One worksheet or matrix should be constructed for each player or community; a *User matrix,* a *Supplier/Handler matrix* and a *Manager matrix.*

Each worksheet should use the same column and row entries for any one organization: *Column* entries (on the horizontal axis) consist primarily of organizational units and sub-units, while the *row* entries (on the vertical axis) consist of the information resource *types* identified by the inventory. Recall that types are the generic groupings of resource entities reflecting the typology you used for classification purposes at the outset of the discovery process (Tables 2-1, 2-5). Thus, to design a worksheet customized for your organization, appropriate column and row entries must be selected.

Figure 4-2. Model of Information Resource Worksheet. Specific matrices should be prepared for each information community: Users, Suppliers/Handlers and Managers (Fig. 2-4).

ORGANIZATIONAL UNITS / INFORMATION RESOURCE TYPES	Unit A	Unit B	Unit C	etc.	TOTALS
SOURCES Type A Type B Type C etc.					
SERVICES Type A Type B Type C etc.					
SYSTEMS Type A Type B Type C etc.					
TOTALS					

4.2.1 Review Typology

First, you should select the row headings listing the resource types. With the benefit of hindsight, you can assess the validity and utility of the classification scheme (typology) for information resources adopted at the beginning of Step One. Having examined a large number of information entities that actually exist, some changes in the typology will probably be called for. For example, some types initially selected may be too broad, others too narrow; new ones may be needed; some expected types may turn out in reality not to exist at all, and so on. Draw up the revised list of information resource types and enter them along the left side of your worksheet.

The main reason for listing resource *types* on the worksheet, and not all of the individual inventory resource entities, is to ensure that the resulting worksheet is compact enough to deal with the entire organization on a single piece of paper or spreadsheet. This will allow for a complete corporate overview and, at the same time, avoid an overwhelming amount of detail.

4.2.2 Select Organizational Units

Next, select the column headings along the horizontal axis. The number of organizational units identified across the top of the worksheet will depend of course on the scope of the survey and on the level of detail sought. However, as with the rows, it is important to restrict the number of columns such that the entire organization can be portrayed on a single page or spreadsheet. The major purpose of the worksheets is to provide a summary or overview of corporate information resources; this purpose might be defeated by a detailed organizational breakdown requiring several pages of columns.

In addition to the organizational units across the top of the worksheet, you can use one or more columns to codify general characteristics of the resource types considered useful in carrying out the analysis. For example, codes (such as those below in parentheses) could be placed in separate columns to distinguish or highlight:

- *External* (E) vs *internal* (I) resources; distinguishes whether the resources are obtained from outside the organization (e.g., government publications) or generated internally (e.g., a personnel system database).
- *Manual* (M) vs *technology-based* (T) resources; distinguishes between types dominantly of a traditional paper-based nature from those that are automated or technology-based, such as microforms, electronic and optical systems.
- *Supplier categories*; indicates whether suppliers are commercial (C), governmental (G), domestic (D), foreign (F), etc. (for Supplier/ Handler Worksheet).
- *User categories*: indicates whether the users are intermediate (I) or "end" users (E), problem solvers (S), production workers (W), top management (M), etc. (for User Worksheet).

Other characteristics useful for analysis could be added. Enter the organizational units and the relevant resource characteristics you have selected across the top of your master worksheet. The same worksheet matrix will be used for each of the three main information communities: Users, Suppliers/Handlers and Managers.

4.2.3 Construct User Worksheet

With your customized master worksheet in hand, you are now ready to plot the worksheet data. Users are the first of the three major information communities or players you will want to locate (Fig. 2-4). The purpose of the User Worksheet is to show you which organizational units use which information resource types, or "who is using what, and where." This is achieved by placing an X in those cells on the User Worksheet which represent the intersection of 1) a particular organizational unit in which a user or users are located, and 2) the resource type being used. The needed information on users is usually obtained from the Description of Contents, Operations and Uses field on the Inventory Data Forms (Appendix 1). The entire preliminary inventory should be scanned to relate *each* information resource type to *all* known users in the organization. A case example is given in Fig. 4-3.

In placing an X on this type of worksheet, we are purposefully making some generalizations. Judgment should be used in deciding whether the *extent* of usage, or *number* of users, warrants placing an X in a particular cell, or not. Usually, we are interested in locating strategic and significant usage, not just any usage, or only casual usage. However, for the moment we eschew qualitative considerations — how effectively the entities are serving their intended purpose. Do not at this point attempt to distinguish "good" from "bad" usage.

A second generalization involved in the placement of an X on the worksheet is that an X could refer to the use of only one, or of two, or of many information resource *entities* (IREs). We are deliberately plotting usage at the level of information resource *type* (Table 2-1) in order to obtain a broad corporate overview. While it might be feasible later on to plot Xs at the more detailed IRE level, say on an electronic worksheet, we do not recommend doing so *at this point* because the resulting matrix would in most cases be too unwieldy for display on a single page or screen.

4.2.4 Construct Supplier/Handler Worksheet

Although our model of information communities (Fig. 2-4) distinguishes suppliers from handlers, for the purposes of most organizations constructing their first information resource worksheets, the two should be combined in one as the Supplier/Handler Worksheet. If desired, two separate worksheets could be prepared. An X should be placed in each of the cells representing an intersection of 1) a particular organizational unit which, or through which, suppliers and/or handlers are located, and 2) the resource type being supplied or handled. Case examples of this worksheet are given in Figs. 4-4 and 4-5.[2]

As for the User Worksheet, information on who the suppliers and handlers are for each resource type usually comes from the Description of Contents, Operations and Users or other fields on the Inventory Data Forms (Appendix 1). If the information is not found here, consult the other supporting documents or contact the resource manager, if there is one.

As with the others, the placement of an X on the Supplier/ Handler Worksheet is a generalization: Judgment must be applied as to *how much* information should be handled or supplied before an X is used; and the X may refer to only one, or to several information resource entities.

4.2.5 Construct Manager Worksheet

Managers are the third community to be plotted on a worksheet. By manager, we usually mean the person responsible for such traditional management functions as planning, organizing, budgeting, directing and controlling: In brief, whoever is accountable for end-result performance of the entity, whatever the level of management. An X should be placed in each of the cells on the Manager Worksheet which represents the intersection of 1) a particular organizational unit in which a manager or managers are located, and 2) the resource type being managed. Do not include here the vast array of information professionals who add value to data products and services but have no managerial responsibilities — people such as indexers, abstractors, statisticians, technical writers, data processors and telecommunication operators.

In some instances it may be difficult or impossible to identify a manager. In such cases leave the cells blank. These findings would be useful in themselves during the analysis. For example, resource entities of the "hidden" category simply may have no identifiable managers. If management responsibility for a particular entity or type is shared or widely dispersed, then Xs should be placed in all appropriate cells. The generalizations implicit in placing Xs on the previous two worksheets apply in a similar manner to the Manager Worksheet. A case example appears in Fig. 4-6.

4.2.6 Analysis of the Worksheets

What can the worksheets tell us about the organization's information resources? First, and most obviously, they convey in summary

Figure 4-3 Information resource worksheet: User matrix for CRA Exploration case.

INFORMATION RESOURCE WORKSHEET

USER MATRIX

INFORMATION RESOURCE CATEGORIES AND TYPES	Resource Characteristics				ORGANIZATIONAL UNITS		
	Internal	External	Manual/ analog	Technology-based	General Manager	Admin & Tech Serv	Basin Study
1. SOURCES							
CRAE Information							
1.1 Bibliographic data	I		M	T		X	
1.2 Drill-log and assay data	I		M			X	X
1.3 Exploration reports	I		M		X	X	X
1.4 Geochemical data	I		M	T			
1.5 Geological samples data	I		M	T			
1.6 Geophysical data	I		M	T			X
1.7 Management information	I		M	T	X	X	X
1.8 Maps and charts	I		M	T		X	X
1.9 Mineral lease data	I		M			X	
1.10 Mining information	I		M		X	X	
1.11 Petroleum information	I		M		X		X
1.12 Prospects data	I		M			X	X
1.13 Remote sensing data	I			T			
1.14 Other	I						
External Organizations							
1.15 Commercial		E	M	T			
1.16 Federal agencies		E	M	T			X
1.17 Other CRA Group		E	M		X	X	
1.18 State agencies		E	M	T		X	X
1.19 Other		E		T			
2. SERVICES							
2.1 Aerial photography		E	M				
2.2 Core/samples curation	I	E	M	T			
2.3 Drafting	I	E	M	T	X	X	X
2.4 Geophysical surveying		E		T			
2.5 Information locating	I	E	M	T		X	X
2.6 Library	I	E	M	T		X	
2.7 Mineral lease information	I	E	M			X	
2.8 Records management							
2.9 Reporting	I		M		X	X	X
2.10 Reprographics	I		M		X	X	X
2.11 Resource evaluation	I		M	T	X	X	
2.12 Systems/programming	I	E	M	T		X	
2.13 Other							
3. SYSTEMS							
3.1 Bibliographic control	I	E		T		X	
3.2 Computing	I	E		T		X	
3.3 Communication		E	M		X	X	X
3.4 Drafting/graphics	I	E		T			
3.5 Geoscience data analysis	I			T			
3.6 Geoscience data management	I			T			
3.7 Image analysis	I			T			
3.8 Mineral lease data	I	E	M	T		X	
3.9 Prospect information	I		M	T			
3.10 Word processing		E		T	X	X	X
3.11 Other							
TOTALS	30	19	29	27	11	23	15

Figure 4-3. (Continued)

Overseas	Research Group	Geo-physics	Diamonds	Northern WA	Southern WA	South Australia	Victoria	New South Wales	East Queensland	TOTALS
X	X	X	X	X	X	X	X	X	X	11
X	X			X	X	X	X	X	X	10
X	X	X	X	X	X	X	X	X	X	13
X	X			X	X	X	X	X	X	8
			X	X	X	X	X	X	X	6
X	X	X	X	X	X	X	X	X	X	11
X	X	X	X	X	X	X	X	X	X	13
X	X	X	X	X	X	X	X	X	X	12
X			X	X	X	X	X	X	X	9
										2
										2
X	X	X	X	X	X	X	X	X	X	12
	X									1
										0
	X	X		X	X	X	X	X	X	8
	X	X		X	X				X	6
						X				3
		X	X	X	X	X	X	X	X	10
	X	X		X	X	X	X	X		7
				X	X			X		3
	X					X	X	X		4
X	X	X	X	X	X	X	X	X	X	13
X		X								2
X	X	X	X	X	X	X	X	X	X	12
	X			X	X	X	X			6
X			X	X	X	X	X	X	X	9
										0
X	X	X	X	X	X	X	X	X	X	13
X	X	X	X	X	X	X	X	X	X	13
										2
	X	X	X	X	X	X	X	X	X	10
										0
	X									2
	X	X	X	X	X	X	X	X	X	10
X	X	X	X	X	X	X	X	X	X	13
	X	X	X	X	X	X	X	X	X	9
	X	X	X	X	X	X	X	X	X	9
				X					X	2
	X									1
X		X	X	X	X	X	X	X	X	10
									X	1
X						X				5
										0
18	25	21	20	28	26	27	27	26	26	293

Figure 4-4. Information resource worksheet: Supplier/Handler matrix for CRA Exploration case.

INFORMATION RESOURCE WORKSHEET

SUPPLIER/HANDLER MATRIX

INFORMATION RESOURCE CATEGORIES AND TYPES	Resource Characteristics				ORGANIZATIONAL UNITS		
	Internal	External	Manual/ analog	Technology-based	General Manager	Admin & Tech Serv	Basin Study
1. SOURCES							
CRAE Information							
1.1 Bibliographic data	I		M	T		X	
1.2 Drill-log and assay data	I		M				X
1.3 Exploration reports	I		M			X	X
1.4 Geochemical data	I		M	T			
1.5 Geological samples data	I		M	T			
1.6 Geophysical data	I		M	T			
1.7 Management information	I		M	T	X	X	
1.8 Maps and charts	I		M	T		X	X
1.9 Mineral lease data	I		M			X	
1.10 Mining information	I		M			X	
1.11 Petroleum information	I		M				X
1.12 Prospects data	I		M				X
1.13 Remote sensing data	I			T			
1.14 Other	I						
External Organizations							
1.15 Commercial		E	M	T			
1.16 Federal agencies		E	M	T			
1.17 Other CRA Group		E	M		X	X	
1.18 State agencies		E	M	T		X	
1.19 Other		E		T			
2. SERVICES							
2.1 Aerial photography		E	M				
2.2 Core/samples curation	I	E	M	T		X	
2.3 Drafting	I	E	M	T		X	
2.4 Geophysical surveying		E		T			
2.5 Information locating	I	E	M	T		X	
2.6 Library	I	E	M	T		X	
2.7 Mineral lease information	I	E	M			X	
2.8 Records management							
2.9 Reporting	I		M			X	X
2.10 Reprographics	I		M			X	
2.11 Resource evaluation	I		M	T		X	
2.12 Systems/programming	I	E	M	T			
2.13 Other							
3. SYSTEMS							
3.1 Bibliographic control	I	E		T		X	
3.2 Computing	I	E		T			
3.3 Communication		E	M				
3.4 Drafting/graphics	I	E		T			
3.5 Geoscience data analysis	I			T			
3.6 Geoscience data management	I			T			
3.7 Image analysis	I			T			
3.8 Mineral lease data	I	E	M	T		X	
3.9 Prospect information	I		M	T			
3.10 Word processing		E		T			
3.11 Other							
TOTALS	30	19	29	27	2	18	6

Figure 4-4. (Continued)

Overseas	Research Group	Geo-physics	Diamonds	Northern WA	Southern WA	South Australia	Victoria	New South Wales	East Queensland	TOTALS
	X									2
X	X		X	X	X	X	X	X	X	10
X	X	X	X	X	X	X	X	X	X	12
X	X		X	X	X	X	X	X	X	9
			X							1
X		X	X	X	X	X	X	X	X	9
		X								3
X	X		X	X	X	X	X	X	X	11
X			X	X	X	X	X	X	X	9
										1
										1
X	X		X	X	X	X	X	X	X	10
	X									1
										0
									X	1
		X								1
										2
		X		X	X					4
	X									1
										0
								X		2
	X			X	X	X	X	X	X	8
										0
	X									2
	X									2
X				X	X	X	X	X	X	8
										0
X	X	X	X	X	X	X	X	X	X	12
	X	X	X	X	X	X	X	X	X	10
										1
	X				X	X				3
										0
	X									2
	X			X	X	X	X	X	X	7
										0
	X			X	X	X	X	X	X	7
	X			X	X	X	X	X	X	7
					X				X	2
	X									1
X				X	X	X	X	X	X	8
							X		X	2
						X				1
										0
10	19	7	10	16	18	17	16	16	18	173

Figure 4-5. Information resource worksheet: Supplier/Handler matrix for Department of Energy, Mines and Resources (Canada) case.

Information Resources	DM's Office		P& E	Science and Technology Sector									
	SADM	Secretariat		ADM, S&T	CANMET	GSC	SMB	EPB	CCRS	PCSP	Explosives	OERD	CCGD
Sources:													
General inquiry centers					x	x	x	x	x				
Sales & distribution centers					x	x	x				x		
Libraries					x	x	x	x	x				
Scientific & technical information centers					x	x	x	x	x	x	x	x	
Record management centers		x			x	x	x	x	x	x	x		
Services:													
Public relations							x						
Publishing					x	x	x		x				
Drafting & cartographic						x	x	x			x		
Photographic						x	x						
Abstracting & indexing				x	x	x			x	x		x	x
Computing						x			x				
Telecommunications						x							x
Copying & duplicating	x	x	x	x	x	x	x	x	x	x	x	x	x
Word processing		x		x	x	x	x	x	x				x
Mail & delivery					x	x	x	x	x				
Systems:													
Scientific & technical data					x	x	x	x	x				
Bibliographic data					x				x				x
Economic data													
Financial data									x				
Personnel data													
Materiel data													
Management information	x	x	x										
Totals: Branch	2	4	2	3	12	14	14	10	13	4	4	3	5
Sector	6		2	82									
Dept.													

Source: Cornelius F. Burk, Jr., "Management of Departmental Information Resources: Report to EMR Executive Committee," (Ottawa, Ont.: Department of Energy, Mines and Resources, March 25, 1980), Table 1. Reproduced with permission.

Figure 4-5. (Continued)

Mineral Policy Sector					Energy Sector						Administration Sector								
ADM, MP	AD	RDD	MMD	ISD	ADM, E	EC	FAS	ADM, P	ADM, CN	ADM, EPA	ADM, A	FS	PB	AS	CSC	OLB	Translation		Totals
						x							x					x	8
														x				x	6
				x															6
				x				x	x	x					x				13
	x											x	x	x		x			14
						x												x	3
	x						x							x				x	8
	x							x						x					7
																		x	3
									x										8
															x				3
														x	x				4
x	x				x	x	x	x	x			x	x	x	x		x	x	25
	x					x	x							x	x		x	x	15
	x						x							x	x				9
				x			x												7
				x						x									3
												x			x				2
													x			x			3
														x					2
																			1
x					x						x								6
2	6	0	0	4	2	4	5	3	3	2	1	3	4	9	7	2	2	7	

12		19		35	

156

Figure 4-6. Information resource worksheet: Manager matrix for CRA Exploration case.

INFORMATION RESOURCE WORKSHEET

MANAGER MATRIX

INFORMATION RESOURCE CATEGORIES AND TYPES	Resource Characteristics				ORGANIZATIONAL UNITS		
	Internal	External	Manual/ analog	Technology-based	General Manager	Admin & Tech Serv	Basin Study
1. SOURCES							
CRAE Information							
1.1 Bibliographic data	I		M	T		X	
1.2 Drill-log and assay data	I		M				
1.3 Exploration reports	I		M			X	X
1.4 Geochemical data	I		M	T			
1.5 Geological samples data	I		M	T			
1.6 Geophysical data	I		M	T			
1.7 Management information	I		M	T	X	X	
1.8 Maps and charts	I		M	T		X	
1.9 Mineral lease data	I		M			X	
1.10 Mining information	I		M			X	
1.11 Petroleum information	I		M				X
1.12 Prospects data	I		M			X	
1.13 Remote sensing data	I			T			
1.14 Other	I						
External Organizations							
1.15 Commercial		E	M	T			
1.16 Federal agencies		E	M	T			
1.17 Other CRA Group		E	M		X	X	
1.18 State agencies		E	M	T		X	X
1.19 Other		E		T			
2. SERVICES							
2.1 Aerial photography		E	M				
2.2 Core/samples curation	I	E	M	T		X	
2.3 Drafting	I	E	M	T		X	
2.4 Geophysical surveying		E		T			
2.5 Information locating	I	E	M	T		X	
2.6 Library	I	E	M	T		X	
2.7 Mineral lease information	I	E	M			X	
2.8 Records management							
2.9 Reporting	I		M		X	X	X
2.10 Reprographics	I		M			X	
2.11 Resource evaluation	I		M	T		X	
2.12 Systems/programming	I	E	M	T		X	
2.13 Other							
3. SYSTEMS							
3.1 Bibliographic control	I	E		T		X	
3.2 Computing	I	E		T			
3.3 Communication		E	M		X	X	X
3.4 Drafting/graphics	I	E		T			
3.5 Geoscience data analysis	I			T			
3.6 Geoscience data management	I			T		X	
3.7 Image analysis	I			T			
3.8 Mineral lease data	I	E	M	T		X	
3.9 Prospect information	I		M	T			
3.10 Word processing		E		T		X	
3.11 Other							
TOTALS	30	19	29	27	4	23	5

Overseas	Research Group	Geo-physics	Diamonds	Northern WA	Southern WA	South Australia	Victoria	New South Wales	East Queensland	TOTALS
	X									2
X			X	X	X	X	X	X	X	8
X	X	X	X	X	X	X	X	X	X	12
X			X	X	X	X	X	X	X	8
			X							1
X		X								2
										2
X	X	X	X	X	X	X	X	X	X	11
X			X	X	X	X	X	X	X	9
										1
										1
X			X	X	X	X	X	X	X	9
	X									1
										0
	X	X		X	X	X	X	X	X	8
	X	X								2
										2
				X	X	X	X	X	X	8
	X	X		X	X	X	X	X	X	7
				X	X			X		3
	X					X	X	X		5
	X			X	X	X	X	X	X	8
		X								1
	X									2
	X									2
X				X	X	X	X	X	X	8
										0
X	X	X	X	X	X	X	X	X	X	13
	X		X	X	X	X	X	X	X	.9
										1
	X	X			X					4
										0
	X									2
	X	X		X	X	X	X	X	X	8
X	X	X	X	X	X	X	X	X	X	13
	X			X	X	X	X	X	X	7
	X	X		X	X	X	X	X	X	8
		X		X	X				X	5
	X									1
X				X	X	X	X	X	X	8
							X		X	2
						X				2
										0
11	19	14	10	20	21	20	20	19	26	206

fashion where in the organization the three information communities are located with reference to the various types of information resources identified by the preliminary inventory. For example, in the CRAE case, only two units (General Manager, Admin. & Tech. Services) are users of *Mining information*, while 12 units are users of *Bibliographic data* (Fig. 4-3); 10 units use external *State agency* information which is supplied through four units (Figs. 4-3, 4-4) and so on. Conversely, the worksheets tell us which units *do not* use, handle or manage various types. For example, no units made use of *Records management* services (Fig. 4-3).

The Xs displayed on the various worksheets paint a broad picture of the distribution of potential resources across the organization. Differences among the User, Supplier/Handler and Manager patterns reflect the divisions of labor, responsibility, use and accountability that actually existed in the company at the time of the inventory. Although generalized, the worksheets are factual. As such, they are useful in their own right, but in addition they can serve as guides or pointers to more detailed information at the entity or lower levels. For example, a particular worksheet pattern might prompt the preparation of a more detailed worksheet for a particular information resource type, by plotting all the component *entities* (IREs) and/or by using a finer organizational breakout.

Totals listed for the rows (information resource types) and columns (organizational units) simply distill and summarize in numeric form the X distribution patterns. Grand totals at the lower right corner give no more than a rough indication of corporate information "busyness." For our purposes here, there is no special significance to the absolute or relative values of any totals: A higher (or lower) number of Xs for one resource type or organizational unit, as compared with another, is not in itself better (or worse). But the worksheet totals may have other meanings, which will be found only when examined in the broader context of more substantive questions.

There are a number of ways we might approach a substantive analysis of the three worksheets. We could, for example, take each of the types (User, Supplier/Handler and Manager) in turn, and proceed that way. Or, we could take a single organizational unit, such as the Basin Study Group, and proceed vertically to evaluate all resource types for all three of the main information communities for that one organizational unit. Finally, we might take a single resource type, such as *Petroleum information*, and proceed horizontally to analyze that type across all organizational lines, and for all three of the information players.

At this point it is useful to re-emphasize that the task at hand is *discovery* of your information resources, not yet finding new or better ways to manage particular functions or holdings. Consequently, *analysis* in this limited context, at this stage of the mapping process, means evaluation of those factors bearing on whether, and how effectively, the organization's information entities are treated and deployed as *resources*; i.e., whether the resource management principles we described in Chapter 1 are being applied. Thus we will not analyze the actual operational flows and utilization of information itself (Fig. 1-4).

User Matrix. We recommend proceeding initially with the User worksheet (e.g., Fig. 4-3), primarily because we strongly believe that the entire information resources management (IRM) process should be driven by actual corporate user requirements (Fig. 1-3). Putting ourselves in the shoes of users, including both individual users and the organization as a whole, we may ask: What considerations are *critical* to finding and using a particular information resource entity? Is it the nature of the medium (paper, electronic, etc.) in which the data, documents and literature are stored? We don't think so. Is it whether or not the resource has been developed in-house or procured externally? Again, we don't think this is the crucial variable.

Our judgment is that only a few basic factors govern the user's perspective of whether or not a particular resource entity has been effectively deployed by the organization. They are:

1. A means of knowing whether or not the resource *exists*;
2. A means of knowing the conditions governing the resource's *availability*;
3. A means of knowing the *procedures and tools* needed to easily access the information held or delivered by the resource;
4. A means of obtaining timely *delivery* of the relevant information, in the right form, at the right time, and in the right place.

All other considerations, we suggest, may be to varying degrees important, but are secondary in our relatively narrow context. Returning to the User matrix example (Fig. 4-3), let's look at Resource Type 1.9: *Mineral lease data*, bearing in mind the four critical factors. These data refer to various legal instruments authorizing exploration and development (exploration licences, rights, claims, etc.), referred to as "tenements" in the Australian mineral industry.

First, is there a means for knowing about the very existence of these data? While the pattern of Xs suggests fairly extensive use across CRAE's organizational units, still, outside of the General Manager's Office, at least three units do not use mineral lease data (Basin Study, Research and Geophysics units). We need to verify that the reason for nonuse is something other than ignorance. In this actual case, it happens that mineral lease data are simply not relevant to work of these three units. However, in other cases it may be that locator tools are missing or deficient. These could include announcements, catalogues, indexes and directories.

Suppose we've verified that nonuse is not because of ignorance of the existence of the resource. What then? Proceeding iteratively, we should next verify that a particular unit does not use these particular data because their availability and accessibility is somehow, either consciously or inadvertently denied or restricted. Perhaps there is some discriminatory rule that precludes their being given access (need-to-know, sensitivity, proprietary controls or similar reasons).

Having assured ourselves that there are no legal, policy or administrative barriers to availability and access, we can then proceed to the third factor: Delivery mechanisms for obtaining the actual data. Perhaps the data are needed in electronic form, but are available only in paper or microform. Or, perhaps there is no technical analysis module for manipulating the data once accessed, thereby creating a gap between expected (theoretical) use and actual use. Or perhaps the quality and reliability of the data itself or its source are suspect, such that users distrust the data. This, then, becomes a quality assurance problem.

We don't mean to infer or suggest here that, in actual fact, any or all of these considerations is (or was) at fault in the case of this particular company's mineral lease data. We do suggest, however, that you proceed with an evaluation of this sort.

The analytical process will highlight strengths and reveal weaknesses relating to our basic four resource factors: Knowing the resource exists; knowing the conditions of availability; knowing procedures and tools for access and having a suitable means for delivery. For example, the organization may either excel, or be found wanting with respect to such areas as:

- Corporate locator tools (indexes, directories, announcements, bulletins, guides) at various levels of detail for various purposes.

- Standards for data identification, data representation and data maintenance.
- Policy and methodology for regularly verifying the reliability and quality of data.
- Policy and methodology for periodically assessing the credibility of data sources.
- Capabilities for graphically displaying data in nontextual forms (pictograms, histograms, statistical tables, etc.).
- Compatibility of databases, data sets, records and files, to allow correlation and analysis of disparate data.
- Data directory/data element dictionary systems, as a single, central, authoritative user tool.

In an era of increasing use of online databases, search tools and services have become increasingly important finding and using aids. Searching strategies, searching methodologies, searching services and off-the-shelf or customized hardware and software that support them, are important. However, a detailed discussion of even a fraction of these is not possible here.

Returning again to the User matrix example (Fig. 4-3), we suggest a type-by-type analysis, proceeding down the entire list of resource categories and types. As we approach the boundaries of each of the three major resource categories (sources, services and systems) and types, some additional questions suggest themselves. First, taking external sources as a whole, we might ask if knowledge of, and ways to use *commercial* sources, is available. What about *government* sources? Or *international* sources? Perhaps what is needed is more training and just plain awareness-raising. It may be that some scientists, engineers, managers and administrators are simply unaware of the existence of important (i.e., strategically valuable) external resources.

Moving to services, one common problem is that charge-back policies and procedures are either non-existent, misunderstood, or otherwise not working effectively. Perhaps they need to be overhauled. But remember, we're primarily interested in discovering resources here and now — not spending an inordinate amount of time exploring how we might make their use more effective and efficient.

In the systems area, many users are pulling away from using large, centralized corporate systems and exploring other configurations such as developing local databases with their own software, using personal computers and distributed networks to support applications. In other situations there may be need for the opposite

— to centralize data sources, application programs and hardware in order to ensure that all users are accessing and using the same data, without unnecessary and expensive duplication or risking oversight of critical data. While the mapping process will not itself resolve such strategic issues, it can expose or help articulate them.

The reader may wish to stop here and review the individual examples of CRAE entity profiles in Appendix 1 for the purpose of trying his or her hand at a more detailed and thorough analysis. However, now we must move on to the second of the three main matrices — the Supplier/Handler matrix, exemplified in Figs. 4-4 and 4-5.

Supplier/Handler Matrix. In a fashion analogous to the way in which we tried to analyze the User matrix, we might now similarly ask: What, from a resource management point of view, are the factors critical to the information supply and handling roles in the organization? Once again, we believe that the number of considerations of critical significance is comparatively limited if we concentrate just on questions of finding and actually using the resources, rather than on strengthening, upgrading, enhancing or replacing them with newer, better and more powerful alternatives. We believe the critical factors to be:

1. A means for the efficient and effective *procurement* of needed external information resources, including means that address make-or-buy, cost-benefit and price-performance considerations;

2. A means for efficient and effective *bench-marking and testing*, so that users can intelligently evaluate the benefits and costs of alternative hardware, software and systems, whether in-house or externally acquired;

3. A means for corporate and individual users to intelligently *compare and judge* the relative efficiency, effectiveness and other *values* of various information products and services, including values such as reliability, selectivity, comprehensiveness, cost savings, time savings, currency, linkage, compatibility, precision, browsability, response speed, interfacing and so on (Table 3-5);

4. A means of promoting and improving *information literacy* — the capacity for seeking, finding and using information resources for achieving bottom-line results. Information literacy includes: Knowledge of the availability of specific information; skill in extracting or obtaining information; skill in evaluating the probable reliability and validity of data; capability to recognize the level and scope of information needed to resolve a problem and competency in articulating, organizing, communicating and presenting information to others.

Following our analytical process, you should then move iteratively down the Supplier/Handler matrix, type by type, and across it, organizational unit by organizational unit.

Manager Matrix. Finally, we come to the third and last of the three matrices, the Manager matrix (e.g., Fig. 4-6). Once again, we ask ourselves: What are the really critical considerations in the information manager's role for proper deployment of information resources, bearing in mind our central purpose — finding and evaluating the resources? We suggest the following critical factors:

1. Identification of an information resource management *role* related to each specific information resource entity (IRE), including specific authorities and responsibilities of the incumbent, clearly articulated in appropriate organizational directives so that accountability can be pinpointed;

2. A corporate information *policy* that spells out the organization's information resources management (IRM) program, as well as policies for the management of its specific information functions, holdings technology, processes and so on;

3. A *common understanding* among all line and staff units of the role of information managers vis-a-vis functional user departments they support and serve;

4. Information managers with the *competencies* (knowledge, skills, attitudes) necessary to play their roles effectively.

In the CRAE case, we might, for example, ask if responsibility for exploration and geoscience data and information services is optimally dispersed throughout the company or whether it might be spread too widely or too narrowly. Or whether the means and machinery exist for periodically inventorying CRAE information resources, and reviewing CRAE information programs in the light of changing company strategies, exploration opportunities and resource constraints. Or whether there is a CRAE corporate information management policy and plan.

In summary, in this the first of three main mapping techniques, we have described how information resource worksheets can be prepared to depict where in the organization the users, suppliers, handlers and managers of information resources are located. The matrices provide an overview of "who is doing what, and where." Then we indicated how the results can be analyzed, by reviewing each resource entity in terms of the critical factors that govern the actual use of such resources. The analysis will serve to pinpoint the organization's relative strengths and weaknesses in deploying information resources for achieving its corporate goals and objectives.

4.3   MAPPING THE SPECTRUM OF INFORMATION RESOURCES

In the previous section we described techniques for locating information resources, expressed in terms of where in the organization those who use, supply, handle and manage information are located. Now we will turn our attention to the *nature* of these resources by describing a technique for mapping the location of resource entities on the corporate terrain map in relation to two spectra of information resource characteristics.

The conventional geographic or road map shows the location of cities, towns, rivers and mountain ranges in relation to each other by plotting them on a global or other grid or coordinate system, defined for example by degrees of latitude for the north-south (or Y) direction, and degrees of longitude for the east-west (or X) direction. Our information resource map will also plot the entities on a grid, but the nature of the coordinate system, illustrated in Fig. 4-7, is of a different sort: In the "north-south" direction we will use information handling *functions* (north) and information *holdings* (south) as two end-members of a spectrum; and in the "east-west" direction we will use information *content* (east) and information *media* or *conduit* (west) as two end-members of another, intersecting spectrum. This grid system is basically the same one we used in Chapter 1 to illustrate the spectrum of information products and services in the marketplace (Fig. 1-5).

When the information resource entities identified in the preliminary inventory are plotted on such a grid, as described below, we can generate a *corporate information resource map*.[3] The map shows, on one page, all of the organization's entities in relation to each other, expressed in terms of the relative proportions of the four end-members each entity represents.

4.3.1   Information Spectra

We pointed out in Chapter 1 that individual information resource entities are combinations of *content* and *medium*, and that if all conceivable IREs were arrayed, they would form a continuous spectrum, ranging from nearly pure content (or meaning) to nearly pure medium (the container). This spectrum defines the information map's horizontal, or "east-west," axis. The notion of content and medium as a special symbiotic combination, first brought to popular attention by Marshall McLuhan's dictum of the early '60s, "the medium is the message," is a useful, even if somewhat abstract

Figure 4-7. Model of the information resource map grid. Entities from the preliminary information resource inventory are plotted to develop a corporate map of potential information resources.

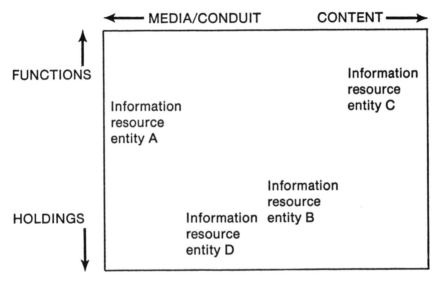

Source: Modified from John F. McLaughlin with Anne E. Birinyi, "Mapping the Information Business," in *Understanding New Media: Trends and Issues in Electronic Distribution of Information*, ed. Benjamin M. Compaine (Cambridge, Mass.: Ballinger Publishing Company, 1984).

construct for viewing information entities. As shown in our diagram of the information resources management (IRM) process (Fig. 1-3), content and media are the two terms we chose to articulate one of the basic components, *information needs.*

The Functions-Holdings axis is the second spectrum, which defines the "north-south" direction of the information map grid. It distinguishes the utilitarian or practical aspects of the IRE. The Functions (north) end-member connotes activities, flows, actions or movements needed for the handling of information, while the Holdings (south) end-member refers to the static physical, electronic or other records in which information itself is preserved. In the context of the overall IRM process (Fig. 1-3), Functions and Holdings can be seen to occupy another of the basic process components, *information resources.*

However, the corporate information resource map is much more than a simple two-dimensional matrix that positions entities along two sets of coordinates. To understand the full potential of the map, let's try to ascertain why these coordinates are important to information resources management. Then we can proceed to describe other insights the map offers us.

First, why have we selected Functions and Holdings as the metaphorical equivalent of the cartographic map's latitudinal degrees, and Content and Media/Conduit as the equivalent of the geographic map's longitudinal degrees?

Most resources can be usefully classified in terms of their temporal status. For example, financial resources may be categorized as either cash-flows or capital assets. Human resources as either turnover (new hires and losses) or on-board strength, and inventories as either work-in-progress or stock-on-hand. So can information resources be thought of in both a flow-through sense and in a stock-on-hand asset sense. We use the term functions to connote the flows, and holdings to connote the permanent on-hand asset. As we said earlier, functions can be further broken down into information services and systems that are provided to users intermittently or continuously. They are the transactional equivalents of a stock receipt or issue in the inventory system, a debit or credit in a financial system or a new-hire or loss in a personnel system.

That is one major way of classifying the information resource and we are using it to define the "north-south" set of latitudinal coordinates. But there is another major way of categorizing the information resources — as there is for other resources. It is the Content:Media/Conduit spectrum.

Once again the other resource areas are helpful to our understanding. In the area of human resources management, for example, the organization not only needs to keep track of turnover and present strength, but it needs to carefully consider the skills of its people and the position requirements of the jobs they encumber. Thus, the organization's position or job descriptions may be viewed as the metaphorical equivalent of the media/conduit end of the spectrum, and the actual skills, knowledge and competencies of its employees as the equivalent of the content end.

Similarly, with the management of financial resources, return-on-investment and profit-contribution might be seen at the Content end, and the type of financial instrument (e.g., cash, loan, securities) at the Media/Conduit end. We do not mean to carry these resource metaphors and parallels too far because they beg almost as many dissimilarity comparisons as they help illuminate similarities.

Nevertheless, we hope they are helpful in explaining and defending why we have chosen the particular two sets of information mapping coordinates here.

In summary, we have selected two spectra — Functions: Holdings and Content: Media/Conduit — as the axes for a map grid upon which information resource entities can be plotted to create a corporate information resource map. The characteristics reflected by these two spectra are closely related to some essential elements of the information resources management (IRM) process; consequently, we can expect the resulting maps to be helpful in grouping or clustering entities in terms of both "information" and "resource-related" characteristics. Let us now construct such a map.

4.3.2 Construct the Information Resource Map

As with construction of the information resource worksheets, the basic source of information for constructing the information resource map is the collection of preliminary inventory data forms described in Chapter 2. However, this source must usually be augmented by the analyst's knowledge of the business and by his or her overall understanding of what the entities really are, how they are used in practice, for what purposes and by whom. Much of this insight is acquired by osmosis in the course of the mapping process, rather than by formal note-taking.

First, a word on the mechanics of preparing an information map. Since trial-and-error is the primary method used, at least to begin with, we recommend using an electronic spreadsheet program. With a large number of entities to plot, you will probably need to try many different configurations before you are satisfied. The "move," "erase" and "print" commands of spreadsheet packages make extensive experimentation, editing and printing and reprinting a practical proposition. For most, preparing such a map with pencil, paper and rubber eraser would be too frustrating to bear.[4]

Now let's try to describe the intellectual process for positioning a particular information resource entity (IRE) on the map, using the CRA Exploration case as an example (Fig. 4-8). To begin, let's take a comparatively simple IRE — *Mail service* (37). First, ask yourself the question: Is mail service primarily concerned with media/conduit or with content? Clearly the purpose of mail service is to deliver a message from a sender to a receiver *without regard to its content*. The postman doesn't need to read the contents of a letter to

Figure 4-8. Map of information resource entities (IREs) identified in preliminary inventory: CRA Exploration case. Numbers in parentheses refer to identification (ID) numbers in Appendix 1.

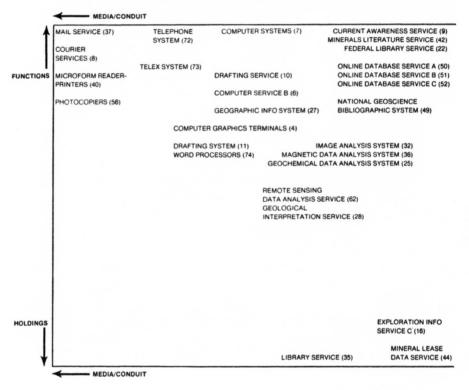

CONTENT ——→

AERIAL PHOTOGRAPHY SERVICE (1)

RESOURCE EVALUATION SERVICE (64)
COMPUTER SERVICE A (5)

RESEARCH INFORMATION SERVICE (63)

FUNCTIONS

BIBLIOGRAPHIC DATA (3)
EXPLORATION REPORTS INDEX (18)
REMOTE SENSING BIBLIO DATABASE (60)

TECHNICAL INFO SERVICE (71)

GEOPHYSICAL SURVEY INDEX (2)
EXPLORATION WELL INDEX (19)
PETROLEUM PERMIT INDEX (53)
EXPLORATION SERVICE B (15)

DRILL-LOG DATA SYSTEM (13)
LABORATORY DATA SERVICE (34)

PROSPECTS REPORTING SYSTEM (59)

IMAGE ANALYSIS SLIDE CATALOGUE (31)
MINERALS EXHIBIT CATALOGUE (45)

FEDERAL GEOSCIENCE AGENCY (20)
STATE GEOSCIENCE AGENCY A (66)
STATE GEOSCIENCE AGENCY B (67)
STATE GEOSCIENCE AGENCY C (68)
STATE GEOSCIENCE AGENCY D (69)
STATE GEOSCIENCE AGENCY E (70)

FIELD DATA CODING SYSTEM (23)
GEOCHEM SAMPLING SYSTEM (26)
PROSPECTS CODING SYSTEM (57)

LABORATORY ANALYSIS SYSTEM (33)
SAMPLE DATA MANAGEMENT SYSTEM (65)

MINERAL DEPOSIT
DATABASE SERVICE (41)
MINERALS INFO
AND DATA SERVICE (46)

GEOCHEMICAL DATA (24)
GEOPHYSICAL DATA (30)
REMOTE SENSING DATA (61)

FEDERAL GEOSCIENCE
DATABASES (21)

GEOLOGICAL SAMPLES DATA (29)
DRILL-LOG & ASSAY DATA (12)

PETROLEUM WELL DATA SERVICE (55)
PROSPECTS DATA (58)
MINERAL LEASE DATA (43)

MINING INFORMATION (47)
PETROLEUM INFORMATION (54)

HOLDINGS

EXPLORATION INFO
SERVICE A (14)

MAPS & CHARTS (39)   EXPLORATION REPORTS (17)

MONTHLY MGT REPTS (48)
MANAGEMENT INFO (38)

CONTENT ——→

know to whom he should deliver it, so long as the address is properly typed or written on the envelope. So, we would say the mail service IRE is primarily media/conduit.

But then we must ask: To what degree is the mail service IRE media/conduit in purpose, versus content? 100% ? 50% ? 25% ? To answer this second question, it's helpful to think of other IREs for comparison. For instance, consider the *Telephone system* (72).

To use the postal services, we need only put a name, address and stamp on an envelope; then the postal system takes over and delivers the letter or parcel "automatically." But the telephone system does a bit more than that. It enables us to put through conference calls, record calls, store and forward messages, recall and much more (at least modern PABX systems do). In short, comparatively, the telephone system is not virtually 100% media/conduit, but is relatively more content-related. We've positioned the *Telephone system* (72) at perhaps the 90% media/conduit: 10% content point along the X ("east-west") axis (Fig. 4-8). But what about the *Current awareness service* (9), to take another example? Clearly, this IRE is even more content-related, so it appears at roughly the 60:40 position. And so on.

Now let's take up the second spectrum — Functions: Holdings. Returning to the *Mail service* (37) IRE, this time ask a different question: Is mail a "permanent asset" (part of our information holdings), or a "transactional instrument" (a function or flow)? Clearly, mail is not intended as something to be immediately put in the vaults, on the shelf, in the bins or into the desk drawer. The value of mail service lies in expeditious delivery of the mail. Once again, we must ask a second question: To what degree is the mail service a transactional flow instrument — 100%, 50%, 25% ? Once again we must say: Probably pretty close to 100%.

What about *Photocopiers* (56)? Their purpose and value, too, lies primarily in their ready availability and accessibility for immediate use. However, modern photocopiers have much more versatility with respect to information packaging (holdings) than does the postal system. For example, modern copiers can now reproduce in color, can enlarge or compress images, can copy on two sides, can staple and can even output microfilm or digitize images for entry into electronic systems. So we've positioned copiers at about the 90:10 point on the "north-south" coordinate.

The reader should now be able to move across the corporate information map and verify the positioning of the full complement of IREs. To achieve consistency in placing the IREs, you should adopt a certain viewpoint. That is, the IREs should be positioned with reference to the perception of a particular user or a defined group, such as top management.[5] In the CRAE case example (Fig. 4-8), we have placed them as we believe they would be viewed by top management.

The most useful questions to ask in determining the position of each IRE are: To what extent is the IRE *valued by* (in this case) top management: 1) For its media/conduit characteristics (e.g., electronic *vs* paper), 2) for its content (the value of the information itself), 3) for its functionality (e.g., taking aerial photographs) or 4) for its holdings capabilities (e.g., retaining mineral lease records)? It is probably best, at this stage, not to assess to what extent the IRE *actually* possesses, or has the *potential* to possess these end-member characteristics. Rather, assess how the value of the IRE is *perceived* by a specific person or group. We hasten to underscore that the reader's judgment may well differ from ours in the relative weighting we have assigned. We make no pretense to suggesting that this technique is wholly objective. But we do contend that placing *all* IREs of an organization on *one* map, to show their *relative* positions, will have some important benefits.

4.3.3 Analysis of the Information Map

Before considering some of these benefits, let's review what maps in general are all about. Melville Bell Grosvenor of the National Geographic Society once said:

> Well do I remember the moment when my eyes first were opened to the magic of maps. I was a boy of 11, and my family was planning a summer trip to Europe. My father spread before me charts of the countries we intended to visit. With his finger he pointed out the figures that gave water depths, and I saw the reasons for the course our Baltic steamer would follow on its ways from Lübeck to Stockholm. He pointed out black markings that meant railroads and contour lines that meant hills, and I understood why our train must snake a way through Sweden. He showed me the patch of white and wiggly blue that stood for glaciers we would skirt, the cross marks that located peaks we would see, the ticked line that revealed the Göta Canal we would travel in crossing from Stockholm to Göteborg.
>
> I learned that day the meaning of map symbols. But more, I gained the realization that the knowledge offered by maps is as full and exciting as the world they portray.[6]

Cartographic maps are packed with information that discloses interesting, useful and insightful details about the history of lands, the geography of areas, something of the inhabitants of those lands and their customs, market locations, transportation grids, power grids, political boundaries, statistical demographic units and much, much more.

What can information maps tell us? They, too, are packed with insights. Let's look at the map of CRA Exploration (Fig. 4-8). Several features seem to stand out. For instance, there is a clearly discernible pattern of IREs scattered from the upper left corner of the map to the lower right. Only a few IREs appear outside this diagonal band (e.g., *Research information service* (63) in the upper right quadrant). This pattern reveals to us that:

- Although CRAE has few entities in the lower left and upper right quadrants, IREs are not only theoretically but even commercially available in these areas. Compare this map with Fig. 1-5, a similar map prepared by Harvard's Center for Information Policy Research, not for an individual organization or company, but for the entire information and communication business in the United States. CRAE might ask itself: Are there any information resource entities, not shown in its map, which the company should be taking advantage of? Or has something important the company actually uses been overlooked by the preliminary inventory?

- The strategic information resource entities for the mineral exploration company appear to be confined to a cluster in the lower right quadrant; i.e., in the polygon formed by *Geochemical data* (24), *Drill-log and assay data* (12), *Maps and charts* (39) and *Exploration reports* (17). Each member of this cluster tends to have one or more systems located in the central part of the map with which it is functionally closely allied; e.g., *Geochemical data* (24) and *Geochemical data analysis system* (25).

- According to its location on the map, the *Library service* (35) is evidently valued only for the holdings it maintains, not for services it provides.

- The major locator tools and services form a prominent diagonal band in the upper-middle part of the map; i.e., in the polygon formed by *Current awareness service* (9), *National geoscience bibliographic data* (49), *Exploration service B* (15) and *Bibliographic data* (3). Metadata and metainformation such as this present a special problem: Should they be positioned with respect to the data or information to which they *refer*, or should they be considered as largely devoid of any "holdings" value? We have adopted the latter approach.

- The company's *Computer systems* (7) are viewed essentially as functional tools, evidently not closely allied with databases, analytical systems or other applications.

Next, there are constellations of IREs — clusters of individual entities in groups of two, three, four or more. We may ask ourselves:

- Can or should these clusters be managed as a group by a single manager?
- Can comparisons be made between and among the IREs in the same constellation, much as we might compare the sales performance of a company's sales offices that are geographically dispersed?
- Can or should we try to reposition individual IREs (or entire constellations) if their responsiveness (as revealed by audits, evaluation studies and assessments and so forth) is found deficient?

Continuing, we might superimpose a dotted-line boundary around a particular "galaxy" of IREs to circumscribe those belonging to a particular department, subsidiary, regional territory or other meaningful unit. Or group them by source, business unit, dependence on high tech and so on. This may help management "see" where shared resource capabilities exist when boundary lines overlap. Or, where they may be disconnected, whether the isolated IREs really support organizational units.

In summary, the construction of a corporate map of the organization's information resource entities allows us to see all of them at once, together on a single page. Their relative positions are dictated by the extent to which each IRE represents or is made up of varying amounts of four end-members from two spectra that characterize the information resource: The Content:Media/Conduit spectrum, and the Information Functions: Information Holdings spectrum. The map reveals natural relationships by clustering like entities. It provides the information manager with an analytical tool relating all IREs to a common framework, much as the explorer's reconnaissance map relates mountains, rivers and lakes to a geographic grid, revealing critical relationships that can lead to discovery.

4.4   LOCATING COST DATA AND FINANCIAL CONTROLS

You have now used mapping techniques to locate the three key players — users, suppliers/handlers and managers — for each of your information types (from the Information Resource Worksheets) and to acquire a deeper understanding of the information resource entities themselves (from the Information Resource Map). From personnel and functional standpoints you now have a much better picture of each IRE. But you still haven't gone quite far enough with your profiling effort. What remains is to determine how each IRE is, or is not, tied into the organization's key financial and accounting systems. Unless you establish the nature of that link, you won't be able to assess accountability, budgeting, controlling and other management issues.

So we turn now to the third leg of the Step Three chart (Fig. 4-1) to deal with corporate cost data and financial controls. Our objective here is modest. We simply want to determine whether, or to what extent, the costs of the information resource entities (IREs) we identified in the preliminary inventory (Step One) are recorded or reflected as such in the organization's chart of accounts, and if so, to determine the nature of the financial controls applied by management to these costs — budgeting, variance analysis, management reporting and the like.

4.4.1   Review Costs of Information Resource Entities

In Step Two (Chapter 3) you did your best to determine the actual costs associated with each IRE and to rank IREs by broad categories of cost (Table 3-3). One purpose was to isolate the costliest IREs and to see, roughly, how the total costs are distributed. Does one system consume most of the costs; are the IRE costs normally distributed or do all IREs cost about the same? For purposes of locating and assessing corporate cost data and controls, you need not review the entire inventory of IREs. A sampling should suffice. However, be sure to include the most costly entities in the sample, at least the top three or four.

4.4.2   Relate IREs to Corporate Financial Systems

You should now turn your attention to the organization's accounting and financial systems. Having used these, or at least become familiar with their existence during the costing exercise in Step Two, you will probably already know, or with help from financial officers and accountants you can determine, whether and to what extent the specific IREs from your sample are represented as such in the corporate accounts and financial systems.

Let's take up the cost accounting machinery. The first task is to match up your sample of IREs with the organization's master chart of accounts and cost-accounting reports. Unfortunately, in most cases there will not be a one-to-one match, for two primary reasons:

1. As we have already contended, the costs of many information resource entities are hidden or buried in overhead or direct accounts.

2. Even where we can see a superficial close match between the line items in the organization's existing cost-accounting system and the IREs in the preliminary inventory, the meaning of the words and terms used may not be the same. One must be on guard and not beguiled into forcing a definitional fit just because the words (labels) may look the same. Look behind the labels. In particular, be sure that an organic IRE, a configured amalgam of input resources, is not confused with a similarly named entity which is more limited in nature and scope; for example, "Computer system X" (an IRE) *vs* "Data processing" (a related support function). Where do "mail service" costs leave off and "communication" costs begin? Or, where do "editorial services" leave off and "publishing services" begin? The examples are many and the answers few, because accounting practices and conventions have not kept pace with the impact of new technology or with related information management concepts and practices.[7]

Your findings on costs and cost controls for your IREs can be categorized as:

1. IRE costs fully and accurately represented in the accounting system(s). List these.
2. IRE costs partially or approximately represented. List these.
3. IRE costs unrepresented or essentially so. List these.

Recall that at this stage, in Step Three: Analysis, you still have made no formal judgments on which of the potential information resource entities are, in fact, your organizational resources. Final decisions will be made later in Step Four: Synthesis. By now, however, you will have become so familiar with most of the IREs that some interim or even strong opinions will have surfaced. In particular, a number of IREs will probably now be clearly seen as nonstarters, perhaps poorly conceived in the first place, or more appropriately combined with some other IRE. For such entities, clearly not candidates for the short list of corporate information resources, there is no need to pursue the minutiae of their place in the company's books.

4.4.3   Review Values of Information Resource Entities

On the value side of the equation, we described in Chapter 3 some possible elements of value, parallel to what we did on the cost side. These values were grouped into five categories: The quality of information itself, the utility of information holdings, impact on organizational productivity, impact on organizational effectiveness and impact on financial position (Table 3-5). We also reviewed Robert Taylor's value-added model, which categorized 23 "added values" among six categories of user needs: Ease of use, reducing noise, quality, adaptability, time-savings and cost-saving (Table 3-6).

Then we described a series of numeric indexes related to information value: Resource Effectiveness (RE) Index, Importance to Activity (IA) Index, Importance to Organization (IO) Index and Value Index. Their use for ranking information resource entities by value in an organization was illustrated with a hypothetical example (Table 3-7). Finally, we suggested various kinds of cost/value ratios that might be determined.

While admittedly crude and approximate measures of value, these descriptors, weightings, indexes and cost/value ratios can serve the present purpose of analyzing your information resource base by offsetting the generally more prevalant information on the corporate *cost* (the accountant's beloved "materiality") with some sense or articulation of *value*. Without at least a feel for the values — better, a relative ranking or measure of values — there is no significance for the resource manager to the copious information on costs. Resource management principles tell us to minimize costs *and* maximize values. Auditors must certify that "value for money" has been received. Value and cost, like content and medium, are inseparable peas in one pod.

Thus, for each of the IREs forming the sample to assess the organization's knowledge of the cost of its information resource entities, list beside each a measure of the value and, if available, the cost/value ratio. Additional value assessments may already be available. You should ask: Has the organization ever assessed the value of the entity in the context of an audit, inspection, evaluation study, computer risk analysis, benefit, cost study, feasibility study and so on? If it has, you should cross-reference the assessment to the IRE. If it has not, you should appropriately annotate your documentation.

Clearly, if the capital investment outlays and operating expenses for a particular IRE are very high, and the organization has never undertaken an assessment or review of its value, management may well elect to direct such a study. But we shouldn't lose sight of our goal here — to simply identify and locate existing cost and value information and financial controls. One outcome of management's attention to the information resource discovery exercise may well be to establish cost and/or profit centers for at least the most critical and strategically valuable entities.

4.4.4   Determine Degree and Nature of Cost Control

Although in Step Two the actual costs for each IRE were determined or estimated, assessing the organization's own knowledge of costs and its ability to control them with its corporate financial systems add other, more general, dimensions to the information resource discovery process. For example, by:

- Establishing the overall goodness of fit or congruency between information resources and the organization's ability to monitor and control costs.

- Locating invisible expenditure sinks — individual IREs that are unrecognized in the financial systems as such — continuously and unobtrusively absorbing a multitude of costs that go unnoticed and unrecorded.

- Comparing the IRE costs as determined by the discovery process to what management routinely knows.

- Distinguishing the critical types of information resources: Those of 1) high cost, 2) high value and 3) strategic value. Are the organization's financial controls focussing on the IREs that matter most?

Assuming your organization knows the costs of some or all of its information resources, how are the costs controlled? Of course if the costs are unknown, they are not under direct control; instead, these costs are subsumed in other (often several) expenditure categories such as overhead and various operating functions. But if known, the costs of major and strategic information resource entities should be included as "line items" in the basic planning, budgeting, reporting and evaluation processes used by your organization to manage its costs.

Again, using the sample of IREs used earlier to test for the presence of cost data in the organization's accounts, examine your financial planning, budgeting and other cost controlling processes to see whether or not the IREs are represented.

4.5   OBSERVATIONS FROM THE INFORMATION CHARTS AND MAPS

Like all good maps, the information resource charts and maps you now have in hand illuminate your organization's information highways and byways. You can now "see" your corporate information resource base in a way that wasn't possible before. You can now discern more clearly the corporate information handling environment, not just in terms of dim outlines — an information technology center there, an information services unit here, graphics somewhere else — but in terms of how they all fit, or don't fit together. You know, for example, who is using what and where. You know who is supplying what, and where. And you know who, if anyone, is being held accountable for results.

Your information resource forms, charts and maps have allowed you to make observations on a wide variety of characteristics, attributes and qualities of your information resources. Among the most obvious observations are:

1. The resource managers and contacts.
2. Purposes supported.
3. Descriptions of contents, operations and uses.
4. Primary inputs and outputs.
5. Storage media used.
6. Preliminary evaluations of some entities.
7. Categories and types of resources.
8. Costs of each entity.
9. Values of each entity.
10. Ratios of cost to value of each entity.
11. Organizational locations of users.
12. Organizational locations of suppliers/handlers.
13. Organizational locations of managers.
14. Internal *vs* external entities.
15. Manual *vs* technology-based entities.
16. Relative degrees of content and media "in" each entity.
17. Relative degrees of holdings and functions "in" each entity.
18. Natural groupings of entities by resource characteristics.

This list is by no means exhaustive. In specific cases, observations of other parameters could also be made, some more general, some more detailed and some of different sorts. In every case, however, the scope and depth of observations made in the course of the discovery process will have succeeded in making the information manager intimately familiar with his or her organization's information resources. This, we submit, is a prerequisite for effective information management.

It is indeed a cliché to observe that, despite our greatly sharpened vision provided by the corporate information map, the completed matrices and the individual data inventory forms, we still only have in our hands a map, some charts and some forms. Now begins the journey. Where do we want to go? How fast? By which route? And if we can't get there from here, do we need new information routes and vehicles to take us?

. . . .

Our information destination and itinerary is a strategic management decision that does not belong to the cartographer. But at least our port of departure has been well surveyed, channel buoys set in plain view, wharves and moles for berthing outlined, floating debris flagged and the areas of open water charted. In Step Four, described in the final chapter, you will consolidate what the maps and charts have indicated, in order to identify and assess your organization's information resource base, expressed in terms of the specific IREs that in fact supply the information critical to your survival and prosperity. This is the metaknowledge base your organization will need to underpin and nurture strategic information planning, enlightened information management and emboldened corporate risk-taking.

NOTES

1. Described originally as "Information Management Worksheets" by Forest W. Horton, Jr., *The Information Management Workbook: IRM Made Simple*, (Washington, D.C.: Information Management Press, 1981), pp. 2-2 - 2-4. The first practical application of this type of matrix appears to have been prepared by Cornelius F. Burk, Jr., "Management of Departmental Information Resources: Report to EMR Executive Committee," (Ottawa, Ontario: Department of Energy, Mines and Resources, March 25, 1980), Table 1 reproduced in Fig. 4-5.

2. Burk, "Management of Departmental Information Resources," Fig. 1.

3. As far as we are aware, the concept of the information resource map originated with: John F. McLaughlin with Anne E. Birinyi, "Mapping the Information Business," in *Understanding New Media: Trends and Issues in Electronic Distribution of Information*, ed. Benjamin M. Compaine (Cambridge, Mass.: Ballinger Publishing Company, 1984), pp. 19-67. To apply their technique to mapping *organizational* information resources, we exchanged their Services-Products axis for a Functions-Holdings axis.

4. The example shown (Fig. 4-8), the result of numerous iterations, was prepared using Lotus 1-2-3 (TM, Lotus Development Corporation). Results were printed in "compressed" print font on 14-inch paper, then photoreduced to provide working copies. It is doubtful that such a map would even have been attempted without the flexibility offered by this package — another good example of the interdependence of medium and message.

5. McLaughlin and Birinyi ("Mapping the Information Business," pp. 22-23) placed entities on their information business map (Fig. 1-5) from the viewpoint of a "customer," but recognized that different customers could place the same item differently. Other important limitations on use of this technique they noted are its two-dimensional nature (items that should be overlapping must be inserted above or below one another; the amount of information that can be conveyed is limited), and the use of particular labels reflects a chosen level of aggregation.

6. Melville Bell Grosvenor, *National Geographic Atlas of the World*, 3rd ed. (Washington, D.C.: National Geographic Society, 1970), p. 4. Reprinted courtesy of the National Geographic Society.

7. Modified from Forest W. Horton, Jr., *Information Resources Management: Harnessing Information Assets for Productivity Gains in the Office, Factory and Laboratory*, (Englewood Cliffs, N.J.: Prentice-Hall, Inc., 1985), p. 198.

5

THE CORPORATE INFORMATION RESOURCE

The reconnaissance exploration of your organization's information landscape is now complete. It is time to synthesize your findings and to place all you have seen and discovered in the context of the organization's business, its strategic plans and its goals and objectives. In brief, to define the corporate information resource. Like the maps and charts produced by Lewis, Clark, Palliser and the other 19th century explorers of western North America, the end product of your exploration is an objective overview of a large, previously uncharted domain containing, potentially, a wealth of resources. This corporate view of your information resources will allow you to see, up front, the most important, the costliest and the most valuable, and to place in the background the trivial, the overhead and the waste.

In addition, you will reap a range of other benefits that inevitably accrue as byproducts of the discovery process. In some cases these benefits may, in the long run, be of even greater significance to the organization than knowledge of the resource base itself. You can expect the mapping exercise to illuminate a variety of management issues, some strategic, concerning one or more of the various elements of the information resources management (IRM) process. Returning to the first of our six Charts that describe the discovery process (Fig. 1-3), we can see that information resource entities (our book's primary focus) affect, or are affected by, a number of basic processes of the corporate information management function. For example:

- Defining corporate information needs.
- Meeting corporate information needs.
- Managing corporate information holdings and information handling functions.
- Accounting and budgeting for information resources.
- Supporting organizational activities, including operations and administration.
- The corporate IRM process as a whole.

Some of these topics, or others related, may have been included in the objectives you set at the beginning of Steps One (Survey) and Three (Analysis) of the discovery process to address the particular conditions and concerns in your organization. In any event, many management issues will, in all likelihood, simply emerge as a matter of course during the discovery process. While we cannot delve into the management issues themselves, Chapter 5 will provide illustrations of topics, issues and problems typically raised.

Chapter 5 Preview. To conclude our book, Chapter 5 describes Step Four, definition of the corporate information resource. First, we set out a range of resource criteria and then apply them to test for and identify your information *resources*. Next we suggest additional criteria which, when applied, will help identify the relative strengths and weaknesses of your resources. Finally, we summarize key results of the discovery process and point to the next stage: Developing a corporate policy and program to strategically manage and deploy your information resources.

5.1   PINPOINTING YOUR INFORMATION RESOURCES

We call Step Four of the discovery process Synthesis (Fig. 5-1). In this context, synthesis means drawing together all of the observations, facts, figures, judgments and preliminary evaluations that bear on two basic aspects of your corporate information resources: 1) What they are, and 2) how adequate they are. The main "drawing together" technique we will use is to develop and apply various criteria and standards designed to test for, in the case of the former, the presence of information resources, and in the case of the latter, their strengths and weaknesses.

Figure 5-1. Synthesis chart: Identify corporate information resources and resource strengths and weaknesses (Step Four).

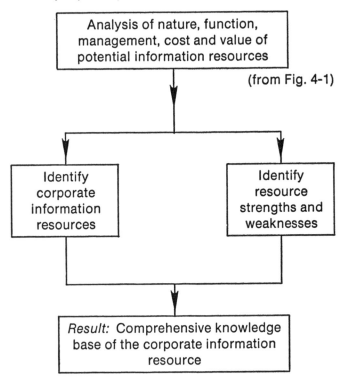

5.1.1 Develop Resource Criteria

In Chapter 1 we looked into the fundamental concept behind the term "resource" and sketched the history of resource management in fields such as personnel and finance. Then we described the similarities and differences between information and the other resources. Out of this we concluded that information, or more precisely, *some* information in *particular* contexts, is an organizational resource by virtue of the role it can or could play in that context, not just because it is information. Not all information is a resource. Conversely, we rejected the argument that information is *not* a resource just because it *is* information and not a tangible "thing" like the other resources.

The three previous Steps of the discovery process (Survey, Cost/Value, Analysis) have provided you with the critical information you need on the role and context of your organization's potential information resources — what we have called information resource entities or IREs. Now, finally, in Step Four, you are in a position to identify your information resources. To make these determinations, you should first develop, then apply, *resource criteria* to each of the IREs listed in your preliminary inventory.

To develop criteria suited to your circumstances, you will need to consider, on one hand, the specific contexts and roles of your IREs, and on the other hand, the generally accepted principles of resource management described in Chapter 1. Thus, the precise criteria statements and how they would be applied must be customized for each organization. But in general terms, all should relate to the three fundamental aspects of information resources management, namely:

1. The nature of the information resources entities (IREs),
2. IRE costs and
3. IRE values.

Let's take up the criteria related to each aspect.

5.1.1.1 Nature of the Information Resource Entities (IREs). During Step One, in the context of conducting the preliminary information resource inventory, while under the pressures of limited time, an uncertain typology and a rudimentary understanding of the total resource base, you recorded (and were encouraged to record) a large number of IREs without prejudice as to their significance, worth or interrelationships. Like the tiny submersible *Alvin* and its robot camera *Jason Jr.* probing the darkness surrounding the silent sunken liner *Titanic*, you made all the observations you could during the limited time available. Analysis, reflection and conclusions would have to come later.[1]

Now, with benefit of having completed Steps Two (Cost/Value) and Three (Analysis), a fuller understanding of the corporate resource base is emerging. It is likely that some of the original IREs, in retrospect, can be likened to isolated steel plates that drifted far from the hull, fragments of a larger structure. Another IRE may have been described originally as, say, "a short rusty deck rail," but with hindsight now recognized as in reality a part of "the liner's entire upper deck." Still other entities are akin to debris on the sea floor — coal, safes, copper kettles and the like. Only now, after all the artifacts have been identified and the thousands of photographs analyzed, plotted and summarized, and the maps and charts prepared, does the enormity of the whole ship and its component parts come into clear focus against a recognizable background.

So you should now test whether each IRE, as originally defined and identified in Step One (Survey), could indeed be a *bona fide* information resource in the sense that it meets our criterion of being a "self-contained" informational entity such as a named source, service or system, and not merely an input resource (Fig. 1-6), or only a disjointed part of another entity. Put another way, you should test for and confirm the "structural integrity" of each IRE inventoried in Step One.

In developing your IRE criteria, the primary sources of information are the information resource worksheets (e.g., Figs. 4-3 to 4-6) and the information resource map (e.g., Fig. 4-8), in conjunction with the supporting inventory data sheets (e.g., Appendix 1). For example, in the *CRA Exploration* case, the following IREs identified in the preliminary inventory (Appendix 1) would, we expect, not now be recognized as *bona fide* resource entities, in the sense that they should more properly be considered as parts of other, better structured IREs:

- *Field data coding system*, ID 23 (*part* of a field data system)
- *Microform reader-printers*, ID 40 (*part* of an office system)
- *Word processors*, ID 74 (*part* of an office system)

We have already described in Chapter 2 the "hidden" resources in the *CRAE* case: Various types of geoscience and exploration data and information — *Geophysical data, Petroleum information* and so on (Table 2-6). Expressed this way, they are not configured entities and so do not meet our "IRE" resource criterion. Yet, as we shall see, they are clearly among the company's strategic information resources.

Even though these IREs lacked "structural integrity," common sense (knowing the business) forces one to make a special case of these entities and to place them in abeyance. The facts are simply brought to management's attention. In CRAE's case, the company reported later that most of these subject-defined data entities had been incorporated in well-structured, user-controlled geoscience databases and computer data management systems.[2]

Those IREs from the preliminary inventory that still meet the "IRE" criterion — those with integrity — should next be assessed against criteria related to the two other resource aspects: Costs and values.

5.1.1.2 Costs of Information Resource Entities. Costs can be used to establish criteria in two ways. One is to consider the absolute cost, in dollars, pounds or whatever. If costs reach a certain level, no matter what the benefits or other considerations may be, management will usually consider such costs as a critical corporate factor. So one resource criterion could reflect a certain threshold cost level (the measure of cost appropriately defined, of course); all IREs exceeding the threshold would be recognized as resources.

Examples of Illustrative Criteria:

- IREs whose total investment costs exceed $500,000 are deemed organizational resources.
- IREs falling in the "high" and "medium" cost categories are deemed organizational resources (Table 3-3).

In the second way, costs can be used by relating them to some other cost, or to some value or other attribute. For example, IRE costs might be related to the costs of other resource types (people, space, cash, etc.), or to overhead costs; or costs might be related to some measure of value, as in our suggested cost/value ratios (Table 3-9). The resource criterion would be some threshold ratio, relationship or condition involving costs as one of the variables.

Examples of Illustrative Criteria:

- IREs whose operating costs exceed the combined salaries of our clerical staff are deemed organizational resources.
- IREs whose "rank order" cost/value ratio exceeds 2 are deemed organizational resources (Table 3-9).
- IREs whose annual operating costs exceed $250,000 and are used by the Sales Department are deemed organizational resources.

5.1.1.3 Values of Information Resource Entities. We have seen in Chapter 3 that values of IREs can be expressed in a number of ways: In terms of the elements of value we identified (Tables 3-5, 3-6), as value indexes (Table 3-7) and value rankings (Table 3-8) and in terms of cost/value ratios (Table 3-9). For purposes of developing resource criteria, we include here also consideration of the strategic roles, business or otherwise, of the IREs. For most organizations, we believe that consideration of strategic roles and values, rather than of costs, should dominate thinking in the development of your resource criteria. Yet the two cannot be separated entirely. Once again, we point to Robert Taylor's seminal work on the value-added model for the help it can provide in determining and articulating your information values.[3]

As with costs, values used in criteria statements can be viewed both as "absolutes" (i.e., any IRE having a particular value is deemed a resource, regardless of cost or other considerations) and in combination with other variables or conditions.

Examples of Illustrative Criteria:

- IREs directly impacting "improved customer satisfaction" are deemed organizational resources (Table 3-5).
- IREs with a Value Index greater than 200 are deemed organizational resources (Table 3-7).
- IREs in the "high" and "medium" value categories are deemed organizational resources (Table 3-8).
- IREs that support our two strategic objectives for the coming five-year planning period are deemed organizational resources.

Each of the above examples of cost and value-related criteria reflect either 1) cost alone, 2) value alone, 3) value and cost combined or 4) relating the cost and/or the value to some condition of the IRE in the organization. Only you can specify the threshold numbers and assessments of cost and value and the conditions. As we are dealing here with *resources*, the criteria you choose should reflect the *strategic* roles played by the IREs. The sorts of questions you should address are: How many expenditure or investment dollars make a cost strategic? Which information values are those of strategic significance? What combinations of cost, value and conditions make a difference in strategic terms to our organization? And so on.

5.1.1.4 Combined Criteria. In most cases, an organization will select a combination of criteria to identify its information resources, rather than depend on criteria based on the nature, cost or value alone. More likely, it would include two, three or more criteria. In the following illustrative example, the first criterion relates to *context*, the second to *financial risk* and the third to *strategic objectives*.

Illustrative Example of Combined Criteria:

IREs deemed corporate information resources must meet all of the following criteria:

1. The entity is an internal or external source, service or system used by, or for benefit of, the Manufacturing or the Research and Development Departments, and

2. The entity has incurred a total investment cost exceeding $1,000,000 and/or annual operating costs exceeding $250,000 and

3. The entity's Value Index ranks it among the five most valuable IREs in the organization.

5.1.2   Identify Your Information Resources

With substance and wording of the resource criteria specified, the next step is simply to apply them to each IRE in the preliminary inventory. Using the information you have already compiled in Steps Ones through Three, test each IRE against each criterion. Those IREs that meet all of the stated criteria are your information resources. It's as simple as that! These are the sources of the information critical to your organization's success.

The consultant's study of CRA Exploration, our main case example, did not include the development or application of resource criteria. This phase was carried out by the company itself. A description of its information resources was later published, including both information holdings and information handling functions. We cannot be certain from the published descriptions exactly how CRAE defined these entities and thus how, precisely, they relate to the IREs that were described four years earlier (Appendix 1); nevertheless, there appears to be a close match. (Some entities do differ; e.g., CRAE recognizes a corporate *library*, whereas the case study recognized the *sources* of the library's holdings, not a library as such.)

For purposes of illustrating our method, we can assume that CRA Exploration's own description of its information resources, given below, reflects the outcome of applying its own resource criteria to the preliminary inventory of 74 IREs detailed in Appendix 1. The resources listed in the first part of CRAE's description represent the company's information holdings, while those listed in the second part (functions performed by CRAE's newly established Central Information Service) are information handling functions (Fig. 1-3). We have added bracketed ID numbers to identify the apparently equivalent IREs of the preliminary inventory. CRAE's Michael Porter and colleagues stated:

CRA Exploration's information resources include:

- 20,000 internal reports detailing the results of all past CRAE exploration and related activity. [ID 17]
- 40,000 internal plan transparencies. [ID 39]
- 1.5 million geochemical/diamond sampling/drill-hole samples and the related assay values, mineralogical observations, sample site information and drill logs. [ID 12, 29]

- Data tapes archiving the results of several million line kilometers of airborne geophysical surveys. [ID 30]
- A comprehensive library of geoscience texts and Mines Department and [Bureau of Mineral Resources] publications and published maps. [ID 20, 21, 66, 67, 68, 69, 70]
- Details of more than 30,000 mineral occurrences throughout Australasia. [ID 16]
- Summaries of past Australian mineral exploration. [ID 16]
- Summaries of Australasian petroleum wells. [ID 54]

The principal functions of the CRAE Central Information Service are to:

- Manage the physical information resources that CRAE holds involving the systematic physical storage and/or cataloguing of each, as appropriate.
- Provide easy-to-use, reliable referencing systems to gain access to CRAE's information resources. [ID 63, 71]
- Provide electronic files of appropriate data — e.g., geochemical results, drilling data, etc. to allow ready retrieval and interpretation.
- Update archiving and retrieval systems and identify new information sources to stay abreast of new technology. [ID 63]
- Obtain other information not provided by the above means at the request of district staff. [ID 71]
- Prepare routine internal reports of companywide activities for distribution to district staff. [ID 48, 71][4]

While CRAE's published description does not necessarily include all entities recognized by the company as its information resources, again, for purposes of illustrating our method we will make this simplifying assumption. Table 5-1 summarizes the 16 information resource entities (IREs) from the preliminary inventory which appear to represent what CRA Exploration itself regards as its information resources. When the 16 IREs are plotted on an information resource map (Fig. 5-2), using the same set of coordinates used earlier to show all 74 IREs (Figs. 4-7, 4-8), the company's information resources can be seen to occupy "resource space" mostly in the lower right portion of the map. We also plotted the apparent location of the Central Information Service (CIS), the major new division created after CRAE completed the discovery process.

The map shows us that CRAE's corporate information resource is characterized mainly by information *content* (as opposed to media), and mainly by information *holdings* (as opposed to handling

Table 5-1. List of information resource entities (IREs) from preliminary inventory (Appendix 1) equivalent or approximately equivalent to information resources later recognized by CRA Exploration Pty. Limited.

ID Numbers	Information Resource Entity Names
12	Drill-log and assay data
16	Exploration information service C
17	Exploration reports
20	Federal geoscience agency
21	Federal geoscience databases
29	Geological samples data
30	Geophysical data
39	Maps and charts
54	Petroleum information
63	Research information service
66	State geoscience agency A
67	State geoscience agency B
68	State geoscience agency C
69	State geoscience agency D
70	State geoscience agency E
71	Technical information service

functions). Not included are the computer systems, database services, analysis systems and other high tech. While CRAE cannot ignore the technology — and clearly it has not — *information itself* is its key information resource. Michael Porter, head of CRAE's Central Information Service, told an international conference:

Information is the raw material of mineral exploration.[5]

What did CRA Exploration discover by applying the information resource mapping process? Were any information "gold mines" located?[6] We don't know. Discovery, someone once said, consists of seeing things that everyone has seen before and thinking what no one else has thought.[7] We cannot know what connections CRAE may have made between their preliminary information resource inventory (the 74 IREs), the information resource charts and so on, and their exploration operations and research. But CRAE has since reported impressive progress in integrating their corporate information resources, building upon, as we have seen, an already substantial base. We will summarize these reported advances in the next section.

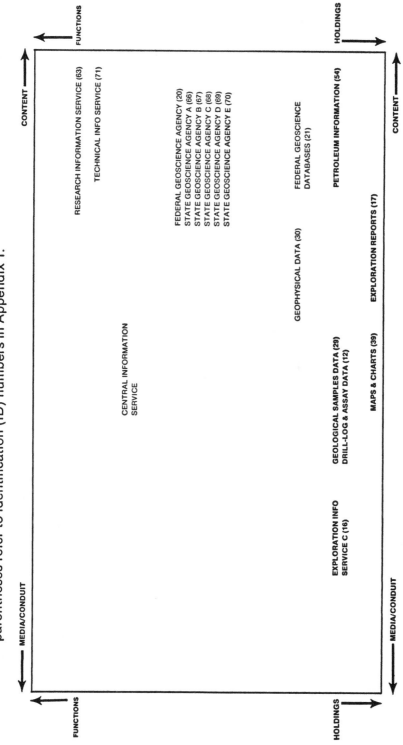

Figure 5-2. Map of corporate information resources reported by CRA Exploration Pty., Limited, expressed in terms of IREs identified in preliminary inventory and the new Central Information Service. Numbers in parentheses refer to identification (ID) numbers in Appendix 1.

5.2 HOW TO IDENTIFY YOUR STRENGTHS AND WEAKNESSES

The information resource maps (Figs. 4-8, 5-2) specify the information resource units identified by the discovery process. You now know what the resources are. Still, something is missing: *Evaluation* — the charts, maps and lists do not indicate, for example, the *quality* of content or functionality, how *accessible* the resources are to users, what their *cost/value* ratios are, *performance* levels, degree of *use*, *effectiveness* in meeting information requirements or any other such strengths or weaknesses. In this section, we will remind you of some of these factors and suggest they be evaluated, so that at the end of the discovery process you will know not only what and where your information resources are, but you will also have acquired a sense of how effective they are.

To assess relative strengths and weaknesses among your IREs, you need first of all to know the business and its competitive environment; and you'll need knowledge of the state of the art of information management in this context. By "relative," you could mean either: 1) relative to other IREs within the organization, 2) relative to equivalent IREs external to the organization or 3) both. For example, you may want to assess which of your corporate resources are the strongest, relative to each other, but you may also want to know how certain of your corporate resources, say your data analysis systems, stack up against the competition. It is one thing to *have* a resource, but something else to have one that outperforms the competition at, say, half the cost — and to know this is the case.

Once again, in the spirit of reconnaissance exploration, we are not interested in making fine distinctions using calipers or other precise measuring tools. You should simply apply generally recognized standards of excellence and performance in the context of whatever business or profession the organization finds itself, and rate the apparent *relative* strengths and weaknesses within the resource base.

However, strengths and weaknesses can be assessed only in specific contexts. One organization's so-called strength may be irrelevant or of little consequence to another. There are no absolutes. While we advocate that you carry out such assessments as part of Step Four, we cannot supply a master checklist of "strengths" and "weaknesses" as such, since we could not possibly generalize all the varied contexts from which these lists might be derived.

Consequently, we will describe certain strengths and weaknesses in a neutral fashion, by providing, in the form of statements or assertions, examples indicating certain conditions or policies, the presence or absence of something, certain management practices and so on, that might suggest, in your context, either a strength *or* a weakness in respect of this factor. The examples are basically a sampling of factors you could consider in assessing the specific relative strengths and weaknesses of your information resources.

For example, one statement (or criterion) reflecting a strength/weakness factor could be: "The organization has effective bibliographic control of its corporate files and reports." This criterion might suggest, in your particular case, either a relative strength, or possibly a relative weakness (i.e., relative to your other IREs, or relative to bibliographic systems in other organizations). The conditions in your organization might be either "control not effective," "adequate system in place," "state-of-the-art system in place," or "poorly done." If the actual condition is say, "state-of-the-art system in place," you might rate this condition as a "strength"; but if the condition was "control not effective" you might rate it as a "weakness." Another possible judgment is that regardless of the actual condition, neither a strength nor a weakness is manifested overall, since bibliographic control of corporate files and reports may be of no strategic significance.

However, in the four sections that follow, we will not provide any examples of specific conditions or judgments — just statements or criteria describing some of the many factors that you could consider in the context of completing the second part of Step Four (Fig. 5-1). The factors listed are limited mainly to a selection from sources, cases and examples we have already cited.

The factor statements (criteria) that follow are grouped according to some of the main components of the IRM process as we described it in Chapter 1; namely, information holdings, information handling function, information accounting and budgeting and, finally, information management. To use our statements, first ask yourself if they are appropriate in the context of your organization, within its business environment. If they are, then you should go on to ask:

"Does this statement reflect a relative *strength* important in the context of my organization? Or, alternatively, would the converse or some other variation of this statement suggest an important *weakness*? Or, is the organization about *average* or normal with respect to this factor?"

The answers (Strength, Weakness or Average) should be related to the appropriate IRE(s) from your preliminary inventory, including of course those selected as your information resources.You might set up a table showing "Strengths" on one side and "Weaknesses" on the other, each related to the IREs involved.

5.2.1 Information Holdings

Under this heading we list a selection of possible strength/weakness factors that deal primarily with aspects of information content or meaning, together with the associated media. The following statements or criteria are drawn from material introduced and referenced earlier in the book. We emphasize that the criteria are samples of possibilities; others more appropriate to identifying *your* organization's strengths and weaknesses should also be considered.

Strength/Weakness Criteria

- Each article or chapter in all books held by the library is keyworded down to the mine or mineral occurrence level using a controlled, in-house thesaurus. Information on all library holdings is accessible immediately to staff via on-line terminals, and paper copies of requested articles are delivered overnight.
- Raw data are always made available in their original, uninterpreted form, even if interpretations have been made.
- Investigators have tools and guides to access all available pertinent data, including both internal and external sources.
- Corporate holdings of charts, maps, plans, reports and samples are controlled by corporate systems that assign and maintain unique identification numbers.
- Corporate information holdings, including literature, reports, maps, charts, tapes and other media containing technical data amassed over the history of the company have been systematically catalogued, stored and archived, and all are currently available for use.
- Requirements for information content, format and presentation are known and carefully documented, and based on thorough consultation with known and potential users.
- The organization provides a convenient means for potential users to know what holdings exist.
- All information holdings are described, categorized and ranked according to their strategic values.

Use this sampling of strength/weakness factors to select similar or like-sounding factors that are significant for evaluation purposes in the context of your organization and its information resources. Then compile your customized list of strengths and weaknesses.

5.2.2 Information Handling Functions

Next, we turn to the other end of the information resource spectrum: Information handling functions. Compile a list of strengths and weaknesses relating to this area. The following examples of criteria are drawn from case examples and materials presented earlier:

Strength/Weakness Criteria

- The organization provides a means for efficient and effective bench-marking and testing so that users can intelligently evaluate the benefits and costs of alternative hardware, software and systems, whether in-house or externally acquired.

- Different classes of data, each with their own processing requirements, users and applications, are handled with software packages designed to meet these requirements, users and applications.

- Systems can be used effectively by professional staff without consulting instructions or manuals.

- Data entered into major databases are available immediately to all staff at all locations.

- Database programs automatically check spelling and validate both data entries and queries.

- The library and internal reports system has full-text storage, retrieval and output capability.

- Specialists are kept up to date in their respective fields by customized current awareness services and products.

- The organization has means for corporate and individual users to intelligently compare and judge the relative efficiency, effectiveness and other values of various information products and services.

- Information holdings of strategic value are subject to corporate policies and practices for ensuring their safekeeping and preservation.

5.2.3 Information Accounting and Budgeting

In Chapter 4 we described the need to locate information cost data and financial controls in order to determine whether, and to what extent, the costs of your IREs are recorded or reflected as such in the organization's chart of accounts, and to determine the nature of financial controls applied by management to these costs. We were not optimistic, since few if any accounting and budgeting systems match up closely with either information resource entities (as we conceive them) or even with the resource inputs (Fig. 1-6).

Yet if information is in fact, and not just in theory or intent, to be managed as a resource — and some recognized as corporate assets — it's axiomatic that the organization's accounting and budgeting systems accommodate and reflect all the dollars spent on, capitalized for, invested in and planned for, information. Our discovery process will not magically rationalize your accounting system with the costs of your information resources. But it can help highlight or isolate problems and issues that may be critical. Here is another sampling of criteria to consider when assessing strengths and weaknesses of your information resources. Again, these samples are drawn from the case examples and material cited earlier.

Strength/Weakness Criteria

- The total costs for major systems development projects are broken down into reasonable categories, then captured, analyzed and reported to management on a regular basis.
- Management recognizes all important information handling activities as corporate cost elements, for which total direct costs are captured and reported, including salaries, equipment purchases, rentals and so forth.
- The organization maintains cost accounting systems for all information products and services provided to external customers and clients.
- Where the total cost is significant, the costs of even routine information handling functions, such as photocopying, are broken down into component elements (e.g., rentals, purchases, full-time operators, user-operators, space).
- Users of computer systems external to and independent of the organization pay for any use made of these systems.
- The benefits of installing new automated office systems are quantified in dollar terms.
- Unnecessary and excess (wasted) costs for information are identified.
- In addition to accounting for costs by Objects of Expenditure, by Activities, by Organizational Unit (Responsibility Center) and by Program, the organization's accounting system accounts for the costs of Information Resources.

- Organizational units responsible for providing information products and services, either to external customers/clients or internally, are designated as corporate Cost Centers and/or Profit Centers, depending on circumstances.

- The costs of information products and services, whether for external sale or internal use, are capitalized if values and benefits are expected to accrue over a period of several years.

- Information assets are included in the organization's financial reports.

The presence (a possible strength) or absence (a possible weakness) of these budgeting and accounting conditions may or may not be relevant or important to your case. If their presence is important, we do not minimize the probable difficulty of meeting the criteria. It may simply not be possible, at least in the near term. However, if David Vincent is correct in his prediction that by the end of the 1980s every enlightened corporation will include information assets in its financial reports, then financial managers and accountants must, somehow, come to grips with how information costs, assets and liabilities will be accounted for (Fig. 3-2).[8]

5.2.4 Corporate Information Management

This is the last of the four areas for which we provide examples of strength/weakness factors. It should be clearly evident by now, as we stated at the outset, that a complete rundown of all possible factors, in all possible contexts, is out of the question. We do not even mean to imply that we believe the specific examples given are necessarily the most relevant to most organizations. Everyone's circumstances are unique. So too are their strengths and weaknesses.

In looking here at the area of corporate information management, we are on the frontier of the information resource discovery process (Steps One through Four), with one foot tentatively placed in the domain of information resources *management*. In terms of our IRM chart (Fig. 1-3), we are examining some of the interaction between the "Information Resource Entities" box and the neighboring functions. However, as we have stressed, this is not a book on "how to manage." The criteria that follow merely suggest topics or areas of information management that may be highlighted by the discovery process, some of which your organization may wish to pursue.

Strength/Weakness Criteria

- Named managers and units are accountable for the economical, efficient and effective use of each of the organization's information resource entities (IREs).

- The organization has a corporate information resources management (IRM) policy.

- The organization has a Chief Information Officer (CIO).

- All line and staff units have a common understanding of the role of information managers and the Chief Information Officer (if there is one) vis-à-vis the functional user departments they support and serve.

- The systematic cataloguing and archiving of corporate information holdings is strongly supported by top management.

- A central information service develops and maintains expertise in new technology, approaches and trends in the information field on behalf of the organization.

- The organization provides a means of promoting and improving "information literacy" — the capacity for seeking, finding and using information resources for achieving bottom-line results.

- The organization's strategic plans for its information resources take a wide range of corporate elements into account (e.g., Table 1-2).

- The organization's business unit plans recognize and take into account the strategic significance of information resources.

- Top management supports the maintenance and advancement of legislation providing for national information standards and systems.

Identifying the strengths and weaknesses of your information resource base is the last phase of Step Four (Fig. 5-1) and thus the end of the information resource discovery process as a whole (Fig. 1-8). For the last phase, we provided a sampling of criteria that could be applied to four aspects of your information resources (no longer qualified with the adjective "potential"); namely, information holdings, information handling functions, accounting and budgeting and corporate information management. Your objective in applying these and other criteria was to establish, objectively, what your organization's information strengths and weaknesses are — here and now.

Solid knowledge of the current baseline position of your information resources will allow your organization to reap the immediate benefits that this new intimacy will bring. But more important, it will set the trajectory of your IRM planning in the strategic direction.

5.3 SUMMARY OF THE INFORMATION RESOURCE DISCOVERY PROCESS

The discovery process is now complete. Your voyage may have been, at different stages, tedious, perplexing, perhaps exasperating and probably time-consuming. Why have you gone to all this trouble? What did you discover or achieve that will make a difference? Did the value of the discovery exercise to your organization exceed its cost? Let's step back now and look at the overall results from each of the Four Steps. Then, you be the judge.

5.3.1 Step One: Survey

The first step (Fig. 2-1) provided a standardized list of all the information sources, services and systems in your organization: The preliminary information resource inventory. Potentially, each of the entities identified could later become recognized as an information resource. To compile and present the inventory data efficiently, you developed a provisional classification scheme for your information resource entities or IREs. The resulting IRE metadatabase would provide the basic input to the remaining three steps of the discovery process.

Your main discovery from this step was probably the surprising number and variety of information entities uncovered — probably much greater than you had anticipated. Which of these entities are important? Which are of strategic value — those that provide the information critical to your organization's success? Which entities are merely waste? Steps Two, Three and Four provide the answers.

5.3.2 Step Two: Cost/Value

In the second step (Fig. 3-1), approaches and methods for costing and valuing were selected and applied, in order to attach a measure of cost, and an assessment of value, to each of the IREs identified by Step One. As a result, you were able to compare, directly, the cost of each IRE with its value. For some entities, cost/value ratios were calculated or expressed.

The discoveries you made in Step Two probably included finding out, for the first time, the total cost of your corporate information, and revelation of high investment and operating costs of particular IREs. Deficiencies in your cost accounting practices may have become apparent. Another probable discovery was the world of information values — what they are, how they are described and measured and how, as with costs, they can and should be managed. You articulated, probably for the first time, the values associated with each of your information resource entities.

5.3.3 Step Three: Analysis

The first result of the third step (Fig. 4-1) was discovery of where your IREs are distributed throughout the organization, as shown on information resource worksheets. Another key result was illumination of the nature and characteristics of your IREs, as portrayed on an information resource map. It displayed all of your IREs on one page, plotted in terms of two spectra expressing the composition of each IRE: 1) the content:media spectrum, and 2) the holdings: handling functions spectrum. Finally, you determined which IREs are reflected in the corporate chart of accounts and the extent to which your IREs are subject to financial controls.

The various information resource charts and maps constructed in Step Three led to numerous discoveries. For example, you may have learned which and how many organizational units actually use a particular information service. Or how many record centers there are. Or how managerial responsibility for information systems is shared (or not shared). You charted the locations within your company of the various information communities: Users, suppliers, handlers and managers (Fig. 2-4).

The information resource map led to the discovery of natural clusters and groupings of your IREs. The positioning and nature of IRE groupings would have implications for how best they should be exploited and managed. Another probable discovery was that very few of your information resource entities appear as such in your accounting and other financial control systems. Thus, there may be no means to track and control individual entity or total information costs.

5.3.4 Step Four: Synthesis

In the final step (Fig. 5-1), all the data and information gathered by the previous steps were marshaled for the purpose of discovering what your information resources are, and how effectively they have performed. To do this, resource criteria were developed and applied to isolate your information resources among the long list of IREs in the preliminary inventory. Then, relative strengths and weaknesses of your information resources were evaluated by testing the performance against criteria statements designed to help determine how your resources compare, both one to another, and with the outside competition.

In addition to discovering which of the IREs identified in the preliminary inventory are, in fact, your information resources — those sources, services and systems that provide the information critical to meeting your corporate goals and objectives — you also discovered (or were re-acquainted with) a host of management issues. Some required immediate attention, others could be addressed over time.

At the end of the discovery process, after all four Steps had been completed, the overall result was a reconnaissance map of previously uncharted terrain — the first of its kind — providing a bird'seye view of your corporate information resources, their identification, location, nature and strategic significance.

5.4   PAYOFFS FROM THE DISCOVERY PROCESS

The discovery process has the potential to chart a passageway through the reefs and lead your organization into a corporate environment in which effective information management is the norm and in which information resources are known, conserved and exploited. Once they have been discovered and mapped from a corporate perspective, top management will be disposed to *think* strategically about their information resources. Only then can you expect them to develop the managerial will, and then the means, to *manage* strategically. So for many, simply raising top management's awareness level would be a major payoff.

As we have stressed, this is not a book on *how* to manage corporate information resources, either individually or collectively, but a book about developing an awareness of *what* to manage. However, the main benefits of specifying the "what" will be manifested later by improving the "how." To conclude, here are some major information management areas in which you can anticipate payoffs in a "how to manage" sense:

1. *Information Holdings and Handling Functions.* You could manage all of the organization's individual information holdings (databases, library collections, corporate records, etc.) together with all of its information handling functions (personal computing, data

processing, office automation, couriers, etc.) as interrelated components of a whole: The corporate information resource. While the needs for specialist skills, knowledge and professionalism in the individual areas are of course essential, you could harness the useful and strategic, and get rid of the nonsense.

2. *Organizational Structure.* You could design and implement an organizational structure that takes account of the actual contribution, here and now, but with an eye on the future, of your strategic information resources and on anticipated future needs for information resources. The new structure would allow the organization to identify and meet its information needs through a process that would take into account, and balance, the cost and value of the resources required. Most organizations lack a structure and process for managing information resources analogous to what has evolved over decades for the management of other corporate resources such as financial and human resources.

3. *Information Architecture.* In addition to a redesigned organization structure, you would be in a position to model and design a corporatewide (enterprise) information architecture that would relate the firm's information resources, flows and uses, to its business model. The architecture could accommodate *all* your information sources, services and systems, not just computer-based information and data.

4. *Accounting and Budgeting.* You could develop and implement accounting and budgeting standards, procedures and systems that would facilitate management of your information dollars. These new financial tools would directly support application of the resource management principles of minimizing costs and maximizing values. Information managers would be provided with information on what the individual and total costs for information resource entities are; with facts on tradeoffs between cost and value and with a basis for forecasting future expenditures and investments for information. Corporate balance sheets could show what the firm's information assets and liabilities are.

5. *Strategic Management of Information Resources.* You could begin or expand the strategic use of your information resources. Here are seven strategies suggested by Donald Marchand and Forest Horton that could be considered — conditional of course on knowledge of what and where your information resources are:

- Using information resources strategically inside the firm.
- Using information resources in new and creative ways.
- Using information resources to offer a new product or service.
- Using information resources to market and distribute a product or service.

- Using information resources in manufacturing.
- Getting into the information management business as a by-product of what you do.
- Engaging in a collaborative information management venture.[9]

6. *IRM Policy and Program.* Success in any of the above "how to manage" areas would depend on your corporate IRM policy and program. Beyond motivating top management to begin thinking strategically about its information resources, the development of corporate IRM policies and programs would probably be among the most rewarding payoffs from the information resource discovery process.

Our annotated biblography lists several works that provide insight into development of IRM polices and programs; for example, the books of Blaise Cronin, John Diebold and Donald Marchand and Forest Horton. Implicit in their discussions, explanations and proposals is that specific resources exist in the organization. As resources, they should be managed. We contend that development of policies and programs for the management of information resources *that work* depend fundamentally on knowledge of what, specifically, the resources are. This is the knowledge base created by the discovery process (Fig. 5-1). Results of the discovery process can serve to motivate and guide your managers into and through development of your corporate IRM policy and program. Initiatives would be soundly based, not just on theory about the need to "manage information as a resource," but on current knowledge of the nature, breadth, depth and deficiencies of your existing information resource base.[10]

Throughout the book we have drawn from the *CRA Exploration Pty. Limited* case to illustrate many aspects of the information resource discovery process. Following its completion, the company took steps to capitalize on what they learned. CRAE's current overall approach, how they have reorganized, where emphasis in their information work lies and what CRAE now sees as important was indicated by Company representatives when they presented the following at an international conference:

> Following a study of CRA Exploration's existing information collection, archiving and distribution facilities [i.e., *this book's main case example*], a decision was taken in mid-1983 to set up a specialized Central Information Service (CIS) unit located in Canberra. CIS is responsible for the physical and electronic storage and management of CRA Exploration's information

resources, the monitoring of available external data and acquisition of such data as is requested by staff geoscientists. To achieve these objectives CIS has planned an integrated company-wide data recording, archiving and retrieval system. Strong emphasis is placed on the development of a system which can easily be used by our geologists without a computing background and with very little training. CIS is also responsible for providing a specialist library, a current awareness service, procurement of documents of all types from various sources such as libraries, etc. and on-line searching of Australian and overseas databases. For the future it is to be hoped that information suppliers will give emphasis to improving the depth of information stored and to vastly improving methods of access so that end-user access can become a reality. In particular, ready access to more source databases to enable explorers to draw their own conclusions from data collected would be most valuable. More efficient access to better quality data will play an important role in the discovery of the next generation of ore deposits.[11]

Obviously, these initiatives by CRAE did not result from a bolt of lightning. In all likelihood the company had for some time been considering steps to take. We think it is fair to say, however, that armed and reinforced with the reconnaissance maps and charts of their information resource entities, the company was in a much stronger position to make its final judgments. We don't know what factors were considered, nor is it important to the presentation of our methodology to have had the anatomy of CRAE's decision-making process exposed to full view. What is important, from our book's standpoint, is that strategic, forward-looking initiatives were taken which led to positive and, from what can be surmised, beneficial results.

· · · · · · · · · · · · · · · · · · · ·

In summary, until the organization's top corporate executives see how information can be used *strategically* to further their many aims — aims which go far beyond functions performed within the walls of the computer room, the information center or the central filing room, the company's information may continue to be viewed merely as "necessary overhead." Once information itself is viewed as a strategic resource, however, management must then provide for information reservoirs, stewardship and safekeeping — like any other resource. Reservoirs must be reliable and cost-effective, just as in the industrial context our reservoirs for energy must be reliable and cost-effective.

We have come full circle with our initial premise: That the information resource is the fuel powering the Information Age. The information resource maps, the various user-handler-manager worksheets and the back-up inventory data sheets are some of the new exploration tools needed to identify, locate and manage your critical information sources — the gold mines of the Information Age. Explore for them. Discover, map and exploit them!

180   THE CORPORATE INFORMATION RESOURCE

NOTES

1. Robert D. Ballard, "A Long Last Look at Titanic," *National Geographic*, 170(6), December 1986, 698-727.

2. T. Michael Porter, J.W. Thorne, S. G. Radke and C.A. Middleton, "An Integrated Approach to Data and Information Management for Mineral Exploration by CRA Exploration Pty. Limited," in *Proceedings of the 3rd International Conference on Geoscience Information*, ed. E. Paul Shelley (Adelaide, Australia: Australian Mineral Foundation, 1986), vol. 1, pp. 192-201.

3. Robert S. Taylor, *Value-Added Processes in Information Systems*, (Norwood, N.J.: Ablex Publishing Corporation, 1986).

4. Porter and others, "An Integrated Approach to Data and Information Management," p. 194.

5. T. Michael Porter, presentation to *3rd International Conference on Geoscience Information*, Adelaide, Australia, June 5, 1986. Reprinted with permission.

6. "The Information Goldmine: The Genius of Making Money Using Information" was the title of a conference sponsored by the Information Industry Association and Associated Information Managers, November 10-12, 1986 in New York, N.Y.

7. This aphorism, apparently a variant of a statement made by Albert Szent-Gyorgyi, Marine Biological Laboratory, Woods Hole, Mass., was brought to our attention by Robert G. Garrett, Geological Survey of Canada, Ottawa, Ontario.

8. David R. Vincent, "Information as Corporate Asset," *Computerworld*, September 26, 1983, p. 1 (In Depth).

9. Donald A. Marchand and Forest W. Horton, Jr., *INFOTRENDS: Profiting from Your Information Resources*, (New York, N.Y.: John Wiley & Sons, 1986), Fig. 4-4. Copyright 1986. John Wiley & Sons, Inc. Reprinted with permission of John Wiley & Sons, Inc.

10. The information manager's role in a governmental IRM context is described by Donald A. Marchand, "A Manager's Guide for Information Resources Management in a State Agency" (Columbia, South Carolina: Institute of Information Management, Technology and Policy, University of South Carolina, February 1984), Project Report PR-83 11.

11. Porter and other, "An Integrated Approach to Data and Information Management," p. 192.

APPENDIX 1

CASE EXAMPLE: CRA EXPLORATION PTY. LIMITED, MELBOURNE, AUSTRALIA

Part 1.1 lists the names of the 74 information resource entities (IREs) identified by the preliminary inventory project. All IREs are given generic names here to better indicate to our readers their scope and nature. Originally, many were labelled with company, agency, local or other proper names. The 74 entities are listed alphabetically and by ID (identification) number.

In Part 1.2, a selection of 48 partially completed data inventory forms illustrate the types of information recorded from individual IREs by the preliminary inventory project. For reasons of company confidentiality, the names of individuals and some original text have been deleted (indicated by . . . . . .). The purpose of the Appendix is not to document CRAE's information resource entities, but to illustrate the nature, types and ranges of textual information that could be compiled in a preliminary inventory project (including the need for conciseness and brevity), and to support various tables, figures, explanations and analyses given in the book.

Part 1.1 List of information resource entities (IREs) identified in preliminary inventory (74 IREs).

ID No.	Entity Name	Inventory Form Included in Part 1.2
1	Aerial photography service	No
2	Airborne geophysical survey index	Yes
3	Bibliographic data	Yes
4	Computer graphics terminals	Yes
5	Computer service bureau A	Yes
6	Computer service bureau B	No
7	Computer systems	Yes
8	Courier services	Yes
9	Current awareness service	Yes
10	Drafting service	Yes
11	Drafting system	Yes
12	Drill-log and assay data	Yes

13	Drill-log data system	Yes
14	Exploration information service A	No
15	Exploration information service B	Yes
16	Exploration information service C	Yes
17	Exploration reports	Yes
18	Exploration reports index	Yes
19	Exploration well index	Yes
20	Federal geoscience agency	Yes
21	Federal geoscience databases	Yes
22	Federal library service	No
23	Field data coding system	Yes
24	Geochemical data	Yes
25	Geochemical data analysis system	Yes
26	Geochemical sampling system	No
27	Geographic information system	Yes
28	Geological interpretation service	No
29	Geological samples data	No
30	Geophysical data	Yes
31	Image analysis slide catalogue	Yes
32	Image analysis system	No
33	Laboratory analysis system	No
34	Laboratory data service	No
35	Library service	No
36	Magnetic data analysis system	Yes
37	Mail service	No
38	Management information	No
39	Maps and charts	Yes
40	Microform reader-printers	Yes
41	Mineral deposit database service	No
42	Mineral exploration literature service	Yes
43	Mineral lease data	Yes
44	Mineral lease data service	No
45	Minerals exhibit catalogue	Yes
46	Minerals information and data service	Yes
47	Mining information	Yes
48	Monthly management reports	No
49	National geoscience bibliographic system	Yes
50	On-line database service A	Yes
51	On-line database service B	Yes
52	On-line database service C	No
53	Petroleum exploration permit index	Yes
54	Petroleum information	Yes
55	Petroleum well data service	No
56	Photocopiers	No
57	Prospects coding system	No
58	Prospects data	Yes
59	Prospects reporting system	No
60	Remote sensing bibliographic database	Yes
61	Remote sensing data	Yes

62	Remote sensing data analysis service	Yes
63	Research information service	Yes
64	Resource evaluation service	Yes
65	Sample data management system	No
66	State geoscience agency A	No
67	State geoscience agency B	No
68	State geoscience agency C	Yes
69	State geoscience agency D	Yes
70	State geoscience agency E	No
71	Technical information service	No
72	Telephone system	Yes
73	Telex system	Yes
74	Word processors	Yes

Part 1.2. Examples of completed preliminary inventory data forms (48 IREs).

ID No:	Category:	Type:	Name:
2	Services	Information locating	Airborne geophysical survey index

Location:	Organ. Unit:	Resource Mgr:	Operating Contact:
Melbourne	Admin & Tech Services	. . . .	. . . .

Concise Statement of Goals/Missions/Purposes Supported:

Management of geophysical data held by CRAE.

Description of Contents, Operations and Uses:

Identification and specifications of about . . . airborne geophysical surveys, including area surveyed, contractor, flying specifications, instrumentation, survey records, processing and presentation.

Current to end of 1981; to be updated annually. Available as CRAE Report . . . .

Used by Geophysics Division to co-ordinate survey activities and by geoscientists to locate geophysical data.

Comments and Observations:

. . . . The entity is a "survey," not an individual observation or report. The index should reduce the risk of duplicate surveys being flown and facilitate access to existing data . . . .

Evaluation:

. . . .

Primary Inputs:	Primary Outputs:	Holdings/Storage Media:
Survey data from districts	Standardized compilation	Paper

Prepared by/Date:	Reviewed by/Date:	Approved by/Date:
CFB 9/4/82	. . . .	. . . .

ID No:	Category:	Type:	Name:
3	Sources	Bibliographic data	Bibliographic data

Location:	Organ. Unit:	Resource Mgr:	Operating Contact:
Various	Various	. . . .	. . . .

Concise Statement of Goals/Missions/Purposes Supported:

Identification and location of specific information contained in reports, literature, photographs and other records.

Description of Contents, Operations and Uses:

The principal generators of CRAE bibliographic data are:

1. Information and Reporting Section, Melbourne in connection with the CRAE Reports Index [ID 17].
2. Research Group, Canberra in connection with corporate bibliographic services and the maintenace of project/personal bibliographies by researchers.

Bibliographic data are scattered in numerous files, reports and publications held by individual geologists and managers.

Computer support has been provided to the CRAE Reports Index (Melbourne) and will be applied to the Image Analysis Slide Collection (Canberra).

Comments and Observations:

Specifications for bibliographic data used for the CRAE Reports Index were established over 10 years ago. . . . .

Evaluation:

. . . .

Primary Inputs:	Primary Outputs:	Holdings/Storage Media:
Document descriptions	Bibliographic lists	Disk, paper, microfilm

Prepared by/Date:	Reviewed by/Date:	Approved by/Date:
CFB 11/4/82	. . . .	. . . .

ID No:	Category:	Type:	Name:
4	Systems	Drafting/ graphics	Computer graphics terminals

Location:	Organ. Unit:	Resource Mgr:	Operating Contact:
Various	Various	District managers	. . . .

Concise Statement of Goals/Missions/Purposes Supported:

Analysis and interpretation of geochemical and geophysical data.

Description of Contents, Operations and Uses:

Most CRAE offices have graphics terminals as part of their computer system configuration. Teletronix 4052s enable on-line representation of histograms, graphs, profiles, maps, etc. produced by analytical programs such as MICRO-GAS [ID 25], MAGMAN [ID 36] and others. The graphics terminals are linked with plotters (e.g., Tektronix 4662, Zeta) to output images in paper form if desired.

Primary Inputs:	Primary Outputs:	Holdings/Storage Media:
Data from analytical programs	VDU display and input to plotters	Microcomputer memory, tape

Prepared by/Date:	Reviewed by/Date:	Approved by/Date:
CFB 11/4/82	. . . .	. . . .

ID No:	Category:	Type:	Name:
5	Services	Systems/ programming	Computer service bureau A

Location:	Organ. Unit:	Resource Mgr:	Operating Contact:
Various	Computer Sciences of Australia P/L	. . . .	. . . .

Concise Statement of Goals/Missions/Purposes Supported:

Computer, systems, programming, networking and automation activities by industry, government and academia.

Description of Contents, Operations and Uses:

[Computer Sciences of Australia Pty., Ltd. (CSA)] is a major Australian computer service bureau providing a wide range of facilities and services. It was used by CRAE more extensively prior to acquisition of the PDP minicomputers. Specific uses by CRAE include COALBOR (coal drill-logs), AUTODRAFT (installed at Perth) [ID 5] and proposals for information systems, e.g.:

1. Requirements survey for a graphics system and a tenement reporting and control system, April 1980.
2. General system design for a field sample analysis and control system, March 1980.
3. Requirements survey and broad system for design for a coal bore data storage and analysis system, May 1981.

Comments and Observations:

. . . .

Evaluation:

. . . .

Primary Inputs:	Primary Outputs:	Holdings/Storage Media:
Various	Various	Tape, disk, other computer-readable media

Prepared by/Date:	Reviewed by/Date:	Approved by/Date:
CFB 9/4/82	. . . .	. . . .

ID No:	Category:	Type:	Name:
7	Systems	Computing	Computer systems

Location:	Organ. Unit:	Resource Mgr:	Operating Contact:
Various	Various	District managers	Various

Concise Statement of Goals/Missions/Purposes Supported:

Analysis, management and display of geoscience data as required by CRAE exploration staff.

Description of Contents, Operations and Uses:

The following computer systems are located in CRAE district offices visited:

Canberra:	PDP 11/34 minicomputer
	COMTAL image processing system
Adelaide:	PDP 11/34 minicomputer
Perth:	VAX 11/780 minicomputer
Preston: Sydney: Karratha: Brisbane:	PDP 11/23 minicomputers

On-site systems staff support is available in Canberra, Adelaide and Perth only.

Comments and Observations:

CRAE geophysicists and geochemists/geologists appear to be well-served and satisfied with the PDP minicomputer systems as tools for the analysis and interpretation of geophysical and geochemical data. Hardware and systems service from the supplier (DEC) has been excellent.

Adequacy of the present hardware in terms of storage capacity, number of ports, word length, processing speed and so on appears to be adequate at all installations visited, except at Perth (Belmont) where the hardware facilities are overtaxed. . . . .

The successful use of the present equipment has been made possible by software and systems support. By themselves, the computers are worthless.

Present capabilities are limited in relation to potential. However, future application areas, such as database management and tele-communications, will be developed successfully to the extent that the necessary investment is made in management, software selection/acquisition and systems support — all matters essentially independent of the hardware.

Evaluation:

Except for the Perth installation, present equipment is adequate for present applications. The potential usefulness of the micro-computers, however, is far greater than actual applications, particularly for data management, office technology and tele-communications applications.

Primary Inputs:	Primary Outputs:	Holdings/Storage Media:
Keyboard, tape	VDU terminal, printed and plotted data	Disk, tape,

Prepared by/Date:	Reviewed by/Date:	Approved by/Date:
CFB 9/4/82	. . . .	. . . .

ID No:	Category:	Type:	Name:
8	Systems	Communication	Courier services

Location:	Organ. Unit:	Resource Mgr:	Operating Contact:
. . . .	Various couriers	. . . .	. . . .

Concise Statement of Goals/Missions/Purposes Supported:

Communication between CRAE offices within Australia.

Description of Contents, Operations and Uses:

Memoranda, letters, reports and other documents destined for CRAE offices are assembled daily in packets, one to each office as required, and physically transported by a courier service. Different couriers are used, depending on local circumstances. Delivery time is expected to be within 24 hours or less.

Primary Inputs:	Primary Outputs:	Holdings/Storage Media:
Documents	Delivered documents	Paper

Prepared by/Date:	Reviewed by/Date:	Approved by/Date:
CFB 11/4/82	. . . .	. . . .

ID No:	Category:	Type:	Name:
9	Services	Information locating	Current awareness service

Location:	Organ. Unit:	Resource Mgr:	Operating Contact:
Canberra	Research Group	. . . .	. . . .

Concise Statement of Goals/Missions/Purposes Supported:

To provide CRAE exploration geologists and managers with current published literature and data on relevant topics.

Description of Contents, Operations and Uses:

A CRAE internal publication, *Current Awareness Service*, is distributed about every six weeks to District offices and staff. Circulation is about 85. The articles listed are selected . . . . . . from about 40 published journals and from about 20 to 60 articles are cited in each issue. Some titles are annotated and certain short articles are reprinted in their entirety.

CRAE staff may obtain photocopies of the articles identified by . . . . . . telephone, telex or mail.

Comments and Observations:

. . . .

Primary Inputs:	Primary Outputs:	Holdings/Storage Media:
Scientific & technical literature	Selected lists of titles	Paper

Prepared by/Date:	Reviewed by/Date:	Approved by/Date:
CFB 10/4/82	. . . .	. . . .

ID No:	Category:	Type:	Name:
10	Systems	Drafting/ graphics	Drafting service

Location:	Organ. Unit:	Resource Mgr:	Operating Contact:
Brisbane	Evans Deakin Industries Ltd.	....	....

Concise Statement of Goals/Missions/Purposes Supported:

Computer graphics support for surveying, mineral exploration and engineering.

Description of Contents, Operations and Uses:

[Computer Drafting Services] provides:

1. Graphics hardware
2. Graphics database
3. Plotting, display of data
4. Digitizing facilities
5. Application services for mineral exploration, cartography and surveying.
6. Training and instruction services.

This bureau has been used to portray results of shallow seismic surveys carried out in eastern Queensland.

Primary Inputs:	Primary Outputs:	Holdings/Storage Media:
Digitized line work	Maps, cross-sections	Disk

Prepared by/Date:	Reviewed by/Date:	Approved by/Date:
CFB 9/4/82	....	....

ID No:	Category:	Type:	Name:
11	Systems	Drafting/ graphics	Drafting system

Location:	Organ. Unit:	Resource Mgr:	Operating Contact:
Perth	SW District Western Region	. . . .	. . . .

Concise Statement of Goals/Missions/Purposes Supported:

Drafting of [maps] prepared by CRAE's Western Region.

Description of Contents, Operations and Uses:

AUTODRAFT is an interactive, general-purpose drafting and graphical editing system, driven by the VAX 11/780 computer. Major features include line-drawing commands, windowing to any part of the drawing, texture and thickness control, choice of units of measurement, text creation and numerous other drafting specifications.

The system is used by the Drafting Section for creating maps, charts, diagrams, etc. based on hand-prepared original sketches. Where base-maps are used repetitively, they can be retrieved from digital storage.

Technical support is provided by Computer Sciences of Australia Pty. Ltd. (CSA).

Comments and Observations:

. . . .

Primary Inputs:	Primary Outputs:	Holdings/Storage Media:
Digitized line drawings	Plotted plans	Disk

Prepared by/Date:	Reviewed by/Date:	Approved by/Date:
CFB 30/3/82	. . . .	. . . .

ID No:	Category:	Type:	Name:
12	Source	Drill-log and assay data	Drill-log and assay data

Location:	Organ. Unit:	Resource Mgr:	Operating Contact:
CRAE offices	CRAE offices	. . . .	. . . .

Concise Statement of Goals/Missions/Purposes Supported:

Exploration for, and definition of, mineral prospects.

Description of Contents, Operations and Uses:

Drill-log data, including assay values, are important, often crucial components of many CRAE Reports. Usually the data are presented in graphical and/or tabular form related to geology, geophysics, tenement boundaries, etc. The descriptive information is usually handwritten or typed on *pro forma* strip charts. Assay values and other analytical results are also stored with "DPO" sheets and to some degree are accessible independently.

. . . .

Drill-log data are in most cases considered to be definitive criteria in the evaluation of mineral prospects.

Comments and Observations

. . . .

Primary Inputs:	Primary Outputs:	Holdings/Storage Media:
Geological descriptions, analytical results	Columnar sections	Paper, disk

Prepared by/Date:	Reviewed by/Date:	Approved by/Date:
CFB 12/4/82	. . . .	. . . .

ID No:	Category:	Type:	Name:
15	Sources	Commercial	Exploration information service B

Location:	Organ. Unit:	Resource Mgr:	Operating Contact:
Sydney	L J Robinson & Partners	. . . .	. . . .

Concise Statement of Goals/Missions/Purposes Supported:

Mineral exploration in New South Wales.

Description of Contents, Operations and Uses:

[The Robinson Exploration Summaries Index is a] manually produced and updated index to determine what minerals were explored for, where, by whom and what reports are available. The five subindexes are:

1. Element
2. Exploration license (EL) number
3. Location
4. Bibliographic
5. Company

Maps consist of transparent overlays for 1:500,000 and 1:250,000 maps, including Exploration License, location of geochemical /geophysical anomalies and drill-hole sites.

About 11 three-ring binders containing all information provided to date are stored and used by the North Sydney CRAE office.

Primary Inputs:	Primary Outputs:	Holdings/Storage Media:
Government open-file reports	Exploration summaries	Paper

Prepared by/Date:	Reviewed by/Date:	Approved by/Date:
CFB 11/4/82	. . . .	. . . .

ID No:	Category:	Type:	Name:
16	Sources	Commercial	Exploration information service C

Location:	Organ. Unit:	Resource Mgr:	Operating Contact:
Crows Nest, NSW	Technical & Field Surveys Pty., Ltd.	. . . .	. . . .

Concise Statement of Goals/Missions/Purposes Supported:

Mineral exploration in Australia.

Description of Contents, Operations and Uses:

The company offers a number of related databases and supporting access and analytical services:

Literature Services

Summaries of exploration projects, abstracts of literature and deposit data compiled in a uniform multiple access system. Database includes:

Mining locality cards	60,000
Stratigraphic unit cards	2,000
Regional exploration tenement summaries	5,000
Literature reference abstracts	25,000
Mines data records	20,000
Maps	3,600

Commodity Distribution

Geographical distribution of mines, prospects and occurrences plotted on 1:250,000 overlays, covering about 25,000 deposits.

LANDSAT Image Archives

Image browse-file, catalogues for Australia; computer-enhancement, color composites, computer tapes.

Primary Inputs:	Primary Outputs:	Holdings/Storage Media:
Government reports, LANDSAT imagery	Organized and compiled data	Disk, paper, map overlays

Prepared by/Date:	Reviewed by/Date:	Approved by/Date:
CFB 21/3/82	. . . .	. . . .

ID No:	Category:	Type:	Name:
17	Sources	Exploration reports	Exploration reports

Location:	Organ. Unit:	Resource Mgr:	Operating Contact:
Melbourne	Admin. & Tech. Services	. . . .	. . . .

Concise Statement of Goals/Missions/Purposes Supported:

To formally document the results of exploration projects and related technical activities.

Description of Contents, Operations and Uses:

About 12,000 technical CRAE reports have been prepared since the mid-'40s. Since the mid-'60s a centrally controlled numbering system and format have been employed. In general, the CRAE Reports constitute the primary repository for all recorded technical information generated by the company, including plans, logs and geoscience data of all types and forms.

A central collection is maintained in Melbourne; copies are available to the districts in microform.

Comments and Observations:

These reports collectively represent the single largest and most significant source of exploration information and data in CRAE. It should be noted that this is so as a result of corporate information management decisions taken during the past 20 years to:

1. Establish a report series for technical information,
2. Assign unique accession numbers to each report,
3. Establish standards for format and presentation of information,
4. Develop a locator tool (CRAE Reports Index) to control the information.

. . . .

Evaluation:

As a mechanism for the presentation, distribution and archiving of technical reports, the CRAE Reports has served the company well.

. . . .

ID No: 17 (Continued)

Primary Inputs:	Primary Outputs:	Holdings/Storage Media:
Results of exploration activities by CRAE	Bound, registered reports	Paper, microfiche

Prepared by/Date:	Reviewed by/Date:	Approved by/Date:
CFB 9/4/82	. . . .	. . . .

ID No:	Category:	Type:	Name:
18	Services	Information locating	Exploration reports index

Location:	Organ. Unit:	Resource Mgr:	Operating Contact:
Melbourne	Admin. & Tech. Services	. . . .	. . . .

Concise Statement of Goals/Missions/Purposes Supported:

Bibliographic control of CRAE Reports [ID 17] and other technical documents held by CRAE Head Office, and access to CRAE technical information.

Description of Contents, Operations and Uses:

The [CRAE Reports] Index identifies about 12,000 documents, indexed by keywords and described in terms of title, author, source and report number. The bibliographic data are managed by software provided by Group Computer Services [ID 34]. Batch updates are performed about twice annually. Output consists of COM indexes by author, keyword and report number. About 30 sets of indexes are distributed to CRAE offices.

Indexing is done centrally in Melbourne, based on a controlled list of keywords covering a wide variety of commodity, geoscience and survey terms.

The indexes are used by exploration staff to locate CRAE reports and the data they contain.

Comments and Observations:

The index is the major CRAE locator tool for technical information and data. . . . . The CRAE Reports Index is used extensively and is highly valued by all CRAE professional staff interviewed.

Evaluation:

The CRAE Reports Index is an important, fundamental information locator tool. However, there is . . . . . . scope for improving its effectiveness in company operations through the use of a modern data management system that would provide for on-line access and Boolean ("coordinate") search.

ID No: 18 (Continued)

Primary Inputs:	Primary Outputs:	Holdings/Storage Media:
Bibliographic data	Author and keyword indexes	Punch cards, disk

Prepared by/Date:	Reviewed by/Date:	Approved by/Date:
CFB 9/4/82	. . . .	. . . .

ID No:	Category:	Type:	Name:
19	Services	Information locating	Exploration well index

Location:	Organ. Unit:	Resource Mgr:	Operating Contact:
Melbourne	Basin Study	. . . .	. . . .

Concise Statement of Goals/Missions/Purposes Supported:

Petroleum exploration activities by CRAE.

Description of Contents, Operations and Uses:

Edge-punched cards contain basic information on individual exploration wells, sorted alphabetically by well name. Information includes well name, location (lat.-long.), total depth, company and status. A separate file for wells currently being drilled contains data provided by the Australian Petroleum Exploration Association (APEA).

Cards also refer to existence of well files maintained in-house (several hundred), which are filed alphabetically by well name. Well data are used for the evaluation of prospects and joint venture proposals. CRAE would have an interest in one or two wells at any one time.

Primary Inputs:	Primary Outputs:	Holdings/Storage Media:
APEA published data	Card file	Paper

Prepared by/Date:	Reviewed by/Date:	Approved by/Date:
CFB 6/4/82	. . . .	. . . .

ID No:	Category:	Type:	Name:
20	Sources	Federal agencies	Federal geoscience agency

Location:	Organ. Unit:	Resource Mgr:	Operating Contact:
Canberra	Bureau of Mineral Resources	. . . .	. . . .

Concise Statement of Goals/Missions/Purposes Supported:

To develop an integrated, comprehensive, scientific understanding of the geology of the Australian continent, the Australian offshore area and Australian administered Territory, as a basis for mineral exploration.

Description of Contents, Operations and Uses:

Included in its objectives, the [Bureau of Mineral Resources] is to serve as "the primary national source of geoscience data and to publish and provide information."

Divisions and branches of BMR comprise:

1. Geophysics
2. Marine geosciences and petroleum geology
3. Continental geology
4. Petrology and geochemistry
5. Geobiological laboratory
6. Resource assessment
   - 6.1 Mineral assessment
   - 6.2 Petroleum assessment
   - 6.3 Geoscience data
7. Special projects and information
8. Operations

Primary Inputs:	Primary Outputs:	Holdings/Storage Media:
Internal research and surveys	Publications, reports, databases	Paper, tape

Prepared by/Date:	Reviewed by/Date:	Approved by/Date:
CFB 3/4/82	. . . .	. . . .

ID No:	Category:	Type:	Name:
21	Sources	Federal agencies	Federal geoscience databases

Location:	Organ. Unit:	Resource Mgr:	Operating Contact:
Canberra	Bureau of Mineral Resources	. . . .	. . . .

Concise Statement of Goals/Missions/Purposes Supported:

The databases support geoscience research activities of [the Bureau of Mineral Resources], which include development of a scientific understanding of the Australian continent, as a basis for mineral exploration; mineral resource assessment programs and the provision of geoscience information.

Description of Contents, Operations and Uses:

BMR has developed a number of small databases covering a wide range of topics, as summarized recently in BMR Record 1981/49. Most appear pertinent to mineral and petroleum exploration.

Reference Databases (8)	*No. of Items*
BMR publications and records index	4,970
Bibliography of digital image processing	700
Bibliography of the geology of the ACT and environs	160
Central register of stratigraphic names	12,500
Library loans system	7,000
Murray Basin bibliography	1,000
Oil shale bibliography	200
Volcanology bibliography	600

Source Databases (26)

Geophysical data (10)
Geochemical data (3)
Geological data (10)
Petroleum exploration data (3)

Primary Inputs:	Primary Outputs:	Holdings/Storage Media:
BMR survey and research activities	Variable	Tape & disk

Prepared by/Date:	Reviewed by/Date:	Approved by/Date:
CFB 2/3/82	. . . .	. . . .

ID No:	Category:	Type:	Name:
23	Systems	Geoscience data management	Field data coding system

Location:	Organ. Unit:	Resource Mgr:	Operating Contact:
Karratha, WA	NW District Western Region	. . . .	. . . .

Concise Statement of Goals/Missions/Purposes Supported:

Mineral exploration in North West District, Western Region.

Description of Contents, Operations and Uses:

A set of codes for the collection, recording and computer storage of stream sediment, rock, geological, geochemical and drilling data, and standardized formats for the collection of stream sediment and rock data.

The system was developed during 1981 and field use is just beginning. The data will be stored as disk files on the Karratha PDP 11/23 [ID 7].

Comments and Observations:

This system represents an attempt to compile a wide range of descriptive geoscience data in a standardized fashion. . . . .

Evaluation:

This project has excellent potential . . . .

Primary Inputs:	Primary Outputs:	Holdings/Storage Media:
Field observations	Sequential listings	Disk

Prepared by/Date:	Reviewed by/Date:	Approved by/Date:
CFB 2/3/82	. . . .	. . . .

ID No:	Category:	Type:	Name:
24	Sources	Geochemical data	Geochemical data

Location:	Organ. Unit:	Resource Mgr:	Operating Contact:
CRAE Offices	CRAE Districts	. . . .	. . . .

Concise Statement of Goals/Missions/Purposes Supported:

Exploration for, and discovery of, mineral deposits.

Description of Contents, Operations and Uses:

Data obtained from exploration geochemical surveys are widely dispersed in CRAE work files, plans and . . . . in computer-based files. . . . . Specific data can . . . . be located by "DPO" numbers. . . . .

The need for improved methods to interpret geochemical data led to implementation of MICRO-GAS in CRAE [ID 25], which in turn was influential in the decision to acquire PDP minicomputers for most offices [ID 7]. However, development of a computer-based system for storage and access began . . . . later.

Geochemical data and their interpretation play a prominent role in prospect search and evaluation.

Comments and Observations:

Exploration geochemical data constitute another major class of data used for exploration. Considerable effort, much of it productive, has been expended by CRAE in recent years to implement systems for the analysis and interpretation of geochemical data (MICRO-GAS), ...

The basic identification control for CRAE geochemical data is the "DPO" (Despatch, Packing and Order) numbering system for requisitioning analyses. . . . .

Primary Inputs:	Primary Outputs:	Holdings/Storage Media:
Geochemical analyses of soils, rocks, etc.	Identification of geochemical background and anomalies	Paper, disk

Prepared by/Date:	Reviewed by/Date:	Approved by/Date:
CFB 11/4/82	. . . .	. . . .

ID No:	Category:	Type:	Name:
25	Systems	Geochemical data analysis	Geochemical data analysis system

Location:	Organ. Unit:	Resource Mgr:	Operating Contact:
Various	Various	. . . .	. . . .

Concise Statement of Goals/Missions/Purposes Supported:

The management, analysis and interpretation of exploration geochemical data.

Description of Contents, Operations and Uses:

[MICRO-GAS is] an interactive, geologist-oriented system to aid in the analysis, synthesis, display and interpretation of exploration geochemical data. Programs perform 11 major functions, the purposes of which are suggested by the program acronyms: CRUNCH, MERGES, MERGV, LISTER, DSTATS, XYPLOT, MAPLOT, PROFILE, MULREG, FACTOR and DISCRM.

The system operates on CRAE minicomputers in Perth, Karratha, Brisbane, Sydney, Canberra, Adelaide and Preston [ID 12], supported by Adelaide. In addition to the treatment of quantitative data, MICRO-GAS can handle descriptive and qualitative data, including commentaries on geochemical projects and drill-core logs. . . . .

Comments and Observations:

This system has had a long history of development and use, going back to the late '60s, which is illustrative of the time, money and expertise actually required to develop a usable, first-class computer-based information system.

MICRO-GAS is well-accepted and used extensively, so far as I could judge, in all CRAE offices visited. . . . .

Primary Inputs:	Primary Outputs:	Holdings/Storage Media:
Geochemical analyses and related data	Statistical and graphic representations of data	Tape and disk storage

Prepared by/Date:	Reviewed by/Date:	Approved by/Date:
CFB 2/3/82	. . . .	. . . .

ID No:	Category:	Type:	Name:
27	Services	Systems/ programming	Geographic information system

Location:	Organ. Unit:	Resource Mgr:	Operating Contact:
West Perth, WA	ESRI — Australia Pty. Ltd.	. . . .	. . . .

Concise Statement of Goals/Missions/Purposes Supported:

Management and analysis of spatial (geographic) information.

Description of Contents, Operations and Uses:

The ESRI system provides for the organization, overlaying and presentation of a wide variety of mapped features, photographic interpretations and field survey data.

Comments and Observations:

An example of an established available data management system for the control, analysis and display of spatially related, multi-parameter geoscience data. Would it meet CRAE's requirements?
. . . .

Primary Inputs:	Primary Outputs:	Holdings/Storage Media:
Spatial data	Maps, results of analysis	Disk

Prepared by/Date:	Reviewed by/Date:	Approved by/Date:
CFB 10/4/82	. . . .	. . . .

ID No:	Category:	Type:	Name:
30	Sources	Geophysical data	Geophysical data

Location:	Organ. Unit:	Resource Mgr:	Operating Contact:
CRAE offices	CRAE offices	. . . .	District geophysicists

Concise Statement of Goals/Missions/Purposes Supported:

Exploration for, and discovery of, mineral deposits.

Description of Contents, Operations and Uses:

Geophysical data of several types are distributed in large quantities among most CRAE District Offices. Airborne magnetic and radiometric data form the largest part, but there are large collections of ground-based survey data. Most data are collected, stored and interpreted in digital forms, since this is the only practical approach to managing such large quantities. Most data are stored on magnetic tapes, collections of which are maintained by the Districts concerned.

Ground survey data are usually keyed into cartridge tapes for computer analysis.

In Perth, microform aperture cards are used for "quick looks" at the large volumes of airborne survey data maintained there.

Comments and Observations:

. . . .

Primary Inputs:	Primary Outputs:	Holdings/Storage Media:
Instrument readings	Located data tapes	Tape

Prepared by/Date:	Reviewed by/Date:	Approved by/Date:
CFB 11/4/82	. . . .	. . . .

ID No:	Category:	Type:	Name:
31	Systems	Bibliographic control	Image analysis slide catalogue

Location:	Organ. Unit:	Resource Mgr:	Operating Contact:
Canberra	Research Group	. . . .	. . . .

Concise Statement of Goals/Missions/Purposes Supported:

Development and application of image processing and remote sensing to CRAE mineral exploration.

Description of Contents, Operations and Uses:

Catalogue of about 3,000 35mm slides of images, photographs, etc. related to projects and research on image processing. The slides are stored sequentially in ring binders.

Primary Inputs:	Primary Outputs:	Holdings/Storage Media:
Descriptions of 35mm slides	Catalogue	Paper

Prepared by/Date:	Reviewed by/Date:	Approved by/Date:
CFB 10/4/82	. . . .	. . . .

ID No:	Category:	Type:	Name:
36	Systems	Geoscience data analysis	Magnetic data analysis system

Location:	Organ. Unit:	Resource Mgr:	Operating Contact:
Various	Various	. . . .	. . . .

Concise Statement of Goals/Missions/Purposes Supported:

Intepretation of airborne and ground magnetic survey data.

Description of Contents, Operations and Uses:

[MAGMAN is] an interactive, menu-driven, modelling system for the storage, analysis and interpretation of magnetic data. Data are stored and input on tape cassettes and the results displayed on a Tektronix graphics screen and/or plotter. The geoscientist can match observed data against values generated by hypothetical models stored in the computer, thus adding to his interpretative capability.

MAGMAN is used by CRAE geophysicists in Adelaide, Perth, Karratha, Sydney, Brisbane, Preston and elsewhere. A scaled-down version called MAGMOD is also used.

Comments and Observations:

This is one of the important weapons in CRAE's arsenal of software tools for the analysis and interpretation of geoscience data — in this case magnetic data. Apparently state-of-the-art technology, MAGMAN gives CRAE a definite competitive edge over those who do not have such a tool.

Primary Inputs:	Primary Outputs:	Holdings/Storage Media:
Magnetic data	Geophysical interpretation	Tape cassettes

Prepared by/Date:	Reviewed by/Date:	Approved by/Date:
CFB 10/4/82	. . . .	. . . .

ID No:	Category:	Type:	Name:
39	Sources	Maps and charts	Maps and charts

Location:	Organ. Unit:	Resource Mgr:	Operating Contact:
CRAE offices	Drafting units	District Managers	Chief Draftsman

Concise Statement of Goals/Missions/Purposes Supported:

To document and portray the spatial relationship of geoscientific, administration, legal or other geographic data.

Description of Contents, Operations and Uses:

Plans are prepared by CRAE drafting units to support and accompany CRAE Reports [ID 17] and to assist in other mineral exploration and administrative activities.

Virtually all geological, geophysical and geochemical data and information collected and used by CRAE is portrayed, directly or indirectly, on the plans. An estimated 40,000 originals are stored and catalogued in the offices that create them. Copies of the registers (catalogues) are sent periodically to Head Office for central storage. . . . .

Comments and Observations:

The archival collections of original plans stored in District offices constitutes a basic information resource of the company, ...

Primary Inputs:	Primary Outputs:	Holdings/Storage Media:
Hand-drawn sketches, maps charts, etc.	Drafted plans	Paper and film

Prepared by/Date:	Reviewed by/Date:	Approved by/Date:
CFB 12/4/82	. . . .	. . . .

ID No:	Category:	Type:	Name:
40	Services	Reprographic	Microform reader-printers

Location:	Organ. Unit:	Resource Mgr:	Operating Contact:
CRAE offices	. . . .	. . . .	. . . .

Concise Statement of Goals/Missions/Purposes Supported:

To read and/or reproduce microfilm and microfiche documents.

Description of Contents, Operations and Uses:

Most CRAE offices have a microform reader-printer (usually a Minolta RP 407) to allow use of the CRAE Reports Index [ID 18], aperture cards, water-bore files and other records stored in microfiche or microfilm form.

They are used by all staff as required.

Primary Inputs:	Primary Outputs:	Holdings/Storage Media:
Microform documents	Visual display and photocopy	Microform

Prepared by/Date:	Reviewed by/Date:	Approved by/Date:
CFB 11/4/82	. . . .	. . . .

ID No:	Category:	Type:	Name:
42	Services	Information locating	Mineral exploration literature service

Location:	Organ. Unit:	Resource Mgr:	Operating Contact:
Falls Church, VA USA	American Geological Institute (AGI)	. . . .	. . . .

Concise Statement of Goals/Missions/Purposes Supported:

Mineral exploration research and activities.

Description of Contents, Operations and Uses:

[Mineral Exploration Alert] is a current awareness service based on the GEOREF database. On a subscription basis, 150-200 references are provided every two weeks, covering mineral-related subjects available in the literature, theses, open file reports and patents. About 3,500 serials written in 57 languages are scanned.

. . . .

Primary Inputs:	Primary Outputs:	Holdings/Storage Media:
GEOREF bibliographical data	Bibliographical lists	Paper

Prepared by/Date:	Reviewed by/Date:	Approved by/Date:
CFB 10/4/82	. . . .	. . . .

ID No:	Category:	Type:	Name:
43	Sources	Mineral lease data	Mineral lease data

Location:	Organ. Unit:	Resource Mgr:	Operating Contact:
CRAE offices	CRAE Admin. Units	District Mgrs.	. . . .

Concise Statement of Goals/Missions/Purposes Supported:

To identify and locate those specific areas in Australia and overseas in which CRAE is authorized to carry out exploration activities.

Description of Contents, Operations and Uses:

[Lease] data concerning the acquisition of exploration rights relate to the following aspects:

1. Information on CRAE mineral prospects.
2. Applications to regulatory agencies for exploration rights.
3. Awarding of rights to CRAE.
4. Maintenance of tenement records in Head Office and District Offices.
5. Timeliness in meeting reporting and other obligations.
6. Relinquishments of rights by CRAE and other obligations.

Responsibilities for [leases] are divided between Head Office and the Districts. Each operates its own "system," but a central file is maintained in Melbourne.

. . . .

Comments and Observations:

. . . .

Primary Inputs:	Primary Outputs:	Holdings/Storage Media:
Government certificates	Plans showing [leases]	Paper

Prepared by/Date:	Reviewed by/Date:	Approved by/Date:
CFB 11/4/82	. . . .	. . . .

ID No:	Category:	Type:	Name:
45	Services	Core/ samples curation	Minerals exhibit catalogue

Location:	Organ. Unit:	Resource Mgr:	Operating Contact:
Melbourne	Admin. & Tech. Services	. . . .	. . . .

Concise Statement of Goals/Missions/Purposes Supported:

Curation of mineral and rock specimens in Melbourne Head Office.

Description of Contents, Operations and Uses:

Card catalogue identifying specimens of minerals and rocks retained in Melbourne. Cards are sequenced by accession numbers and cross-referenced by a second set of cards sorted by country of origin.

. . . .

Comments and Observations:

. . . .

Primary Inputs:	Primary Outputs:	Holdings/Storage Media:
Data on specimens	Card catalogue	Paper

Prepared by/Date:	Reviewed by/Date:	Approved by/Date:
CFB 10/4/82	. . . .	. . . .

ID No:	Category:	Type:	Name:
46	Services	Information locating	Minerals information and data service

Location:	Organ. Unit:	Resource Mgr:	Operating Contact:
London, UK	Geosystems	. . . .	. . . .

Concise Statement of Goals/Missions/Purposes Supported:

Mineral exploration research and activities and mining.

Description of Contents, Operations and Uses:

MINSYS is a database, accessible on a subscription basis, containing literature citations, mining industry information and mineral data (reserves, production, etc). The database is searchable on-line from a mainframe in Denver, Colorado.

Subject coverage is broad: Exploration, mine development, production, processing, extractive metallurgy, equipment, environment, management, marketing and government.

. . . .

Primary Inputs:	Primary Outputs:	Holdings/Storage Media:
Literature, mining industry sources	On-line retrievals and printouts	Disk

Prepared by/Date:	Reviewed by/Date:	Approved by/Date:
CFB 10/4/82	. . . .	. . . .

ID No:	Category:	Type:	Name:
47	Sources	Mining information	Mining information

Location:	Organ. Unit:	Resource Mgr:	Operating Contact:
Melbourne	Evaluation Group	. . . .	. . . .

Concise Statement of Goals/Missions/Purposes Supported:

To support CRAE evaluation studies and ancillary support to mineral exploration activities.

Description of Contents, Operations and Uses:

Information on mining methods, costs, reserves/resources assessment, drilling and technology is used and created by the Evaluation Group in Head Office.

From time to time exploration geologists and managers require basic information on the nature, magnitude and profitability of existing mines in Australia and elsewhere. Current information from the press and trade journals is also used on occasion.

(Evaluation Group not interviewed).

Primary Inputs:	Primary Outputs:	Holdings/Storage Media:
Evaluation work, press, trade journals	Criteria for evaluation of prospects or mines	Paper

Prepared by/Date:	Reviewed by/Date:	Approved by/Date:
CFB 11/4/82	. . . .	. . . .

ID No:	Category:	Type:	Name:
49	Systems	Bibliographic control	National geoscience bibliographic system

Location:	Organ. Unit:	Resource Mgr:	Operating Contact:
Adelaide	Australian Mineral Foundation (AMF)	. . . .	. . . .

Concise Statement of Goals/Missions/Purposes Supported:

The [Australian Earth Sciences Information System (AESIS)] supports mineral and petroleum exploration and development in Australia, including the activities of exploration companies, government research and administration, and university research.

Description of Contents, Operations and Uses:

AESIS is a reference (bibliographic) database containing about 16,000 records dealing mainly with the Australian landmass in the fields of geology, geochemistry, mineral/petroleum exploration, mining, mineral processing and related topics. About 40 per cent of the database comprises unpublished, government-held reports.

The system is operated by the Australian Mineral Foundation as a national program, with participation and support from the Bureau of Mineral Resources, CSIRO, the National Library of Australia, all State geoscience agencies and member companies of AMF.

The AESIS database is available in three modes: on-line access through AUSINET, batch retrievals from AMF (via CSIRO) and in hardcopy form (*AESIS Quarterly* , *AESIS Cumulation* and *Special Lists*). The main users are mineral/petroleum exploration companies and government research agencies.

Primary Inputs:	Primary Outputs:	Holdings/Storage Media:
Indexing data by AMF & State agencies	Online access; batch retrievals; publications	Disk, tape, COM, paper

Prepared by/Date:	Reviewed by/Date:	Approved by/Date:
CFB 2/3/82	. . . .	. . . .

ID No:	Category:	Type:	Name:
50	Services	Information locating	On-line database service A

Location:	Organ. Unit:	Resource Mgr:	Operating Contact:
Canberra	ACI Computer Services P/L	. . . .	. . . .

Concise Statement of Goals/Missions/Purposes Supported:

Service providing online access to a wide range of databases.

Description of Contents, Operations and Uses:

Databases accessed through [the AUSINET] network, provided by ACI Computer Services, include:

> AESIS   (Australian Earth Sciences Information System)
> ASI   (Australian Science Index)

Access is also available to 15 other databases.

Use by CRAE staff is available through the Research Group Information Officer . . . ., and is used to locate scientific and technical literature.

Primary Inputs:	Primary Outputs:	Holdings/Storage Media:
Computer-readable bibliographic databases	Printed results from on-line searches	Disk, mass storage

Prepared by/Date:	Reviewed by/Date:	Approved by/Date:
CFB 9/4/82	. . . .	. . . .

ID No:	Category:	Type:	Name:
51	Systems	Bibliographic control	On-line database service B

Location:	Organ. Unit:	Resource Mgr:	Operating Contact:
Sydney	Insearch DIAL .... Services		....

Concise Statement of Goals/Missions/Purposes Supported:

Provide online access to a wide range of publicly available reference databases.

Description of Contents, Operations and Uses:

Among the over 100 databases available through DIALOG, those of particular interest to CRAE are:

GEOARCHIVE   (UK-produced geoscience database)
GEOREF   (USA-produced geoscience database)
PATENTS
CHEMICAL ABSTRACTS
ENERGYLINE

These databases are available to CRAE staff through the Research Information Service in Canberra [ID 63].

Primary Inputs:	Primary Outputs:	Holdings/Storage Media:
Computer-based reference databases	Bibliographic lists	Disk, mass storage

Prepared by/Date:	Reviewed by/Date:	Approved by/Date:
CFB 10/4/82	....	....

ID No:	Category:	Type:	Name:
53	Services	Petroleum information	Petroleum exploration index

Location:	Organ. Unit:	Resource Mgr:	Operating Contact:
Sydney	Aust. Petroleum Exploration Association	. . . .	. . . .

Concise Statement of Goals/Missions/Purposes Supported:

Petroleum exploration activities in Australia.

Description of Contents, Operations and Uses:

List of petroleum exploration wells drilled in Australia from 1885 to present, listed chronologically by states. Cross-referenced alphabetically by well name and geological basin. Current exploration tenements or permits listed with accompanying location maps. Updated quarterly.

Used by Basin Study group to support prospect evaluation work.

Primary Inputs:	Primary Outputs:	Holdings/Storage Media:
State and Federal regulatory services	Printed lists	Paper

Prepared by/Date:	Reviewed by/Date:	Approved by/Date:
CFB 6/4/82	. . . .	. . . .

ID No:	Category:	Type:	Name:
54	Sources	Petroleum information	Petroleum information

Location:	Organ. Unit:	Resource Mgr:	Operating Contact:
Melbourne	Basin Study	. . . .	. . . .

Concise Statement of Goals/Missions/Purposes Supported:

Evaluation of petroleum exploration and development prospects.

Description of Contents, Operations and Uses:

A wide assortment of reports, files and other documents accumulated over the past 35 years that relate to petroleum exploration by [CRA petroleum exploration subsidiaries] is located in CRA Archives . . . . and at Head Office. . . . .

Information on petroleum matters of immediate interest is obtained by scanning about 15 trade journals and 3 newspapers.

Comments and Observations:

. . . .

Primary Inputs:	Primary Outputs:	Holdings/Storage Media:
Government reports and data, internal files	Prospect evaluation criteria	Paper, microfilm

Prepared by/Date:	Reviewed by/Date:	Approved by/Date:
CFB 11/4/82	. . . .	. . . .

ID No:	Category:	Type:	Name:
58	Sources	Prospects data	Prospects data

Location:	Organ. Unit:	Resource Mgr:	Operating Contact:
CRAE offices	. . . .	District managers	District managers

Concise Statement of Goals/Missions/Purposes Supported:

Exploration for, and discovery of, mineral deposits in regions being explored by CRAE.

Description of Contents, Operations and Uses:

. . . .

Comments and Observations:

. . . .

Primary Inputs:	Primary Outputs:	Holdings/Storage Media:
Geoscience data and concepts	Record of a potential mine	Paper

Prepared by/Date:	Reviewed by/Date:	Approved by/Date:
CFB 11/4/82	. . . .	. . . .

ID No:	Category:	Type:	Name:
60	Systems	Bibliographic control	Remote sensing bibliographic database

Location:	Organ. Unit:	Resource Mgr:	Operating Contact:
Canberra	Research Group	. . . .	. . . .

Concise Statement of Goals/Missions/Purposes Supported:

To support the development and application of remote sensing and image processing technology for CRAE mineral exploration.

Description of Contents, Operations and Uses:

Bibliographic data on published and unpublished reports dealing with various aspects of remote sensing and image processing, worldwide. Aspects identified include subject, wave length, data type, platform, vehicle, application, field, method, commodity association, country and Australian state.

Input data have been compiled on cards for about 1,200 references and about 400 input to the local PDP 11/34 computer, using DEC file management utilities. New items are to be added from proceedings, etc.

Comments and Observations:

This system is well-conceived and thoughtfully designed. . . . .

Primary Inputs:	Primary Outputs:	Holdings/Storage Media:
Bibliographic data	Bibliographic lists	Card, disk

Prepared by/Date:	Reviewed by/Date:	Approved by/Date:
CFB 11/4/82	. . . .	. . . .

ID No:	Category:	Type:	Name:
61	Sources	Remote sensing data	Remote sensing data

Location:	Organ. Unit:	Resource Mgr:	Operating Contact:
Canberra	Research Group	. . . .	. . . .

Concise Statement of Goals/Missions/Purposes Supported:

Applied research projects for development of new exploration techniques and concepts.

Description of Contents, Operations and Uses:

Remote sensing data are obtained from LANDSAT and related satellite cameras, received by tracking stations in Australia, USA and Europe. CRAE data are stored on 9-inch, 1,600 bpi magnetic tapes . . . .

Data are organized in a standardized format, sequenced geographically (by row and path numbers), with about 30 megabytes per tape; about 420 tapes have been collected, controlled by a catalogue.

Comments and Observations:

As with [geological samples] data, remote sensing data are controlled and physically stored centrally. . . . . The data are received in computer-processable form from essentially a single source (LANDSAT satellite). The benefits from this high degree of standardization and centralization, for interpretive purposes and applications, are manifest in the sophistication of various image processing techniques (see [Image Analysis System (32)].

Primary Inputs:	Primary Outputs:	Holdings/Storage Media:
Satellite imagery	COMTAL system	Tape

Prepared by/Date:	Reviewed by/Date:	Approved by/Date:
CFB 11/4/82	. . . .	. . . .

ID No:	Category:	Type:	Name:
62	Services	Systems/ programming	Remote sensing data analysis service

Location:	Organ. Unit:	Resource Mgr:	Operating Contact:
Crows Nest, NSW	Earthsat (Computing) P/L	. . . .	. . . .

Concise Statement of Goals/Missions/Purposes Supported:

Analysis of LANDSAT and other [remotely sensed] digital imagery.

Description of Contents, Operations and Uses:

Service offers analysis and enhancement using Dipix LCT-11 and Dunn Camera for application in fields of geology, agriculture, environmental monitoring and water resources.

Not presently being used by CRAE.

Primary Inputs:	Primary Outputs:	Holdings/Storage Media:
LANDSAT imagery data	VDU images, photographs, slides	Tapes

Prepared by/Date:	Reviewed by/Date:	Approved by/Date:
CFB 10/4/82	. . . .	. . . .

ID No:	Category:	Type:	Name:
63	Services	Information locating	Research information service

Location:	Organ. Unit:	Resource Mgr:	Operating Contact:
Canberra	Research Group	. . . .	. . . .

Concise Statement of Goals/Missions/Purposes Supported:

Exploration operations and research carried out by CRAE.

Description of Contents, Operations and Uses:

This resource provides a one-man scientific and technical information literature/data service, divided about evenly between the Research Group (Canberra) and exploration districts throughout Australia. The main functions are provision of a Current Awareness Service [ID 20], notifying staff of the release of technical data by BMR, distribution of technical literature, doing on-line searches of bibliographic databases via ORBIT [ID 52], DIALOG [ID 51] and AUSINET [ID 50] and obtaining information from a wide variety of public sources.

Comments and Observations:

Many staff expressed appreciation with the services provided.

. . . .

Primary Inputs:	Primary Outputs:	Holdings/Storage Media:
Public STI sources and services	Specific reports and bibliographic listings	Hardcopy & electronic library resources

Prepared by/Date:	Reviewed by/Date:	Approved by/Date:
CFB 10/4/82	. . . .	. . . .

ID No:	Category:	Type:	Name:
64	Services	Resource evaluation	Resource evaluation service

Location:	Organ. Unit:	Resource Mgr:	Operating Contact:
Edmonton, Canada	Summus Resource Evaluations, Ltd.	. . . .	. . . .

Concise Statement of Goals/Missions/Purposes Supported:

Coal, petroleum, oil sands, sand/gravel exploration; terrain analysis and environmental geology programs.

Description of Contents, Operations and Uses:

Service provides computer techniques to solution of geological mapping and resource evaluation problems, including:

1. Design and supervision of exploration and evaluation programs.
2. Complete computer-based geological and engineering data management services.
3. Estimation of commodity reserves and resources.
4. Geological modelling and simulation.
5. Computer-based geological mapping.

. . . .

Comments and Observations:

Though modest in appearance, this company offers the most conceptually sound and technically imaginative solutions I have encountered for the application of computer technology to the development of resource inventories and borehole-related data management systems.

Primary Inputs:	Primary Outputs:	Holdings/Storage Media:
Company geoscience data	Custom maps, plans and reports	Disk, diskette

Prepared by/Date:	Reviewed by/Date:	Approved by/Date:
CFB 11/4/82	. . . .	. . . .

ID No:	Category:	Type:	Name:
68	Sources	State agency	State geoscience agency C

Location:	Organ. Unit:	Resource Mgr:	Operating Contact:
Adelaide	South Australia Department of Mines and Energy	. . . .	. . . .

Concise Statement of Goals/Missions/Purposes Supported:

To provide government with the knowledge and organization to ensure the orderly development of the mineral and energy resources of the state, which are regarded as the new materials of industry, to be utilized in the public interest.

Description of Contents, Operations and Uses:

Information services and systems made available by [the South Australia Department of Mines and Energy] include:

1. Publication of reports and records related to mining, petroleum and extractive industries.
2. Provision of specialized resource data.
3. Control of mineral and mining tenements, including exploration titles.
4. Provision of a storage and retrieval system for geoscience information and data.

Among the specific sources are a bibliographic database (SADMEB) and a "Water Bore" file of microfiche aperture cards covering all drilling results from South Australia, including mineral, petroleum, water and geotechnical boreholes, and an index to samples and cores held by the Department.

Primary Inputs:	Primary Outputs:	Holdings/Storage Media:
Government surveys, research and industry activity.	Publications, reports, indexes, data files.	Library, files, tapes, cabinets, aperture cards.

Prepared by/Date:	Reviewed by/Date:	Approved by/Date:
CFB 2/3/82	. . . .	. . . .

ID No:	Category:	Type:	Name:
69	Sources	State agencies	State geoscience agency D

Location:	Organ. Unit:	Resource Mgr:	Operating Contact:
Melbourne	Victoria Geological Survey	. . . .	. . . .

Concise Statement of Goals/Missions/Purposes Supported:

To carry out geological surveys, provide geological input to administrative activities, provide advice to government, industry and the public, to manage the state's natural resources and to act as a central repository for geological information.

Description of Contents, Operations and Uses:

[The Victoria Geological Survey's] library provides public access to literature, unpublished Survey Reports and Exploration License Reports. A microfiche water-bore file includes about 40,000 records.

. . . .

The Survey is used mainly by the Preston Office.

Primary Inputs:	Primary Outputs:	Holdings/Storage Media:
Geological surveys, research	Publications, open-file reports	Paper, microfiche

Prepared by/Date:	Reviewed by/Date:	Approved by/Date:
CFB 11/4/82	. . . .	. . . .

ID No:	Category:	Type:	Name:
72	Systems	Communica-tions	Telephone system

Location:	Organ. Unit:	Resource Mgr:	Operating Contact:
CRAE offices	Telecom Australia	. . . .	. . . .

Concise Statement of Goals/Missions/Purposes Supported:

Voice and digital data communication in Australia and overseas.

Description of Contents, Operations and Uses:

The telephone network, national and worldwide, is the most basic and widely used means for person-to-person communication and for the transmission of digital data between terminals and computer facilities. The network utilizes copper wire, fibre optics, microwave and satellite technology and can be used to transmit a wide range of information beyond voice messages. PABX systems have greatly enhanced the power of telephone equipment in the office.

Primary Inputs:	Primary Outputs:	Holdings/Storage Media:
Voice, digital data	Voice, digital data	Wire, optics, electronics

Prepared by/Date:	Reviewed by/Date:	Approved by/Date:
CFB 11/4/82	. . . .	. . . .

ID No:	Category:	Type:	Name:
73	Systems	Communications	Telex system

Location:	Organ. Unit:	Resource Mgr:	Operating Contact:
CRAE offices	CRA Services	District managers	. . . .

Concise Statement of Goals/Missions/Purposes Supported:

Communication of messages between offices within CRAE and elsewhere.

Description of Contents, Operations and Uses:

Telex terminals provide direct office-to-office communication of messages and text. A worldwide network allows communication with many companies, government agencies and other organizations, independent of time zones and the availability of people.

The system is usually operated and controlled at a central site within the organization, and the messages received and sent by the operator by internal mail.

Primary Inputs:	Primary Outputs:	Holdings/Storage Media:
Text, messages	Text, messages	Paper

Prepared by/Date:	Reviewed by/Date:	Approved by/Date:
CFB 11/4/82	. . . .	. . . .

ID No:	Category:	Type:	Name:
74	Systems	Word processing	Word processors

Location:	Organ. Unit:	Resource Mgr:	Operating Contact:
Melbourne	Admin. & Tech. Services	. . . .	Secretaries

Concise Statement of Goals/Missions/Purposes Supported:

To facilitate the preparation, editing, storage and printing of letters, reports and other textual, alphanumeric or tabular information.

Description of Contents, Operations and Uses:

. . . .

Comments and Observations

. . . .

Primary Inputs:	Primary Outputs:	Holdings/Storage Media:
Keyboarded text	Letters, reports	Disk

Prepared by/Date:	Reviewed by/Date:	Approved by/Date:
CFB 11/4/82	. . . .	. . . .

ANNOTATED
BIBLIOGRAPHY

BEDELL, EUGENE F., *The Computer Solution: Strategies for Success in the Information Age.* Homewood, Illinois: Dow Jones-Irwin, 1985. Includes description of techniques to assess the effectiveness and strategic significance of computer-based information systems in an organization. As illustrated in Chapter 3, the approach can be applied to other types of information resource entities.

CRONIN, BLAISE, Editor, *Information Management: From Strategies to Action.* London: Aslib, 1985. A useful collection of original papers by information management professionals in the United Kingdom. In many ways, the idea of managing information as a resource has caught on in the U.K. with even greater vigor than in North America.

CLEVELAND, HARLAN, *The Knowledge Executive: Leadership in an Information Society.* New York, N.Y.: E.P. Dutton, 1985. A broadly experienced executive's view of the impact of the Information Age on leadership and management of both public institutions and private companies. Includes a vivid description of the unique characteristics of information, the "new, intangible resource."

DANIEL, EVELYN, H., *Information Resource Management: An Overview for Educators*, Syracuse, N.Y.: Eric Clearinghouse on Information Resources, Syracuse University, IR-58, 1981. Former Dean of Syracuse University's School of Information Studies presents a lucid case for the basic IRM essentials educators should note.

DIEBOLD, JOHN, *Managing Information: The Challenge and the Opportunity*, New York, N.Y.: Amacom, 1985. As a pioneer in advancing the IRM and CIO (Chief Information Officer) concepts, John Diebold's perspective is particularly valuable. He has for two decades been at the forefront of information technology and management developments.

HORTON, FOREST W., JR., *Information Resources Management: Concept and Cases.* Cleveland, Ohio: Association for Systems Management, 1979. The first complete description of the information resources management (IRM) concept and its application. Includes a chapter on the evolution of resource management and an account on resource management principles.

HORTON, FOREST W., JR., *The Information Management Workbook: IRM Made Simple.* Washington, D.C.: Information Management Press, 1985. The original presentation of the information resource discovery methodology is described in this book. Includes numerous checklists, diagrams and sources of additional information on IRM.

LANDAU, ROBERT M., *Information Resources Management.* New York, N.Y.: Amacom, 1980. This short monograph is valuable for the business executive who wants a quick overview of IRM.

LYTLE, RICHARD H., "Information Resource Management: 1981-1986," in Martha E. Williams, ed., *Annual Review of Information Science and Technology,* vol. 21, Washington, D.C.: Knowledge Industries Publications, Inc. for American Society for Information Science, 1986, pp. 309-336. A review of developments, concepts, published works and professional activities in the IRM field, providing good continuity with an earlier comprehensive IRM review done in the same series by Karen Levitan. An excellent summary of the background and context for this book.

MARCHAND, DONALD A., AND FOREST W. HORTON, JR., *INFOTRENDS: Profiting from Your Information Resources.* New York, N.Y.: John Wiley & Sons, 1986. Analysis of the transition from doing business in an industrial economy to doing business in an information economy. Provides a framework and rationale for the management of corporate information resources, and describes how the resources can be used to advance strategic business goals and objectives.

MELTZER, MORTON F., *Information: The Ultimate Management Resource. How to Find, Use and Manage It.* New York, N.Y.: Amacom, 1981. Includes descriptions of information in resource terms: As an economic, personal, organizational and a national resource. The author, an experienced private-sector information manager, shows how management principles can and should be applied to information.

PORTER, T. MICHAEL and others, "An Integrated Approach to Data and Information Management for Mineral Exploration by CRA Exploration Pty. Limited," in *Proceedings of the 3rd International Conference on Geoscience Information*, ed. E. Paul Shelley. Adelaide, Australia: Australian Mineral Foundation, 1986, vol. 1, pp. 192-201. An account of IRM progress and plans of the Australian mineral exploration company whose pioneering application of the information resource discovery process provided our main case example.

STRASSMAN, PAUL A., *Information Payoff: The Transformation of Work in the Electronic Age*. New York, N.Y.: The Free Press, 1985. In-depth analysis and summary of the use of information technology in the office, with emphasis on productivity issues. Unique recommendations on how the knowledge worker's output can be defined and measured in traditional macroeconomic terms.

SYNNOTT, WILLIAM R., AND WILLIAM H. GRUBER, *Information Resource Management: Opportunities and Strategies for the 1980s*. New York, N.Y.: John Wiley & Sons, 1981. Application of IRM concepts to the management of computing and computer-based systems.

TAYLOR, ROBERT S., *Value-Added Processes in Information Systems*. Norwood, N.J.: Ablex Publishing Corporation, 1986. A scholarly analysis of the meaning and measurement of information values. A seminal work, opening up new opportunities for understanding and managing information content values. Introduces the idea of "value-added" from a research-hypothesis standpoint, and points to avenues of practical application of the hypothesis.

U.S. COMMISSION ON FEDERAL PAPERWORK, *A Report of the Commission on Federal Paperwork: Information Resources Management*. Washington, D.C.: Government Printing Office, Stock No. 052-003-00464-0/ catalog no. Y 3.P 19:2 In3, September 9, 1977. The studies of this U.S. Congressional Commission underpin the theoretical basis for IRM.

GLOSSARY

benefit Something that promotes well-being. An advantage. Useful assistance. Something worthwhile, rewarding or profitable. Expected return on investment.

categories See information resource categories.

corporate information resources Information resources owned by, or accessible to, an organization; e.g., company, government department, not-for-profit agency.

cost An outlay, expenditure or price paid to acquire, construct or manufacture capital assets and commodities, as well as other expenses incurred for running an organization and accomplishing institutional missions, goals and objectives.

data 1. The smallest indivisible units of information utilized or produced in a specific context. 2. The raw facts from which information is derived.

IM See information management.

importance to activity (IA) index A rating, on a scale of 0 to 10, of the strategic significance of an activity in an organization. Activity categories and their numeric ratings include: "Strategic factor" (10), "major support factor" (5), "minor support factor" (1) and "not useful" (0). IA indexes are used to determine the Value Index of an information resource entity (Table 3-7).

importance to organization (IO) index A rating, on a scale of 0 to 10, of the strategic importance of an information resource entity to the activity or activities it is intended to support. Importance categories and their numeric ratings include: "Critically strategic" (10), "strategic" (8), "contributory" (6), "support" (4), "overhead" (2) and "detrimental" (0). IO indexes are used to determine the Value Index of an information resource entity (Table 3-7).

information 1. That which informs or has the potential to inform. 2. Meaning communicated or received. 3. A combination of content or meaning represented by symbols, and media or conduit, used or useable in a particular context. Use of the expression "information itself" makes the content or meaning component of information explicit (Fig. 1-4).

information assets 1. Information of value in the circumstances. 2. Information owned by an organization, person or other entity which has a monetary exchange value.

information benefit The long-term gain or ultimate purpose to be derived from the production/acquisition and use of an information product or service.

information costs The costs incurred in acquiring and/or producing information, as well as costs incurred at any of the other stages of the information life-cycle, such as storing and maintaining it, using it, communicating it and disposing of it.

information cost/value ratios Any expression of the cost of an information resource entity directly related to any expression of its value. Numeric ratios can be derived only from expressions of cost and value that are quantitative and comparable, but semi-quantitative and qualitative "ratios" may also be useful measures; e.g., monetary ratios, rank-order ratios, activity ratios, descriptive "ratios" (Table 3-9).

information communities Any of the five general groups of people playing a role in information management: Information Suppliers, Information Handlers, Information Users, Information Managers and Information Counselors (Fig. 2-4).

information counselors One of the five main communities playing a role in information management (Fig. 2-4).

information handling functions Any of the individual specialized activities for acquiring, storing, documenting, processing, duplicating, organizing, compressing, transmitting or disposing of information. For example:

— collecting statistics	— storing/retrieving records
— recording technical data	— archiving records
— translating	— transmitting documents
— publishing	— inventorying holdings
— advertising	— computing
— printing	— maintaining databases
— photocopying	— word processing
— microfilming	— telecommunications

information functions management (IFM) Application of the traditional management processes to one or more individual specialized functional areas; e.g., data processing, micrographics, records (Fig. 1-2).

information handlers One of the five main communities playing a role in information management (Fig. 2-4).

information holdings   Any of the media containing information under the control of, or accessible to, an organization, together with the information itself (content). For example:

Media	*Information Itself*
— paper files:	profit-and-loss statements
— manuals:	policy statements
— serials:	scientific measurements
— unpublished reports:	patents
— diskettes:	audit findings
— online databases:	bank account balances
— photographs:	wheat crop conditions
— maps:	mineral deposit locations
— videodiscs:	TV newscasts

information inventory data form   A data recording form for compiling summary data on an individual information resource entity (IRE), used in conducting a preliminary inventory of information resources (Fig. 2-2).

information life-cycle   The concept that information is created, passes through various stages of development and ultimately is destroyed; stages usually recognized are requirements definition, acquisition, transmission, processing, storage, dissemination, use and disposal.

information life-cycle management (ILCM)   Application of the traditional management processes to one or more or all stages of the information life-cycle, such as acquisition, storage, processing and disposal (Fig. 1-2).

information management (IM)   The application of one or more of the traditional management processes such as planning, organizing, staffing, directing and controlling, to an information entity or entities; e.g., information functions, information life-cycle stages, information resources (Fig. 1-2).

information manager   The individual in an organizational unit responsible for acquiring, maintaining, using and disposing of information resources economically and efficiently, and for applying those resources effectively to help the organization fulfill its mission and achieve its goals and objectives.

information managers   One of the five main communities playing a role in information management (Fig. 2-4).

information price   The price attached to an information product, service, system or source, either produced in-house or acquired externally.

information products   One of the two primary forms of output from an information-providing organization, usually a tangible, readable record produced by an information process or system; e.g., book, newspaper, directory, database; see also, information services.

information resource categories The highest level of a three-level hierarchy of information resources (the other two levels are "information resource types" and "information resource entities"). The three main categories are information sources, information services and information systems (Table 2-1).

information resource entities (IREs) The lowest level of a three-level hierarchy of information resources (the other two levels are "information resource categories" and "information resource types") (Table 2-1). IREs are specific information sources, services, systems or like configurations of input resources (people, hardware, space, etc.) that comprise the information holdings and information handling functions used by or available to an organization (Fig. 1-3). IREs could be elements of a preliminary inventory (Fig. 2-1), elements of the corporate information resource (Fig. 5-1) or elements in some other context.

information resource inventory An itemized list of those information resource entities (IREs), or other configurations of content and media, held either internally by the organization or available externally, that are recognized by management as actual or potential organizational resources. A *preliminary* information resource inventory, the output of Step One of the discovery process (e.g., Table 5-1), lists all IREs, some, none or all of which may later, in Step Four, become recognized as organizational resources.

information resource maps Any graphical representation of information resource entities plotted on two or more sets of coordinates or spectra; for example, the content:media spectrum and the holdings:functions spectrum (e.g., Figs. 4-8, 5-2).

information resource types The middle level of a three-level hierarchy of information resources (the other two levels are "information resource categories" and "information resource entities"). Each "type" is a generic grouping of information resource entities (IREs) (Table 2-1).

information resource worksheets Any two-dimensional matrices showing the location within an organization (branch, department, division, etc.) of information resource types (or some other resource entity) in terms of who uses, handles, supplies or manages them. Each information community is depicted on a separate worksheet matrix; i.e., user matrix, supplier/handler matrix, manager matrix, etc. (e.g., Figs. 4-3 to 4-6).

information resources 1. In general, the information holdings and information handling functions within or available to an organization (Fig. 1-3). 2. Those information sources, services and systems under the control of, or available to, an organization, which constitute significant sources of supply, support or aid in fulfilling its mission or in achieving its goals and objectives.

information resources management (IRM)   A management process in which traditional management processes and resource management principles are applied to the stewardship of an organization's information resources and assets (Fig. 1-3).

information services   1. One of the three broad categories of information resources, referring to any activity helpful in acquiring, processing or transmitting information (Table 2-1). 2. One of the two primary forms of output from an information-providing organization, usually a utility or other helpful activity depending on human intervention; e.g., accounting, printing, surveying, electronic mail; see also, information products.

information sources   One of the three broad categories of information resources, referring to the information holdings available to the organization or to any aggregated form of holdings, such as a library or records center (Table 2-1).

information suppliers   One of the five main communities playing a role in information management (Fig. 2-4).

information systems   1. One of the three broad categories of information resources, referring to any definable, systematic processes for handling data or information (Table 2-1). 2. The structures, processes and technologies used to generate, process and transmit formal messages (products) or to support services. 3. A series of formal processes by which the potential usefulness of specific input messages being processed is enhanced; e.g., office, library, data processing, management information, decision-support, information retrieval systems.

information users   One of the five main communities playing a role in information management (Fig. 2-4).

information values   The values attributed to information products or services. Two main categories of information values are exchange value (e.g., as evidenced by a monetary or other price paid to acquire something) and use value (e.g., as evidenced by a productivity gain) (Table 3-5).

IREs   See information resource entities.

IRM   See information resources management.

management processes   The functions of planning, organizing, staffing, directing and controlling, carried out by or on behalf of an organization.

manager matrix   See information resource worksheets.

mapping information resources The process of identifying, evaluating and portraying an organization's known and potential information resource entities in sufficient breadth and depth to provide an overview of its information resource base for planning, accountability and other corporate management purposes (Fig. 1-8).

preliminary information resource inventory See information resource inventory.

price The quantity of one thing that is exchanged or demanded in barter or sale for another.

resource 1. A source of supply, support or aid, especially one held in reserve. 2. Any of the four types of resources: Human, physical (land, facilities, equipment, materials, energy), financial or informational (sources, services, systems).

resource criteria Statements of reasonable standards against which information or other entities can be judged to be resources.

resource effectiveness (RE) index A rating, on a scale of 0 to 10, of the effectiveness with which an information resource entity supports the activity or activities intended. Effectiveness categories and their numeric ratings include: "Highly effective" (10), "moderately effective" (5), "ineffective" (1) and "no support" (0). RE indexes are used to determine the Value Index of an information resource entity (Table 3-7).

resource management The set of all activities involved in the optimal allocation and administration of an organization's human, financial, physical and/or informational resources, to fulfill the organization's mission and achieve its goals and objectives. The basic objectives of resource management are:
- To maximize the values and benefits from use of the resource(s);
- To minimize the costs of acquiring, processing, using and disposing of the resource(s); and
- To fix accountability for the economical, efficient and effective use of the resource(s) on named officers and specific departments.

supplier/handler matrix See information resource worksheets.

types See information resource types.

user matrix See information resource worksheets.

value Monetary, attributed, intrinsic and/or relative worth, merit, usefulness, importance and/or utility of a good, service, product, principle, item or entity.

value index A rating of the value to an organization of an information resource entity based on three other ratings: Resource Effectiveness (RE) Index, Importance to Activity (IA) Index and Importance to Organization (IO) Index. The Value Index is the product of the RE, IA and IO Indexes, and can range from 0 to 1,000 (Table 3-7).

INDEX

A

Accounting and budgeting, 19, 24, 30, 45, 76-90, 148-151, 156, 169-171, 176
ACI Computer Services Pty. Ltd., 219
Alvin, 158
American Geological Institute (AGI), 213
Arthur Young & Company, 82
Assets, information (*see* Information assets)
Ausinet, 218-219, 227
Australia:
    Bureau of Mineral Resources, 163, 202-203, 218
    CSIRO, 218
    National Library of, 218
Australian Earth Sciences Information System (AESIS), 218-219
Australian Mineral Foundation (AMF), 218
Australian Petroleum Exploration Association (APEA), 201, 221
Australian Science Index, 219

B

Bedell, Eugene F., 99-101, 104-105, 235
Bibliography, annotated, 235-237
Birinyi, Anne E., 23, 139
Browning, Robert, 76
Burk, Cornelius F., Jr., 89, 128
Business-competitor intelligence, 6-7

C

Canada, Auditor General of, 82
Canada, Department of Energy, Mines and Resources (EMR):
    information center costs, 87-89
    information resource types, 52
    order of magnitude of information costs, 87
    preliminary information resource inventory, 44
    supplier/handler matrix, 128-129
Canada, Federal Government:
    accounting and reporting standards, lack of, 45
    "information" expenditures defined, 30
    photocopying costs of, 82-83
Cancer, unlocking the secrets of, 68

Center for Information Policy Research, 22, 146
Chemical Abstracts, 220
Chick, Morey J., 111
Chief information officer (CIO), 4, 172, 235
Clean Water Act of 1972, 90
Cleveland Harlan, 19-20, 235
Compaine, Benjamin M., 23, 139
Computer Sciences of Australia Pty. Ltd., 187, 193
The Computer Solution, 99-100, 235 (*see also* Bedell, Eugene F.)
Computer systems, 71-72, 87-90, 99, 135-136 142-143, 146, 164, 170, 178
Conserver society, 15
Content, information (*see* Information content)
Corporate (organizational) information resources, 2-4, 6-9, 68, 75, 98, 121, 138, 149, 151-153, 155-157, 161-165, 168, 175-176, 236, 239
Corporate information resources management, 7, 171-173
Cost and value, relating information (*see* Information cost and value, relating)
Costs, information (*see* Information costs)
CRA Exploration Pty. Limited (CRAE):
    Administrative and Technical Services, 184, 197, 199, 215
    approach to information management, 177-178
    Basin Study Group, 132, 201, 221-222
    Central Information Service, 162-165, 177-178
    classification of information resources, 71-72
    collecting inventory data, 66-67
    Current Awareness Service, 191
    description of, 34
    Evaluation Group, 217
    Geophysics Division, 184
    geoscience information and data, 55, 68-70, 101, 106-107, 124-127, 130-133, 137, 142-143, 146, 159, 162-165
    hidden resources of, 68, 70, 159
    importance to activity (IA) indexes, 102-104

CRA Exploration Pty. Limited (CRAE):
 cont'd.
  importance to organization (IO)
   indexes, 102-103, 105
  information management review,
   43-44, 66-67, 162, 177
  information resource criteria, 159
  information resource maps, 141-43,
   146, 165
  information resource types, 52-53
  information resource worksheets, 124-
   127, 130-137
  information resources entities (IREs)
   listed, 181-183
  information resources identified,
   162-165
  main case example, 33, 70, 162, 177,
   181-183, 237
  manager matrix, 130-131
  map of information resource entities
   (IREs), 142-143
  map of information resources, 165
  preliminary information resource
   inventory, 67, 69, 181-233
  rank ordering IREs by information
   values, 107
  Research Group, 185, 191, 209, 224-
   225, 227
  resource effectiveness (RE) indexes,
   101-103
  supplier/handler matrix, 126-127
  user matrix, 124-125
  value indexes, 102-103, 106-107
CRA Limited, 34
CRA Services, 232
Cronin, Blaise, 177, 235

D

Daniel, Evelyn H., 235
Data *vs* information, 26-27, 168, 239
Delphi method, 110
Dewey decimal system, 46
Dialog, 220, 227
Diebold, John, 177, 235
Discovery, nature of, 1, 3, 147, 164

E

Earthsat (Computing) Pty. Ltd., 226
Eddison, Elizabeth Bole, 49

Energy resources, 1-3
Energy resources management, 2-3, 15, 178
Energyline, 220
ESRI — Australia Pty. Ltd., 207
Evans Deakin Industries Ltd., 192
Exploration:
  geographic, 1, 36, 91, 115, 147, 155
  information resources, 1, 3, 36, 51, 115-
   116, 135, 155, 164-166, 179
  mineral resources, 3, 26-28, 34, 68, 105-
   106, 162-164, 177-178
  petroleum resources, 2, 26-28, 163-164

F

Financial management, 12, 15, 39, 44, 73,
 76, 97-99, 108, 140, 148-149, 151, 169-
 171, 176

G

Geoarchive, 220
Georef, 213, 220
Geosystems, 216
Glossary, 239-245
Grosvenor, Melville Bell, 145
Gruber, William H., 237

H

Handling functions, information (*see*
 Information handling functions)
Harvard University, 22, 146
Hedonic wage model, 97
Hidden resources, 66-68, 70-72, 123, 159
Holdings, information (*see* Information
 holdings)
Horton, Forest W., Jr., 5-6, 15, 46, 50-51, 65,
 176-177, 236
Human resources management, 12, 15, 39,
 45, 140, 176
Humphrey, Hubert, 68

I

Implementing the discovery process,
options for:
  complete journey, 35
  quick trip, 35
  scenic route, 35
InfoMap, summaries of the four steps:
  overview chart, 32

InfoMap, summaries of the four steps: cont'd.
    step one: survey, 32, 41, 173
    step two: cost/value, 32, 77, 173
    step three: analysis, 32-33, 118, 174
    step four: synthesis, 33, 157, 174-175
Information:
    definition, 239
    information and data hierarchy, 26-27
    national standards for, 172
    as overhead, 16, 24, 31, 75, 82, 87, 105, 148, 151, 160, 178
    as a resource, 8, 18-21, 42, 91, 170, 177, 236
    scope of the term, 10, 91
    as a strategic resource, 5, 176, 178
    see also Information itself
Information architecture, 176
Information assets:
    capitalized assets, 30, 111, 171
    definition, 240
    illustration, 98
    management's perceptions, 8
    need to know, 8, 171
    reported/unreported in corporate financial reports, 8, 19, 76, 98, 171, 176
    role of context in identifying, 26
Information benefits, 66, 76, 78-79, 86, 97, 103, 108, 136, 160, 169-171, 240
Information business map, 22-23, 138
Information communities, model of, 65
Information content, 11, 13, 16-17, 21-22, 24, 40, 68, 71-73, 91, 100, 138-145, 147, 163-166, 168
Information cost and value, relating:
    activity ratios, 109-110
    cost/value ratios, 108-110, 160, 166, 240
    descriptive "ratios", 109-110
    juxtaposing cost and value, 8, 106, 108, 176
    monetary ratios, 108-109
    rank order ratios, 109, 160
    unnecessary and excess costs, 111, 170
    value-for-money auditing, 150
    value/burden study, U.S. Paperwork Commission, 96
Information costs:
    adsorption (imputed) costing, 85

Information costs: cont'd.
    analysis, 148-149, 170-171
    cost accounting, 19, 30, 80-86, 90, 148-149, 170-171
    cost categories, 81, 88
    cost elements, 80-81, 83, 90, 170-171
    cost estimating, 86
    cost finding, 86
    costing objectives, 84
    cost/profit centers, 171
    definitions, 78-79, 240
    direct costing, 85
    expenditure sinks, 151
    fixed (sunk) costs, 111
    full costs of information, 75, 84, 87, 90, 170, 176
    functional cost elements, 81
    information centers, examples of, 89
    life-cycle costing, 86
    measurement problems, 30
    measuring and ranking costs, 86-90
    need to know, 78
    opportunity costs, 86
    qualitative (nonfinancial) costs, 86
    resource cost elements, 81
    standard costing, 85
    temporal cost elements, 81
    unnecessary and excess costs, 111-112
    use costs, 87
Information costs, rank ordering by (*see* Rank ordering by information costs)
Information counselors, 65
Information functions management, 10-11, 240
Information functions, model of, 65
Information handling functions, 13, 17, 18, 24, 138-141, 156, 162, 169-171, 175-176, 240
Information holdings, 13, 17-18, 24, 48-49, 138-141, 146, 156, 162-163, 168-169, 172, 175-176, 241
Information itself:
    as the basic information resource, 24, 164
    definition, 239
    as "finished goods", 17
    fundamental nature, 18
    quality of, 92-94
    as a resource, 16, 68, 178

Information liabilities:
  on corporate balance sheets, 176
  need to know, 44, 171
Information life-cycle management, 10-11,
  19, 30-31, 84-86, 94, 241
Information literacy, 136, 172
Information management:
  areas highlighted by discovery process,
    171
  definition, 10, 241
  evolution, 6
  holistic approach to, 31
  how *vs* what, 117, 133, 171, 175
  model of roles and functions, 65
  model of scope, 10-11
  prerequisites for success, 2, 152-153,
    175, 178
  problems, 8-9, 111-112
  see also Information functions manage-
    ment, Information life-cycle
    management and Information
    resources management
Information media, 11, 13, 17, 21, 24, 40, 73,
  91, 94, 100, 117, 133, 138-143, 150, 152,
  165, 168
Information price, 19, 43, 72, 78-79, 98-99,
  108, 241
Information products and services, 5, 12, 18,
  22-23, 47, 50-51, 66, 79, 88, 90, 97-99,
  108, 136, 138, 169-171, 176, 241-243
Information resource categories, 45-47, 52-
  53, 55, 57-58, 82, 184-233, 242
Information resource discovery process:
  benefits, 4, 36, 116-117, 155, 173, 175-
    178
  case examples, 33, 237
  costs to implement, 35
  implementation options, 34-35
  knowledge base created by, 157, 177
  objectives, 116-117
  original presentation of, 236
  overview chart, 32
  related to corporate information
    management, 171
  step one: survey chart, 41
  step two: cost/value chart, 77
  step three: analysis chart, 118
  step four: synthesis chart, 157
  summary, 173-175

Information resource entities (IREs):
  accountability for use of, 172
  biological metaphor, 21, 24
  characteristics revealed by discovery
    process, 152
  classification approach, 45-46, 68, 71
  concept, 8, 21-25
  costs of, 8, 148, 160
  definition, 21, 242
  difficulty of locating, 119
  as elements of the IRM process, 13
  examples, 70-72, 142-143, 165, 181-233
  labels and boundaries, 51-54, 71-72, 149
  management context of, 12, 141
  parallels in the information business,
    22-23
  as "raw materials", 17, 78
  related to resource inputs, 24-25
  represented in charts of account, 148,
    151, 170
  source *vs* service, 54
  strategic roles, 160-161
  values of, 160-161
Information resource maps:
  analysis of, 145-147
  benefits, 145, 147
  constructing maps, 141, 144-145
  content-medium spectrum, 22-23, 138-
    141, 147
  criteria for positioning IREs, 145
  definition, 138, 142
  examples, 142-143, 146-147, 165
  explorer's task to prepare, 73, 115
  functions-holdings spectrum, 138-141,
    144-145, 147
  intellectual processes for preparing,
    141, 144-145
  map coordinates for, 115, 138-141, 163
  map legends, 30
  mechanics of preparing, 141
  model of map grid, 139
  need for mapping methods, 28, 30-31
  product-service spectrum, 22-23
  relation to IRM process, 141
  resource space, 163
Information resource types:
  classification approach, 45-46
  definition, 242
  description, 51-54, 58

Information resource types: cont'd.
  examples, 52-53
  inventory data forms, 57-58, 184-233
  need to revise, 120-121
Information resource worksheets:
  analysis of, 123, 132-137
  constructing worksheets, 119, 122-123
  criteria for analysis of, 133, 136-137
  definition, 242
  examples, 124-131
  internal *vs* external resources, 70, 121
  manager matrix, 123, 130-131, 137
  manual *vs* technology-based resources,
    121
  model of, 120
  selecting organizational units, 121
  supplier categories, 121
  supplier/handler matrix, 122-123, 126-
    129, 136-137
  typology for, 120
  user categories, 121
  user matrix, 122, 124-125, 133, 135-136
Information resources:
  alternative concepts of, 22, 24, 157
  classification of, 44-47, 51-56
  conceptual and semantic distinctions,
    16-17
  context, importance of understanding,
    25-28
  criteria for recognizing, 157-162
  definition, 242-243
  differences with other resources, 19-20,
    157, 235
  hidden resources, 66-68, 70-71, 123, 159
  horizontal *vs* vertical views of, 30
  identification of, 162-164
  internal *vs* external, 8, 40, 47, 66-67, 70,
    121, 135, 152, 161, 169, 178
  inventories of, 4, 8, 24, 39, 72-73, 162
  nature *vs* location, 138
  relation to other resources, 24-25
  scope, model of, 17
  selected from preliminary inventory, 164
  similarities with other resources, 18-19,
    140-141, 157
  strategic management of, 176-177
  strategic role of, 5, 161, 178, 236
  see also Corporate information
    resources and Information
    resource entities (IREs)

Information resources management (IRM):
  definition, 9-14, 243
  description, 9-14, 236
  educational requirements for, 235
  how *vs* what, 175, 177
  management issues, 8, 156, 172-173
  model of IRM process, 13, 171
  policies and programs, 4, 12, 22, 33,
    117, 137, 171-172, 177-178
  problems, 8, 111-112, 134-135
  relationship to "information manage-
    ment", 10-12
  as a resource management function,
    15-16
  state-of-the-art reviews of, 236
  strategic planning for, 26, 28-29, 173
  terminology, 10-12, 14, 31, 239-245
  theoretical basis for, 237
  three fundamental aspects of, 158
Information roles, model of, 65
Information services, 1, 3, 4, 22-25, 31, 40,
  45-47, 50-56, 68-71, 84, 115, 132, 135,
  137, 140-141, 144, 146, 159, 161, 172,
  176, 243
Information sources, 1-4, 22, 24, 31-32, 40,
  45-56, 66-72, 101, 115, 135, 159, 161-
  163, 168, 176, 178, 243
Information spectra, 21, 30, 138-141, 144,
  147, 169
Information systems, 2-4, 9, 22, 24, 29, 31-
  32, 40, 45-47, 51-56, 60-64, 68-72, 90,
  112, 115, 135, 140, 144, 146, 159, 161,
  163, 169, 170, 176, 178, 243
  see also Computer systems and Tele-
    phone systems
Information systems résumé form, 61-64
Information technology, 7, 22, 163-164, 237
Information technology facilities, 22, 82, 84
Information technology management, 6-7,
  235
Information values:
  approach to assessing, 91, 95, 237
  assessing and ranking, 99-106
  categories and elements of value,
    examples, 92-93, 95
  commercial values, 98-99
  criteria for information values, 92-93,
    95
  definition, 79, 243

Information values: cont'd.
 exchange value, 108
 hierarchy of values, 92
 impact on financial position, 93, 97-99
 impact on organizational effectiveness, 93, 97
 impact on organizational productivity, 93-94, 96-97
 of information products and services, 169
 of information resource entities (IREs), 160-161
 investment value, 97-98
 measurement problems, 30
 nature of values, 91
 need to articulate, 76
 need to know, 78
 quality of information itself, 92-94
 quantitative measures of value, 96-97
 rank ordering by value indexes, 105-107
 relative values of IREs, 91
 review of IRE values, 149-151
 social values, 79, 96-97
 utility of information holdings, 93-94
 value categories, 92-93
 value elements, 92-93, 96, 160
 value index, 102-103, 105, 160-162
Information values, rank ordering by (*see* Rank ordering by information values)
Infotrends, 5, 236, (*see also* Horton, Forest W., Jr. and Marchand, Donald A.)
Insearch DIAL Services, 220
Institute for Information Management, 75
Inuit language, 10
Inventories:
 definition, 39
 reported on balance sheets, 98
 resource, 39
 strategic significance of, 73
 supermarket, 72
 see also Preliminary information resource inventories
Inventory data forms, 56-60, 66, 68, 72, 122-123, 141, 181, 185-233
Inventory management, 45, 140

J

James, Philip N., 26, 29

Jason, Jr., 158

K

Knowledge management, 15, 44, 153

L

Landau, Robert M., 236
LANDSAT satellite, 196, 225-226
Levitan, Karen B., 236
Lewis and Clark expedition, 1, 36, 155
Liabilities, information (*see* Information liabilities)
Libraries, 24, 52-54, 83, 87, 89, 102, 107, 119, 124-131, 142, 146, 162-163, 168-169, 178
Lytle, Richard H., 236

M

Mail services, 144
Map, information business (*see* Information business map)
Maps and mapping methods, 1, 22-23, 26, 28, 30-31, 115-116, 138-147, 151-153, 165, 178
Maps, information resource (*see* Information resource maps)
Marchand, Donald A., 5-6, 176-177, 236
Management (*see* Corporate Information resources, Energy resources, Financial, Human resources, Information, Information resources, Information technology, Inventory, Knowledge, Materiel, Paperwork, Real property, Records, Resource, Strategic information and Water quality management)
Management of information resources (*see* Information resources management)
Materiel management, 12, 15, 39, 73
McLaughlin, John F., 23, 139
McLuhan, Marshall, 24, 138
Media, information (*see* Information media)
Meltzer, Morton F., 236
Metadata, 44, 146, 173
Metainformation, 146
Metaknowledge, 153
Mineral Exploration Alert, 213
Mineral resources, 3, 34, 68, 91, 178

Minsys, 216

N

National Geographic Society, 145

O

Office automation, 96-97, 108, 170, 237
Orbit, 227
Organizational structure, 176
Organizational strengths and weaknesses:
   in corporate information management,
     171-173
   criteria for identifying, 134-135, 167-
     173
   example, 167
   how to identify, 166-168
   in information accounting and
     budgeting, 169
   in information handling functions, 169-
     171
   in information holdings, 168-169
   need to identify, 29

P

Palliser expedition, 1, 36, 155
Paperwork management, 6, 83
Paperwork Reduction Act of 1980, 22
Patents, 220
Petroleum resources, 2, 40
Photocopiers, 82-83, 142, 144
Porter, T. Michael, 162, 164, 237
Preliminary information resource
   inventory:
   classification scheme, 44-47, 51-56
   collecting data, 56-67
   contents of, 73
   of CRA Exploration Pty. Limited, 69-
     72, 162-163, 181-233
   inventory data form, 56-60
   part of strategic plans, 43
   purpose and scope, 42-44
   top management's support, 42
   use of inventory data in worksheets,
     122-123
Products and services, information (see
   Information products and services)

R

Rank ordering by information costs, 86-88,
   160
Rank ordering by information values:
   assessing and ranking IREs by value,
     99, 105-106
   effectiveness of IREs, 100-101
   example, 107
   importance to activity (IA) index, 101-
     104, 106, 239
   importance to organization (IO) index,
     102-105, 239
   resource effectiveness (RE) index, 100-
     103, 106, 244
   strategic role of activity, 104-105
   strategic role of IRE, 101, 103-104
   value index, 102-103, 105-107, 161-162,
     245
Real property management, 12, 15, 39, 73,
   84
Records management, 11, 52-53, 69, 71, 83,
   132
Resource management:
   concept, 3
   definition, 244
   evolution of functions, 15-16, 157, 236
   principles of, 13-15, 76, 133, 150, 176,
     236, 244
Resources:
   classification by temporal status, 140
   corporate (organizational) resources, 4,
     12-13, 16, 20-21, 28, 40, 91, 116-117,
     149, 157, 160-165
   definition, 2, 14-15, 244
   evolution of classification schemes, 45
   as inputs to information resource en-
     tities (IREs), 17, 24-25, 46, 82, 119,
     160, 170
   see also Energy, Information, Mineral
     and Petroleum resources
Resources, information (*see* Information
   resources)
Robinson, L.J. & Partners, 195
Royal Observatory at Greenwich, 30

S

Sassone, Peter, 96, 108

School of Information Studies, Syracuse
    University, 235
Schwartz, Perry, 96, 108
Shelley, E. Paul, 237
Smithsonian Institution:
    information resource directory, 44
    information resource types, 52-53
    Museums Program, 52-53
South Australia Department of Mines and
    Energy, 229
STORET information system, 90
Strassman, Paul A., 237
Strategic information management, 6-7,
    176
Strategic planning, 4, 26, 28-29, 42-43, 153,
    155, 172-173, 177
Strengths and weaknesses, organizational
    (*see* Organizational strengths and
    weaknesses)
Summus Resource Evaluations, Ltd., 228
Synnott, William R., 237
Syracuse University, 235
Services, information (*see* Information
    services)
Sources, information (*see* Information
    sources)
Systems, information (*see* Information
    systems)

T

Taylor, Robert S., 26, 94-95, 108, 150, 160,
    237
Technical & Field Surveys Pty. Ltd., 196
Telecom Australia, 231
Telephone systems, 119, 144
Titanic, 158

U

United Kingdom, IRM in the, 235
U.S. Commission on Federal Paperwork:
    information resources management
        report, 237

U.S. Commission on Federal Paperwork:
    cont'd.
    value/burden study, 96
U.S. Department of the Army Head-
    quarters:
    Arthur Young & Company study, 82
    information cost elements, 82
U.S. Environmental Protection Agency:
    Clean Water Act of 1972, 90
    information resource types, 52-53
    information systems résumé form,
        61-64
    STORET information system costs, 90
U.S. Federal Government:
    accounting and reporting standards,
        lack of, 45
    definitions used by, 22
    "free" services to the states, 90
    "full costs" of information defined, 84
    information resource concept of, 22
U.S. General Accounting Office (GAO):
    information management problems
        revealed by, 111-112
    see also Chick, Morey J.
U.S. Office of Management and Budget
    (OMB), 84

V

Value-added model, 95, 160, 237
Value and cost, relating (*see* Cost and value,
    relating information)
Values, information (*see* Information
    values)
Victoria Geological Survey, 230
Vincent, David R., 97-98, 171

W

Water quality management, 90
Williams, Gordon D., 26-27
Williams, Martha E., 236
Work profile analysis, 96
Worksheets, information resource (*see*
    Information resource worksheets)